Making Your Primary School E-safe

Making Your
Primary School E-safe

Whole School Cyberbullying
and E-safety Strategies for
Meeting Ofsted Requirements

ADRIENNE KATZ

Jessica Kingsley *Publishers*
London and Philadelphia

Figure 1.1 on p.10 reproduced with kind permission from Ofcom.
BYOD list on p.47 adapted with kind permission, from a ten point guide by Lightspeed systems for NAACE.
Cybersurvey infographics on p.12 and results throughout are reproduced with kind permission from e-Safer Suffolk.
Contains public sector information licensed under the Open Government Licence v3.0.

First published in 2015
by Jessica Kingsley Publishers
73 Collier Street
London N1 9BE, UK
and
400 Market Street, Suite 400
Philadelphia, PA 19106, USA

www.jkp.com

Library of Congress Cataloging in Publication Data
Katz, Adrienne, 1946-
  Making your primary school e-safe : whole school cyberbullying and e-safety strategies for meeting Ofsted requirements / Adrienne Katz.
       pages cm
  Includes bibliographical references and index.
  ISBN 978-1-84905-542-0 (alk. paper)
  1. Cyberbullying--Great Britain--Prevention. 2. Bullying in schools--Great Britain--Prevention. 3. Education--Standards--Great Britain. 4. Great Britain. Office for Standards in Education. I. Title.
  LB3013.34.G7K37 2015
  371.5'8--dc23

                              2015016758

British Library Cataloguing in Publication Data
A CIP catalogue record for this book is available from the British Library

ISBN 978 1 84905 542 0
eISBN 978 0 85700 966 1

Printed and bound in the United States

Contents

1

What Do We Mean by E-safety for Primary Children?

What is e-safety?

Put at its simplest, e-safety is the school's ability to:

- protect and educate pupils and staff in their use of technology
- have the appropriate mechanisms to intervene and support pupils and staff when necessary.

The breadth of issues classified within e-safety is considerable, but can be categorised into three areas of risk:

- *content*: being exposed to illegal, inappropriate or harmful material
- *contact*: being subjected to harmful online interaction with other users
- *conduct*: personal online behaviour that increases the likelihood of, or causes, harm.

These words, 'content, contact and conduct', outline how e-safety is viewed in convenient categories. But there is so much more to it.

Lives lived online and future lives imagined

Young children in our schools are going to live their lives online: their jobs are likely to require good digital skills, and their personal and social lives most certainly will. Being digitally skilled and safe online is a must for them. They can expect to bank online, book holidays, talk to friends, do their shopping, play games and download movies and music if they are not already doing several of these. They will search for information for their schoolwork and simply to find out interesting facts. They will book tickets for a concert, find out how to get there and follow news of their favourite band. They will follow exciting scientific breakthroughs like the Rosetta spacecraft online and view their favourite TV programmes online too.

Technology enables those who have a disability to be equal to anyone when online, connects people in remote areas with millions of others who have the same hobby or interest, and changes how we monitor our health and even how we are diagnosed.

The digital revolution demands that we do more than police children's behaviour – it is a gateway to the most enabling technology that is also disrupting the way we do things, and we need to give them the skills and confidence to navigate it.

Risks and downsides

Nevertheless, despite all the exciting opportunities, there are risks and downsides. What we post online may stay there for years to come, only to turn up in some future search. Images uploaded innocently can be 'harvested' and misused by merchants of pornography. Fundamentally, our privacy and the way we think about our privacy have changed too, and the question of how to retain some privacy and safety while everything is put out there lies at the heart of e-safety work with children and young people. Much of their behaviour is driven by emotion; many say 'I forget about the rules when I go online' and will return again and again to the site where they are hurt. Lonely, isolated people search for friendship and intimacy online, ignoring the safety advice they have received, while others, in the age-old way of youth, feel invincible.

Cyberbullying is thought to be even more hurtful and cruel than face-to-face bullying. It makes it possible to follow a target 24 hours a day, reach them in the privacy of their bedroom, and hurt or humiliate them in front of an audience of people they know. Photos can be misused to embarrass at best, or humiliate and blackmail at worst. Trolls and haters spread racism, misogyny and prejudice.

The intensity of cyberbullying is what amplifies the impact. Victims are polyvictimised as the attacks can now come in so many varied forms, including the old ways in school, on the bus to school and on the playing field, or in school corridors or toilets. The victim is often photographed having a bad time and the image shared to compound or amplify the shame, or taunt him further. The rumour mill is enhanced by technology that allows anonymity and easy ways to reach lots of people with a click.

The worrying message may not be linked with bullying: ten-year-olds report receiving chain letters on their mobiles with threats describing what will happen if they do not pass it on and keep it going. Others are worried by phishing or spam, unsure how to react.

Beyond bullying

Of course, there is much content online that is anything but benign. Sites urge people to harm or kill themselves and tell them how to do things they would previously only have imagined in their wildest dreams. Anorexics compare the size of the 'thigh gap' and bully others into losing even more weight. Adults with ill intent groom children into thinking they are their age and urge them to meet up or send a photo. The spectre of child sexual exploitation is so serious that there is a lot of media emphasis on it, although in fact it is only a small percentage of children who are targeted in this way – but they tend to be the most vulnerable children and the crime is so horrific that the headlines make many parents too scared to let their child go online instead of teaching them how to be safe.

Recent reports such as *Can I Tell You Something?* and the *Health Behaviour in School-Aged Children* report suggest that self-harm and cyberbullying have increased alarmingly. Twenty per cent of teenagers in England have hurt themselves in the previous year,[1] while the percentage of children reporting cyberbullying has risen sharply – up 87 per cent in January 2014 on the previous year.[2]

Do tablets protect younger children?

The Cybersurvey, an annual online survey of young people's online lives I have undertaken since 2008, finds that cyberbullying among mid-teens is rising steadily but among 10–11-year-olds appears stable. We think this is partly because parents tended to buy tablets for the family rather than individual mobile phones for this younger age group at Christmas 2013–2014. It may also be linked to the fact that ten-year-olds are the age group most likely to follow the e-safety advice they have received and they are also good at helping friends out, whereas teenagers are less likely to follow the e-safety advice they have been taught, or to ask for help. The competence in the answers from 10–11-year-olds is typified by the responses from the two young pupils below. The first responded:

> *Well my friend was on xbox (I also know him in person) his account was used by another person and his mum's credit card was being used because it was on his xbox, so I told him to take his mum's credit card off and put a password on his account and it worked.*

Another 10–11-year-old protected her sister:

> *Someone had asked to meet my sister and she had put back yes because she thought it was a new girl moving to her school, but it turned out to be someone she had never met before so I blocked the girl's page before she could send her any more, and I reported it so it wouldn't happen to anyone else.*

It would be a worthy goal to see e-safety as creating competent, confident digital citizens such as these two, and this book has them in mind throughout.

Do we fully recognise the online lives of primary-school children?

'This doesn't happen at our small rural school,' said one primary headteacher when I asked about how he prevented cyberbullying and taught children to be safe online.

This seems pure wishful thinking. Gone are the days when a geographical location could keep children unaware or protected from the big bad world of the cities. Children go online wherever they are in the UK whether it is rural or urban and have mostly the same sort of experiences. Yet the Cybersurvey shows that some parents in rural areas are slow to talk to their children about staying safe online and this could put them at greater risk. These parents clearly have similar views to the headteacher quoted above, but perhaps they should have asked their six-year-olds. In August 2014, Ofcom's 11th *Communications Market* report found that six-year-olds had the same Digital Quotient score as 45-year olds; in other words, six-year-olds claim to have the same understanding of communications technology as 45-year-olds![3]

So while almost all schools actively teach their pupils about staying safe online, primary teachers often expressed anxiety in my training sessions about whether they were actually delivering what was needed in this fast-developing area. They worried when parents did not turn up to e-safety evenings or take an interest in their child's online life. Indeed, some say parents of children in their class are playing games intended for adults with their primary-age child! Teachers claimed to be running out of ideas, or felt they did not have a coherent picture of what they should be covering, while for some the issue was that they could not keep up with the fast-changing scenario. They asked for help with putting in place a good policy and procedures. Many left it all to the school's ICT manager and did not feel they had to 'get my head round it'.

There were also those who thought that policy and procedure could be left to the senior management team, meaning that they did not feel responsibility for, or ownership of, them. One troubling feature of primary schools' e-safety education was that they tended to invite a guest to deliver the messages and, once this person left, the 'box was ticked' and there was nobody there the following day or in the weeks to come to whom children could go with their questions about the session, and little follow-up or embedded work.

Taking these discussions on board and looking at the views of the children in our surveys, it seemed a good moment to share excellent and innovative ideas that some schools were using and to offer a few more. I started by looking at what ten-year-olds were saying in the online survey I have run since 2008, because unless our responses are meeting the rapidly changing needs of our children, we are talking to ourselves in offices far from the front line.

These messages from ten-year-olds give a flavour of their lives online and on their mobiles, wherever they are in England.

What happened to you?

Someone I didn't know sent me this: 'Why did you do this to me?' and then hacked into my account and sent a message to my friend saying 'I'm not your friend any more.'

I got...
 messages telling me to go and kill myself
 scary threats about my family dying and people coming to get you in the night
 people putting statuses about me that aren't true and turning my best friends against me
 I get called a pathetic diabetic
 a list of horrible things about me
 chain messages that make you scared
 someone said I was a shit stain on the underwear of life
 people taking the mickey out of me cos I'm adopted.

Then there are the other risks to young children, involving content, contact, gaming and grooming.

Figure 1.1 shows how digitally active younger children are and should convince you that it is never too early to start teaching them to be safe online and on all mobile connected devices.

Figure 1.1 Digital Quotient Chart
Source: http://media.ofcom.org.uk/news/2014/cmr-uk-2014

What do children do online?

Asked in the Cybersurvey what they go online to do, 80 per cent of children aged 10–11 watched videos or films, 78 per cent were gaming, 72 per cent got information for their homework, 60 per cent were messaging friends, 28 per cent were posting photos, 26 per cent were shopping, 17 per cent were using chat rooms or forums and 16 per cent were posting 'about what I am doing'. Fifteen per cent were finding out about gigs, matches or tickets, 5 per cent went online to plan travel and 4 per cent were looking at pages meant for adults.

What do they go online to do?

Sixty per cent said they spent one to two hours a day online and 24 per cent said three to four hours a day. Another 16 per cent said more than five hours a day. Forty-one per cent said their parents limit how many hours they spend online.

Where are they when they go online?

After home (90%) the second most commonly cited location where they accessed the net was at a friend's house, mentioned by half the children. Forty per cent said they did so when 'out and about on my phone'.

What do they experience?

Fifteen per cent said they experienced online aggression, including homophobia, racist bullying and other bullying. Seven per cent had had their personal details hacked or stolen; 11 per cent said they had their social media account hacked. A few had been tricked into buying fake goods, or paying money for something they did not want, but two thirds said none of these had happened to them. Fourteen per cent admit they 'sometimes' try to get round blocks set up to stop them using certain websites. Sixty-four per cent said they always follow the e-safety guidelines they have been taught, more than twice as many as their mid-teen counterparts. It is hoped that if good habits and skills can be instilled at the age of ten there is a better chance they will be competent and safe at 15, but we know that adherence to e-safety advice drops away as they get older. This upper primary moment may be the key age to make a difference and impart problem-solving skills.

Among these 10–11-year-olds, one in five alarmingly reported coming across websites talking about people 'trying to kill themselves', a quarter said they had come across websites 'urging you to be very thin' and 28 per cent had come across 'very violent pictures or videos that you did not want to see'. A similar percentage came across 'nude pictures or videos that you did not search for'. Almost a third had seen websites giving 'advice they thought might be dangerous', and 17 per cent said that they had experienced 'someone who makes you believe that they are a young person, interested in you but they turn out to be someone quite different'. Twenty-three per cent had seen 'websites trying to sell you stuff that might be illegal'. One in five had come across websites promoting hatred or racist views. Only 8 per cent said they had not come across any of these. Twenty-three per cent had been cyberbullied personally.[4]

2014 Cybersurvey stats

responses of 2988 children and young people in Suffolk
www.esafersuffolk.org

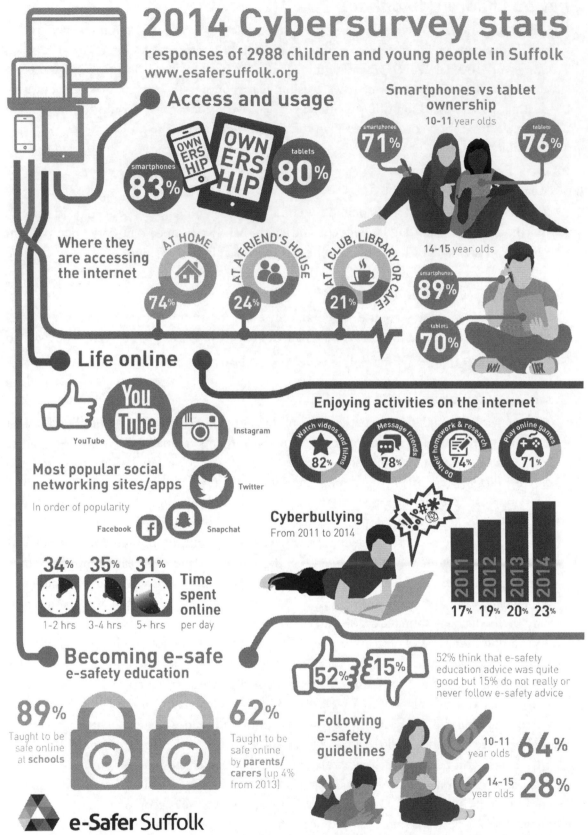

Access and usage

OWNERSHIP
smartphones **83%**

OWNERSHIP
tablets **80%**

Smartphones vs tablet ownership
10-11 year olds

smartphones **71%**

tablets **76%**

14-15 year olds

smartphones **89%**

tablets **70%**

Where they are accessing the internet

AT HOME **74%**

AT A FRIEND'S HOUSE **24%**

AT A CLUB, LIBRARY OR CAFE **21%**

Life online

YouTube

Instagram

Most popular social networking sites/apps
In order of popularity

Facebook   Twitter   Snapchat

Enjoying activities on the internet

Watch videos and films **82%**

Message friends **78%**

Do their homework & research **74%**

Play online games **71%**

Cyberbullying
From 2011 to 2014

2011 **17%** 2012 **19%** 2013 **20%** 2014 **23%**

34% 1-2 hrs
35% 3-4 hrs
31% 5+ hrs

Time spent online per day

Becoming e-safe
e-safety education

89% Taught to be safe online at **schools**

62% Taught to be safe online by **parents/carers** (up 4% from 2013)

52%   **15%**

52% think that e-safety education advice was quite good but 15% do not really or never follow e-safety advice

Following e-safety guidelines

10-11 year olds **64%**

14-15 year olds **28%**

e-Safer Suffolk

The New Context for Teachers

New risks and inspection targets

The new context for teachers, non-teaching staff and social/care workers contains a challenge never encountered before. The country is concerned about radicalisation of young people as war rages in Syria and Iraq, and the Internet is very often the arena in which this plays out. One well-known school failed an inspection because, among other findings, sixth formers were active online with a page said to be linked to various 'extremists'.

Inspectors do an online search before visiting a school. How often does your school do an online search for everything linked to your school? What are parents saying about your school and what are pupils doing online that could be linked to your school? Other current preoccupations with identity are unexpectedly reflected in inspections, which seek to find out if 'students are prepared for life in a modern, diverse, British society', although it is often unclear what this means.

Changes in children's behaviour

On top of this we see how the behaviour of children is changing rapidly. Those aged 9–12 show increased patterns of Internet activity that look like the behaviour of teenagers five to six years ago. Younger school-age children are now doing what 9–12-year-olds used to do, using touch-screen phones and tablets.[5]

Against a backdrop of pop stars making increasingly sexualised videos, it remains true that unwanted sexual jokes or threats are described as the most distressing experiences online when children and young people were asked in the Cybersurvey about the impact of forms of aggressive behaviour. Children aged 10–11 describe their lives in Habbo Hotel, playing in virtual worlds, and 46 per cent having a Facebook page, although they are officially too young as the age group it is intended for is 13+.

One in five has had humiliating photos posted or shared behind their back and 41 per cent claim that rumours were circulated about them. Few are aware of blocks or filters adults may have set up to protect them, yet almost one in five claims to be able to get round these, while a few say they have siblings and friends who can do so. When playing games online they are called names and insulted, but some seem to shrug this off. The more adventurous among them look at videos on YouTube, download music or games, seek out material online for homework, and they begin to hang out with friends online. They read about their favourite sports stars and look at Tumblr, Instagram, Snapchat and Twitter.

At friends' homes they are often online without an adult present. One in five says they have been cyberbullied. They talk below about how it made them feel:

> *It makes you feel no one wants you.*
> *I hated myself.*
> *I couldn't eat or sleep.*
> *It made me feel scared when I went out or when I went to school.*
> *I felt scared and unsure if I should tell anyone, and sad cos I knew it was all true.*

As the last speaker implies, they can begin to believe what is said about them or internalise the position of victim.

Sophisticated grooming attempts

At the extremes, the most vulnerable children can be lured into agreeing to meet someone who might promise to teach them how to win at their favourite game, or find themselves manipulated by clever adults claiming to love and protect them when they need it most, then grooming them for their own purpose over many months of apparent friendship. Are some adults pretending to be children and joining in on Moshi Monsters or Club Penguin? Many people think that paedophiles tend to hang around where children congregate, talk their language and study their likes and dislikes, the better to be able to interact with them convincingly on various platforms.

Children should not be scared away from using the Internet by frightening stories like this, but they should be taught to be alert, never to give their contact details and never to agree to meet someone they have met online. It is good advice to play games with friends you know in the real world and display your faces to one another in the game. If someone unknown to the group joins the game with only an avatar, it should alert everyone to the fact that a new risk has appeared as they do not know who this person is. But groomers can be very plausible, as we saw in the tragic case of Breck Bednar whose mother was suspicious about just such a player. Her conscientious attempts to report her concerns to the police and to talk to her son as she noticed changes in his behaviour were sadly not enough to prevent him secretly going off to meet this man after telling his mother he was going to a friend's house. These cases are not common, but are so dreadful that we need to be on a high state of alert to anything that gives a suggestion that this could be taking place. Educating children walks a fine line between scaring them and making them competent and aware.

A lack of training persists

Schools are finding that pupils' online life intrudes into the life of the school. Their safeguarding and e-safety obligations are rapidly changing, yet staff training appears to be one of the weakest elements of their practice, according to Ofsted.[6]

A fragmented environment

English schools are also working in a new, more fragmented context, as the academies and free schools programme means large numbers of schools are outside the local authority family. While all schools have responsibilities for safeguarding, the responsibility for making the school's IT system safe lies with the proprietor and trust of an academy and not with the local authority. Support services that used to be available to all state schools are now reduced, or offering a lesser or traded service. This can mean a school is only willing to buy a fixed number of sessions, while a child might require more. This increased independence from local authorities, and the loss of considerable amounts of guidance, means a wider variation in threshold levels, varying support and, in many areas, too few places in child and adolescent mental health services, educational psychology, speech therapy and dwindling youth services alongside over-stretched social care services. Even CEOP, the police agency working on online child sexual exploitation, claims to be overwhelmed with cases.

This environment can make referral difficult, but schools must be tenacious in taking a case to the local authority designated officer where required. Safeguarding remains everyone's responsibility.

Helping staff feel more confident

This is an area that training personnel such as pastoral leads and ICT managers will need to consider when providing in-house staff training. If staff feel unsure or anxious about the rapid pace of change in the digital world it can help to anchor this feeling of being out of their depth by discussing the changes they see. By naming these changes, they will soon realise they already have many skills to help guide the children and do not have to 'leave it all to the ICT manager or the geeks'.

Many are reassured to realise that their counselling skills and empathy are just as needed to help children navigate in cyberspace as they are in the real world. Indeed, being someone to trust is an essential role, as long as you know what to do if you receive a disclosure. That is why every single member of staff should be trained. Nobody knows which person will seem right to a desperate child; they will choose a person they have decided to trust; not on the basis of their knowledge, but on their warmth, decency, kindness and general friendliness. The challenge is not to fail them by not knowing what to do and how to preserve evidence.

Start with this discussion as an opener to staff training.

Discussion for teachers and non-teaching staff on rapid change

The following discussion tool can be used by training organisers to help teachers reflect on how rapid the changes have been. It allows people to identify what areas they feel they know a lot about and where they feel they would like to know more.

Put people into small groups and give each group one of the questions in the handout 'Keeping an eye on change' (p.17). They have a discussion for ten minutes and then all the groups report back on what they have discussed. Together they will have an overview of the changes and will have aired their concerns, which can be gathered together by the facilitator.

Before they begin, ask them to put any concerns onto sticky notes.

While they are discussing amongst themselves, sort through the sticky notes and group the queries, putting similar issues together.

Ask the groups to feed back on each of the 'squares' in the diagram, adding in any further items from the answer sheet or suggested additions.

After the feedback discussion, turn to the issues from the sticky notes and ask the groups:

- how well they feel the school's policies and procedures work in cases of this type, and whether changes are needed

- whether they would like training on the issues raised.

Discuss any issues raised that you are able to answer/explain now and plan how to respond to those you cannot address now.

Immediate answers

Short-term plan

Medium-term plan

Longer-term plan

After the discussion it can help to use the staff training needs questionnaire (see below), which gives a snapshot of where to go from here with planning your structured staff training programme in the months ahead, rather than simply inviting in a trainer in an ad hoc way to be able to tick off the issue.

Keeping an eye on changes – questions and answers

What are the changes you see that affect cyberbullying and risky online/mobile phone behaviour?	
What changes in **technology** affect cyberbullying and risky online behaviour?	What changes in **youth culture/icons/music** impact on or are revealed in online cases?
What changes in **provider packages** have had an impact on young people's behaviour?	**Stories in the news** heavily influence youth behaviour. Which have an impact on bullying, hate crime and risky behaviour?
What are the **family issues** you see that affect young people's behaviour?	What are local **neighbourhood issues** you see turning up in youth conflict or abusive cases?
Any other changes? For example, focused grooming, new tactics of abusers, new sites…	

What are the changes you see that affect cyberbullying and risky online/mobile phone behaviour?	
What changes in **technology** affect cyberbullying and risky online behaviour? Mobiles have changed dramatically in very few years: cameras and videos, Internet access, GPS location, apps, services. Webcams, games consoles with Internet access, powerful wi-fi widespread, high-speed downloads. Huge power in the palm of the hand.	What changes in **youth culture/icons/music** impact on or are revealed in online cases? High-profile suicides, sexting. Magazines push images of sex and thinness. Friends move to new SNS or apps – they all go.
What changes in **provider packages** have had an impact on young people's behaviour? 'All you can eat' versus the old dial-up, and pay per minute or GB allows access 24/7.	**Stories in the news** heavily influence youth behaviour. Which have an impact on bullying, hate crime and risky behaviour? Stories about Muslims, war, Middle East, stories about Travellers locally. Anti-Semitism. Public debate about immigration. Denigrating certain groups, disablism. High-profile cases, parents in prison.
What are the **family issues** you see that affect young people's behaviour? Young carers and children in care. Domestic violence. Overstressed parents, or long working hours. Parenting by text, parents break up, bereavement, money worries. Lack of filters, support and knowledge.	What are local **neighbourhood issues** you see turning up in youth conflict or abusive cases? Inter-estate feuds. Local gangs. Fights on buses or at bus stops/between schools. Local substance misuse patterns. Prejudice and racism.
Any other changes? For example, focused grooming, new tactics of abusers, new sites… Self-deleting messages, Snapchat, and apps to save images on Snapchat. Ask.fm, or other anonymous sites.	

Questionnaire for school staff to identify training needs

(This can be adapted to suit the needs of the school.)

Dear Colleague

Thank you for your help with these questions. This is to help us understand your training needs and to aid us in reviewing policy and strategy relating to e-safety and the use of our ICT systems.

The school's Acceptable Use Policy relating to all ITC use

Please circle the number of the statement that most closely reflects your view

1. I have seen it but not used it
2. I have seen it and used it
3. I have seen it but not fully understood it
4. I saw it a long time ago
5. I don't think it applies to me
6. I have not seen it
7. I refer to it frequently in my role
8. I teach it to pupils
9. I teach it to staff

Other:

If you have seen it or used it, please answer the following: (1 = least, 5 = most)

How well does it suit our purpose?	1	2	3	4	5
Is it still up to date?	1	2	3	4	5
Is it comprehensive and thorough?	1	2	3	4	5
Is it easy to understand and act upon?	1	2	3	4	5

Please tell us the aspects of the AUP that require reviewing or updating.

	Yes	Maybe	No
Would you be willing to be involved with a policy review?			
Would you be willing to lead pupils in a policy review?			
Would you be able to lead staff in a learning session?			

How confident are you in the following actions? (1 = not at all, 5 = very)

	1	2	3	4	5
Reporting abuse					
Putting Serious Incident Protocols into action					
Demonstrating privacy settings to pupils					
Tracking incidents/monitoring					
Responding when pupils report cyberbullying					

How aware are you of the following? (1 = not at all, 5 = very)

	1	2	3	4	5
How the school wants you to act in a serious incident					
Advice to staff on contacts with pupils via SNS, mobiles or email					
How professionals can get help if they are bullied online by parents or students					
Protecting your own privacy					
External agencies that can help in cases of cyberbullying, sexting or exploitation of children or young people					
Protecting data/encryption/removing data from school premises					
Taking photographs of school events within the guidelines					
Keeping/saving evidence if a pupil reports incidents of bullying or harassment					
How to get an image removed from a website					
The risks of location software					
Issues of plagiarism and copyright					
The Equality Act 2010					

My training needs

Please identify your priorities for training on a scale of 1–5 (1 = of interest, 5 = priority need). You may add your suggestions in the blank rows.

	1	2	3	4	5
Updates in e-safety advice (e.g. hand-held devices and games consoles with Internet access, BYOD)					
Trends we have noticed within the school and how we might respond					
How to respond to cyberbullying incidents, with case examples					
E-safety for staff					
Embedding our AUP in ICT					
Our anti-bullying policy and strategies					
How to help students with special needs or disabilities to use the Internet safely					
Appropriate responses to cyber-homophobia and other prejudice-related bullying					
Appropriate responses when pupils access sites encouraging anorexia, self-harm or suicidal actions					
Discussions following pupil surveys or incident-monitoring results, e.g. 'How effective is our strategy and how do we know?'					
How to work with parents (our proactive approach) and how to respond when incidents occur (real-life cases)					
My own digital skills					
The Serious Incident Protocol					

Thank you for your response.

What are the risks primary-school children encounter and how well are they prepared?

When planning your e-safety lessons it is good to be aware of messages from young people that show age and gender differences. Not because we want to diminish the message for any group, but rather that we have to find ways to make the e-safety advice relevant and age appropriate. We also need to consider how patterns change fast. Bullying behaviour once seen commonly in girls may spread to boys for example and vice versa. Children with disabilities or special needs may be singled out and you will need to tailor your e-safety lesson to include prejudice-driven behaviour plus support for pupils who may be slower to understand the advice or require it in another format.

The following data are taken from the 2014 Cybersurvey. There are 265 pupils in the primary age group in this sample (slightly more girls than boys). The Cybersurvey has run every year since 2008 in different areas of England. We watch changing trends, gender differences and changes in behaviour. There are currently over 20,000 responses from young people over the life of the survey. Here we look at some recent messages from primary-age children.

Access to the Internet

The way children access the Internet shows a couple of marked gender differences and yet at the same time there are some methods of access on which there is no gender difference at all. These children were all aged 10–11 in the spring of 2014. The major change in recent months can be seen in the shift to tablets. Many families purchased their 10–11-year-olds a smartphone at Christmas 2012–2013, but the following year they were more likely to buy a tablet used by the whole family.

This in turn may be the reason for a slight curb on cyberbullying. Figures remained steady for younger children in 2013–2014 while rising amongst the mid to late teens. A smartphone is more individualised and private, and easier to use to send someone a malicious message, whereas a tablet is shared in the family and not in your pocket on the bus.

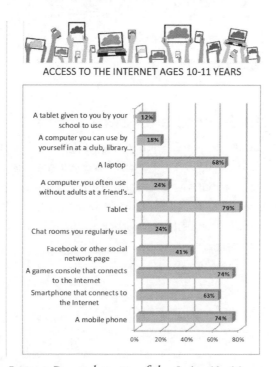

Figure 2.1 Access to the Internet: Do you have any of these? Age 10–11 years

Are there differences between boys and girls?

On the use of tablets and computers 'you can use by yourself' there was no gender difference found, but boys are far more likely to have games consoles and smartphones than girls. There is also no gender difference in the use of chat rooms, which about a quarter of children in this age group claimed they used 'often'. Girls were more likely than boys to use a computer unsupervised at a friend's house (27% vs 21%) and also more likely than boys to use laptops.

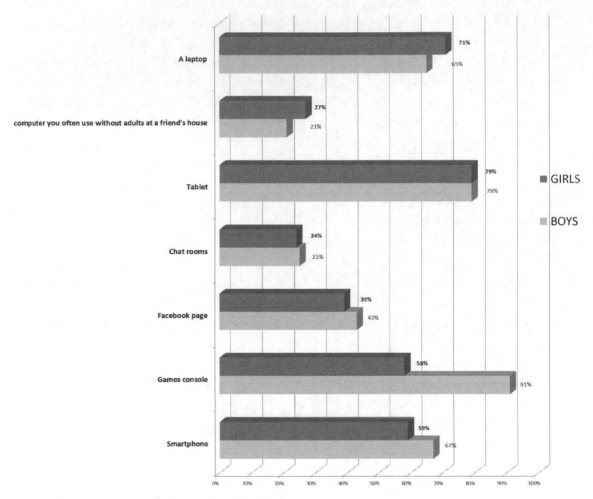

Figure 2.2 Access to the Internet: age 10–11 years

Have you been taught how to stay safe online?

Parents are still more likely to teach their daughters to stay safe online than their sons, but the discrepancy has reduced over the past five years. Girls clearly learn from friends more than boys tend to do, but both girls and boys are using websites to learn about e-safety. This finding could be used in lessons by having girls work in pairs and look up information on recommended websites, and then explain it to each other.

Table 2.1 If you have been taught about e-safety, who taught you?

	Boys (%)	Girls (%)
At school	91	90
By parents	78	83
Another relative	31	32
A friend	23	32
A website	30	29

If you were taught how to stay safe online, how good was this information?

Girls were slightly less likely than boys to think that their e-safety education was very good (69% compared to 73%), but more than a quarter of both boys and girls say it was only 'quite good', and a tiny minority say it was not good enough or useless.

Girls are more likely to say they were taught too late (11% vs 3% of boys). Ninety-two per cent of boys think they were taught at the right time, but girls are less likely to agree (83%).

Do you actually follow the guidelines?

Girls are more compliant than boys and none said they 'never' followed the e-safety guidelines, but when asked for their reasons, these 10–11-year old girls are very fear driven, which seems unfortunate when we want them to enjoy all that the Internet offers.

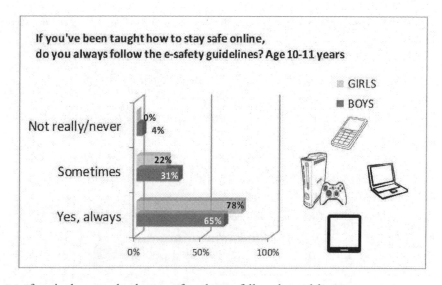

Figure 2.3 If you've been taught about e-safety, do you follow the guidelines?

Reasons boys gave to explain why they do or don't follow the e-safety guidelines

Reasons boys gave for their choices were a mix of understanding that the guidelines helped keep you safe, a recognition of risky situations and also the idea that, to enjoy what the

Internet offers, following the guidelines was worth doing. Below is a selection of answers in their own unedited words.

Because i was taught it at the age of 7
Yes, because if I get into trouble with strangers or someone knows my details
Because I obey the law
Because sometimes i say bad stuff
I only talk to people i know and tell someone if something nasty comes on the screen
It's good to be safe online
When people try to talk to me
Because i want to stay safe online
Sometimes if I'm in trouble
Cause I always Am on computer
Some times and sometimes not
No, I don't now
On the playstation
To make sure that i am safe
Because I want to play/watch things
You could get a scam on a fake site
Always, because it's for your safety
i chose yes always because i know right from wrong
you never know who you are talking to
Because it is dangerous on the Internet but I know what i'm going on
Because it is safe to use. (I don't follow the guidelines all the time)
Because some people are EVIL
Because it keeps you safe
i dont add people on facebook or follow people on twitter if i dont know them
Because it helps me know what to do when i get bullied online
Because there's bad stuff out there
On my console my friends just send me messages sometimes which i dont like sometimes but i just forgive them
Yes because i could get in trouble
Because sometimes I am with my friend I know in real life
I think it is safe but sometimes I can trust the website
Because sometimes people like to be friendly online and sometimes disobey what to do
i always follow the rules of e safety
I always follow these Guidelines, because my settings are friends of friends and when someone i don't know friend requests me i ignore
BECAUSE I NEED TO CONTACT SOMEBODY
Because my mom and dad said not to accept friend requests from strangers
Because there could be strangers on the Internet
Because sometimes it's good to interact with other people

Girls' reasons for their choices

Reasons girls gave for their choices were almost universally connected with perceived danger and keeping safe.

if you get a nasty text
because i want to stay safe for all of my life if I can
i want to stay safe for all of my life and not get in trouble

because you are meant to follow the guide line

because it is very unsafe and i learnt that you should never trust someone online

because I think I'd just forget – there's too much to remember

Because I'm not always in trouble online

i never talk to strangers and i don't give out any personal information

because i feel that i can put photos on the Internet

because i want to put photos on skype and snapchat

To keep safe

because you could always be in trouble at anytime online

i don't want anything bad to happen

i dont share any personal information on any chat rooms

i do because i know it can keep me safe

because then i can be safe online

Danger

I do because I can remember them

So I stay safe

because you can never be sure

I do have an occasion to say which country I am from

because if you don't use e-safety you can be in danger

Because it keeps me safe from scams and viruses

to stay safe

I follow them [the guidelines] because I don't want anything happening to me on the Internet

Because i know if i didint i could be in danger

yes i always follow the guidelines because i know that if i dont i will not be safe!

because i just forget about what they have tought me [she said she only sometimes followed the guidelines]

because they keep me safe and if i didnt i could be in danger

because it keeps me safe

because it will keep me safe on the Internet

so I can be safe

because it keeps me safe

because i know in school teachers can trace back what sites i have visited on the school system

because its important to listen in case you are in danger

because i know that i wouldnt like to be bullied myself if i bullied anyone else

because will feel safer if follow these rules

I always try to and never ever give anyone information about myself

because i feel safer

because if you don't, you wouldn't know what to do if you were bullied or how to stop it and what to do if you see someone else being bullied

on my phone i do not accept unknown numbers or texts

Because if I don't then i could be cyber bullied

I do and i will keep to my word in the future

I follow the guidelines by not going on any website that i have been told not to

YES I ALWAYS DO

i forget

Adult Body Fun Google Internet Mom
Parents
School Teacher

Figure 2.4 Where boys would prefer to get their e-safety information from (Cybersurvey responses)

Google Internet Lesson Look Mom
Parents Safe Safety School Siblings
Friends Teachers Telling Trust Understand

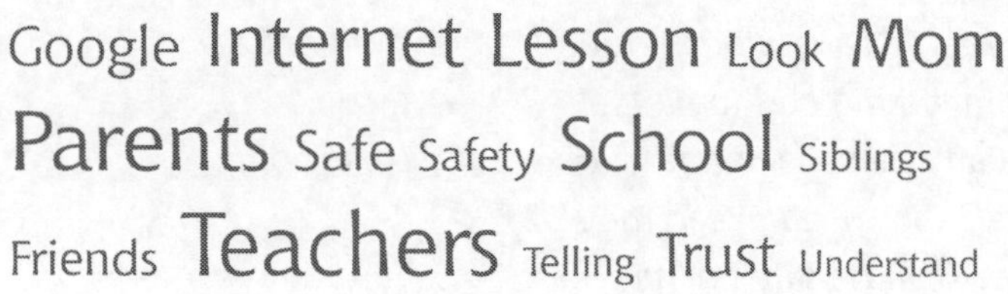

Figure 2.5 Where girls would prefer to get their e-safety information from (Cybersurvey responses)

If you were worried about something you or your friend had experienced online, would you know where to go to get help?

Table 2.2 Seeking help

	Boys (%)	Girls (%)
Yes	81	85
Not sure/No	19	15

What have they experienced by the age of 10–11?

The Internet is a wonderful, exciting place, but just like the real world there are some unpleasant things or people. Have you ever come across the following?

Table 2.3 Internet Experiences

Have you ever come across…	Often		Once or twice	
	Boys (%)	Girls (%)	Boys (%)	Girls (%)
Websites urging you to be very thin?	4	10	12	22
Websites talking about people hurting or trying to kill themselves?	11	13	12	22
Nude pictures or videos that you did not search for?	5	13	23	24
Very violent pictures or videos that you did not want to see?	8	13	26	21
Websites promoting hatred or racist views?	9	14	15	12
Websites giving advice that you think might be dangerous?	13	13	20	21

Someone who makes you believe they are a young person interested in you, but they turn out to be someone quite different?	5	7	9	16
Websites trying to sell you stuff that might be illegal?	11	14	16	15

Sexting

Four boys out of 125 had posted a personal or nude picture they would not want their family to see. Seven girls out of 137 had done the same. Asked if they were pressured into doing this or posted it for fun or in a relationship, one boy wrote, 'Even though i did feel forced I responded as if I was older than him or her and said no.' One girl wrote, 'I always fell scared everyday', and two girls wrote that they had been threatened or bullied because of a selfie like this that they uploaded or sent to someone. Three girls said nothing at all happened after they did this, and two said they were not prepared for what happened when their selfie was shared with other people. Two girls said they had been blackmailed and were told that if they did not send more photos or videos 'they would send them to my family and friends'. Two said, 'I have had a lot of drama over sexy selfies.'

The brutal world of these young children

By the age of 10–11 some of these children had experienced a shocking array of aggressive messages. Some laugh it off; others try to get used to it. Some become very distressed. It is regarded as a test among boys particularly, but increasingly for girls too – that you must be able 'to take it'.

Here is an illustration of racism, homophobia, unwanted sexual jokes, comments and people saying nasty things about you that these young children are beginning to experience. Nearly one in five girls have already been called a 'slut' or 'slag' because of how they dress or behave. While one in ten report requests from strangers to meet up or to provide their location, most are aware of this risk and know what to do. They are more likely to feel devastated by bullying which migrates from life in school to their mobiles or the Internet. Seventeen per cent of girls reported that this had happened to them. More than one in five girls said they got messages showing that people were talking about them nastily online. These are the pupils they will see the next morning and have to sit next to in class, wondering who among them is alienating her friends and alliance building in order to shut her out.

Prejudice should be tackled early

By listening to their experiences, we can shape the e-safety advice we offer and integrate it into Relationships and Social and Emotional Aspects of Learning.

Most of this is not stranger danger but emanates from people in their class, from children they know. Effective whole-school anti-bullying interventions can reduce cyberbullying by half, while all schools should be working to stop racism and homophobia whether online or in the real world.

Almost one in five of these young boys received homophobic insults. This is not going to be addressed fully in an e-safety lesson without work on relationships. Sensitive work is needed to explore stereotypes and prejudice, insults and hurtful behaviour, the stuff of everyday school bullying intervention. If not addressed at this age, we find that prejudice becomes more entrenched as pupils get older and it becomes harder to challenge.

The Internet is seen by many women as a misogynistic environment. This will not change until children of ten are no longer subjected to these insults and cruelty.

Under the Equality Act 2010 every school and public service must be proactive in tackling discrimination. This can mean re-thinking your approach – the anti-bullying policy should interact with equality and e-safety policies and curriculum.

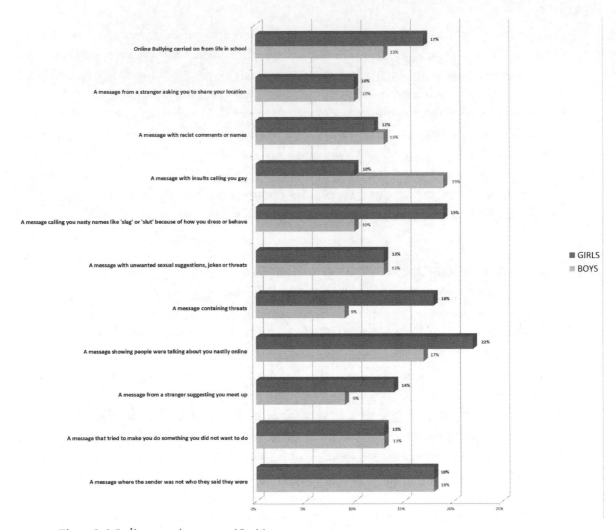

Figure 2.6 Online experiences: age 10–11 years

High-risk messages for 10–11-year-olds

- Eighteen per cent had received a message where the sender was not who they said they were, with a few receiving such a message 'lots of times'.

- Thirteen per cent had received a message that tried to make them do something they did not want to do.

- Fourteen per cent of girls and nine per cent of boys had received a message from a stranger suggesting they meet up.

Types of risk online

	Commercial	Aggressive	Sexual	Values
Content	Adverts Spam So-called 'free' content Personal information	Violent/hateful content Misused images	Pornographic/ unwelcome sexual content	Prejudice: linked to race/disability/ sexual orientation Misleading information/advice, manipulation
Contact	Tracking Harvesting Personal information	Being bullied, harassed, stalked	Meeting strangers Being groomed	Self-harm Unwelcome coercion or pressure to do things or meet up
Conduct	Illegal downloading Hacking, gambling Financial scams Phishing	Bullying or harassing another Threats Rumours Terrorism	Creating and uploading inappropriate/ abusive material 'Sexting' Blackmail about images	Providing misleading information/advice Uploading pro-anorexic photos urging thinness Promoting self-harm

© Adrienne Katz

Figure 2.7 Types of risk online

3

What Do Children Need to Know?

Children as young as two are using tablets and their parents' smartphones to access TV programmes, children's cartoons, games and familiar characters from favourite stories and Disney. At five they are using Club Penguin and finding their TV content, games and music. By eight there are many experienced gamers who are using clubs like Moshi Monsters. Those aged 9–12 show increased patterns of Internet activity that look like the behaviour of teenagers five to six years ago. Younger school-age children are now doing what 9–12-year-olds used to do, using touch-screen phones and tablets. They are going online younger. They tend to begin with club-type sites, virtual pets and purchasing extras for games. They use video-sharing sites, play games, search for information, look for help with homework and socialise with friends. They enjoy virtual worlds.

There is a risk they could compromise their privacy and safety; they could give away their parents' credit card details and identity when using online services unsupervised (e.g. accessing sites such as Amazon where credit card details can be remembered). They could inadvertently come across violence or pornography. They are building up a digital identity from a very young age – they could even have an online presence before they are born, as a photo of them in utero might exist on their parents' Facebook page!

But while staying safe through all of this can seem complicated to adults, it needs to be made simple, consistent and clear for the sake of young children. Don't be the voice of doom! Most children are actually OK online. Many value their sense of autonomy and enjoy solving problems. We need to teach them how to do this in an enjoyable way. The Internet is thrilling; it offers endless possibilities. It represents their future leisure, entertainment, education and social lives and most probably their work life too.

- *Make it simple*: Use easy, enjoyable ways for children to remember messages.

- *Be consistent*: Too much information and different messages are a turn-off.

- *Be practical*: Practical demonstrations deliver the message and ensure children understand and get a chance to test and practise their skills.

- *Make it relevant*: Children want to know why they have to learn these things when all they want to do is enjoy the fun online.

One way would be to try to scare them into doing what we ask. This way failure lies. The Internet is not only thrilling and exciting, it is an enabling, creative and communicative world in which they are going to live and earn their living. Help them to explore, to reason and to make decisions about how they will manage this online environment. It is a dialogue or partnership between adult and child, not a command–control approach.

Components of e-safety for primary-age children

The curriculum for England sets out eight themes:

- Internet safety
- Privacy and security
- Relationships and communication
- Cyberbullying
- Digital footprint and online reputation
- Self-image and identity
- Information literacy
- Creative credit and copyright.

When thinking about translating these themes into the everyday lives of young children I have suggested the components below, along with the idea of colour-coding the information given about each one and using that colour consistently in classroom displays materials, helping children to understand the themes in a coherent way.

Too many children say they are overwhelmed with too much information or confused when learning about different elements of e-safety all in one lesson. Others ask us to make it more practical! So having asked them what they actually do online, here are some components of their lives online.

E-safety

Children learn that, to enjoy and explore what the Internet can offer and to collaborate with others, they need some basic rules about staying safe. Children learn about the SMART rules to help them do this.[7] Their understanding and recognition of risk grows and develops with age.

Privacy

Children learn several ways to keep their privacy protected. They understand what constitutes personal information and they learn about usernames and passwords. They understand why they need to take these steps.

Safe search

Children learn to search for information and to question the credibility and accuracy of search results and information they obtain online.

Copyright

Children learn to acknowledge the owner of the work and not to copy and paste information as if it is their own work. They learn to interpret what they find in their own words and credit the original where needed.

Digital footprint

Children learn to be careful about what they upload or say online and respect their own and others' privacy. They understand that material they post or upload can be around for others to find, leaving a permanent digital footprint. They learn to protect photos they decide to upload or post.

Cyberbullying

Children learn about treating one another with respect, they understand what to do if they experience aggression or cyberbullying online and they help their friends if they experience this. They work to prevent bullying in their setting.

Safe relationships

Children learn to make safe relationships, understanding that friendship online can be very different to real friends offline. They learn to edit friends' lists on social networks and to behave safely as good digital citizens. They understand the risks of unsafe contact. They learn to use the appropriate language for the circumstance. They know how to get help if anything worries them or makes them uncomfortable online.

Downloads

Children learn about download risks and how to be aware of scams, phishing and unsafe attachments. They begin to recognise and become more skilled at distinguishing adverts from content.

Uploads

Children learn to post photos and comments online selectively and with care and to take steps to ensure photos are protected. They understand privacy settings and tags. They do not use photos of other people disrespectfully.

Play safe

Children learn of risks when playing online games, they understand about contact with players they have never met and can confidently take themselves out of a game or chat room and report any problems to an adult. They play games appropriate to their age.

Safe shopping

Children learn to look for trusted online retailers, checking security symbols and the URL before using a family credit card. They learn that apps and games could have hidden costs although they seem free at first.

Safe phones

Children learn to use their mobile phones safely. Location services should be off. Texting others is fun but there are some things that we should not do. Never pass on chain letters, rumours about other people or threatening messages. If they are contacted by anyone they do not know or feel uncomfortable about anything, they know how to seek help. Phones should not be used for cyberbullying.

Safe talk

Safe talk covers all forms of communication including texting, messaging, emailing, chat and apps as well as chat in games and phone calls. Children learn to communicate and collaborate safely and appropriately with others online. They learn to recognise risky situations and know how to block a sender, save evidence and get help.

Secure users

All these components contribute to children becoming secure, competent and confident web users, taking on new devices, software and apps, and conducting themselves safely.

1. WHAT IS E-SAFETY?

Do you think it is A, B or C? Circle the one you think it is.

A. It teaches you how electric gadgets can be safely used

B. It teaches you about health and safety when using an electronic tablet, laptop or mobile

C. It teaches you how to be safe online or on your smartphone

2. WHO SHOULD BE RESPONSIBLE FOR E-SAFETY?

A. Parents

B. My school

C. Me

D. My older brother or sister

E. All of us together

3. WHICH OF THESE DO YOU THINK IS TRUE?

A. I only play games online so I don't have to worry about e-safety

B. I keep all my documents and photos in a cloud so I don't need e-safety

C. My parents trust me so I don't need e-safety

D. I do not have a Facebook page so I don't need e-safety

If you did not think any of these statements above are true, please explain in your groups why you thought this.

4. ## ONLINE THERE ARE WONDERFUL THINGS WE CAN DO BUT THERE ARE ALSO SOME RISKS. PLEASE THINK ABOUT THIS AND PREPARE TO EXPLAIN YOUR IDEAS ABOUT THE RISKS TO THE GROUP OR CLASS.

A. There are risks from other people

B. There are risks from hackers who use software to find out passwords

C. Everything you post online could hang around for ever or get shared

D. I might meet someone online who is not who they say they are

WHAT OTHER RISKS CAN YOU SUGGEST?

How can you protect yourself from harm? You learn to cross the road safely, so what do you think you need to learn to use the Internet safely?

Share your ideas with the group.

List them and put them into order, with the most important ones at the top.

Give them to your teacher.

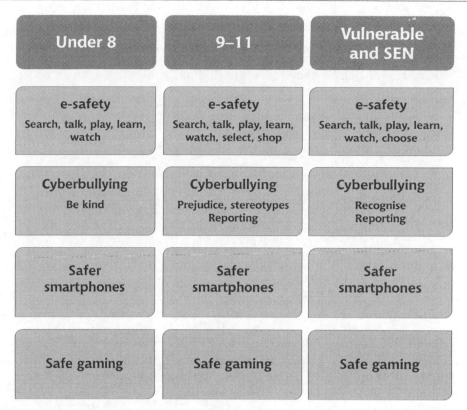

Under 8	9–11	Vulnerable and SEN
e-safety Search, talk, play, learn, watch	**e-safety** Search, talk, play, learn, watch, select, shop	**e-safety** Search, talk, play, learn, watch, choose
Cyberbullying Be kind	**Cyberbullying** Prejudice, stereotypes Reporting	**Cyberbullying** Recognise Reporting
Safer smartphones	**Safer smartphones**	**Safer smartphones**
Safe gaming	**Safe gaming**	**Safe gaming**

Figure 3.1 Build incrementally on what has gone before

The curriculum

Early years foundation stage

Children should learn:

- to talk appropriately and share information and photos, by email, Google Hangout, texts or messaging to communicate with real people within their schools, families and communities.
- to play games on cbeebies or suitable apps on phones
- to learn and find out about things with a grownup they trust
- to watch tv programmes and favourite film or video
- to look for things we want to know, watch or listen to, with a grownup
- to be careful to tell a grownup about anything you don't like seeing online
- to take photos with a mobile phone or tablet

Key Stage 1

Children should learn:

- to respect others
- friendship attributes
- that the Internet offers exciting and positive opportunities to learn and play
- to use technology safely and respectfully
- to behave positively online

- to keep personal information private

- to know where to go for help and support

- where to get help if they are worried about content or contact on any device or online

- safe searching using keywords and sites they like

- to use caution when opening files

- why personal information should be kept private

- safe contact: how to communicate with others online and on mobiles.

Key Stage 2

Children should learn:

- *to use search technologies effectively*: understand how to use key words, appreciate how results are selected and ranked, be discerning in evaluating digital content

- *to use technology safely, respectfully and responsibly*: recognise acceptable and unacceptable behaviour, identify a range of ways to report concerns about content or contact, behave positively online

- *what we mean by personal information*: what it is, what to share and what not to share, that photos and videos can share information, that they could be sharing other people's personal information.

In Upper Key Stage 2, children should learn:

- that many sites have settings that allow a user to restrict what information can be seen publicly

- about unwanted contact and identity theft

- about copyright and ownership

- that everything we say or share online can hang around forever, this is our digital footprint.

Sex and relationships education in the age of the smartphone

It has always been a challenge to prepare children for positive and healthy relationships in a gradual and appropriate way. But whereas it once meant the dreaded talk from a parent on the birds and bees, or the 'how to respect yourself' school lesson, in today's world it is all this and more. Now this task must include paying attention to relationship etiquette online too.

Children's physical, moral and social development needs to be supported so that they can understand themselves, respect others and eventually sustain healthy adult relationships. But along the way they will be negotiating friendships and relationships online and via their mobiles. First love, friendship breakdowns, rejection and prejudice are today all played out in cyberspace, often in front of an audience.

Most children and young people are engaged in managing and tweaking their reputation as they present to the world the sunlit or rose-tinted image of themselves they choose to display – usually showing them to be popular, having a stunning time, always at the heart of things and most certainly not bored and lonely at home.

But here lies risk: take the girl in the Cybersurvey who listed 'lover' among her hobbies and love of fluffy kittens, or the boy who felt his opening move in a relationship with a girl would be aided by sending a photo of his penis. These examples demonstrate how immaturity can lead to long-term risks and problems that could hang around in a digital footprint until the day a prospective employer or partner finds it in a search.

In a risk-averse but sexualised era when even adverts or pop videos reveal more than would have been deemed OK in the swinging sixties, we learn of young people seeking or sharing pornography at a rate never before researched. Headlines tell us that this will affect young people's expectations and be extremely damaging to their future relationships.

Against this backdrop, children and young people need to be prepared for life in a digital future we cannot even imagine. So where do you start? For one thing, personal, social, health and economic education (PSHE) is not a statutorily required subject despite the fact that the DfE expects all schools to teach it.[8] For another, the curriculum has been thought by many to be outdated with regard to the Internet for years. For example, a recent subject report by Ofsted found that 'PSHE education required improvement or was inadequate in 40%' of cases.[9] But there is a glimmer of light. The PSHE Association has created a sample curriculum,[10] and there is new sex and relationships education (SRE) guidance that takes account of the Internet.[11]

Whilst I recommend you explore these, I would also say it is necessary to integrate the e-safety advice in a natural way into every area of the curriculum, especially into anti-bullying work and work on relationships and friendships. The old idea of discrete subjects is not valid. All of these interact and work together to give guidance to a young person on how to conduct themselves in the 21st century.

No 'one size fits all' in e-safety: a three-tier strategy is needed

For more vulnerable pupils extra support will need to be given. Children with special needs may not understand or remember the e-safety rules, while for children in care there may be other risks they take in their efforts to locate family members or to be in touch with people from their old neighbourhood. Research has shown that young carers are particularly vulnerable to being cyberbullied and they say that the e-safety education they have received was not good enough.

Responses from young people to the Cybersurvey, now in its seventh year, show us that delivering one universal format of e-safety education is simply not enough. While this universal level is suitable for the majority, there is a sizable group for whom it does not do enough. I propose a three-tier strategy, as illustrated in Figure 3.3.

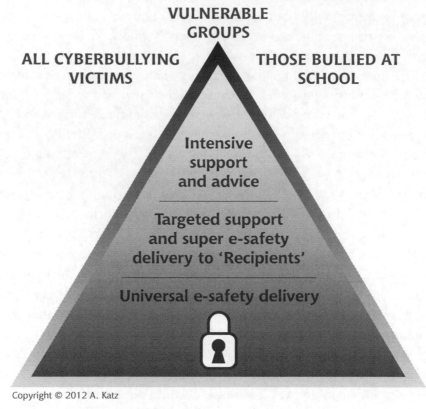

Figure 3.3 Three-tier approach to e-safety education

'Recipients' are children receiving abuse or aggression, including cyberbullying, online. They are possibly bullied in school and there is a risk that this might migrate to cyberbullying. This group also includes people with special educational needs and anyone who for whatever reason may require a top-up on universal delivery.

Intensive support and advice is for those few children who are cause for concern. Their online behaviour is high risk, they may self-harm or be an anorexic, they may be depressed or anxious and they might of course have any other major worry due to home life. They are often known to be vulnerable and the school may be providing some form of support to them already, but does this include advice and help to stay safe online? These may be the very children who are seeking intimacy or friendship online. They may also be easily persuaded or coerced into doing things they do not want to do. If a student has once shared a nude selfie and you are aware of this, they are candidates for the intensive support group. At any time they could be blackmailed. If a child has a parent in prison, they could be harmed by hateful messages sent by local people who know this.

Considering the needs of different pupil groups and pupils with additional needs

The approaches below are suggestions only; no single one will work for every group of children. Some children will need reasonable adjustments to help them access e-safety advice in ways that are adapted for them. E-safety advice may be given in an illustrated format – see Mencap's advice for creating this type of instruction sheet.[12]

Visually impaired children

Among the difficulties that visually impaired students may experience are problems in identifying logos, report buttons and on-screen instructions. They could fail to identify inappropriate content. They might need further help in identifying certain types of risk online, such as when something might look suspicious. Recorded voice-overs with PowerPoint slides can be useful as they can listen and enlarge the slides and play and replay them at their own pace. The ability to enlarge the text and images on screen may be a boon to them.

Behavioural, emotional and social difficulties

Pupils with behavioural, emotional and social difficulties (BESD) tell us that they are often online more hours per day than their peers. They may be left to play games in their room by parents or introduced to activities online in school because they are thought to be engaged or simply 'less trouble' that way. But there are many risks to navigate to ensure they are operating safely so that they can be engaged positively in their learning and development. They can be introduced to blogging and social media in safe ways, use technology to help each other and make safe searches to find out information on staying safe. Parents need to be alerted to PEGI ratings on games so that they can check whether a game is suitable for their child or not. They may be bullied or bully others and will need support to calmly apply their e-safety advice and guidance. Social stories may be useful to help them understand their e-safety education.

Speech, language and communication needs

For pupils with speech, language and communication needs (SLCN), information and communication technology (ICT) can unlock communication and help students develop written communication as well as make videos.[13] While the use of social media can have an impact on the development of writing and communication, it is important to get the right assistive technology for the student and also to watch out for excessive use, as some people develop repetitive strain injuries or posture problems. Some students with SLCN who are badly bullied may turn to the Internet and social media to retaliate. Online they could find the power they lack in social situations. This can be risky and lead them into situations where there is flaming, retaliation and trolling.[14]

Autistic spectrum disorder

In general, ICT can be used as a positive tool for students with autistic spectrum disorders, some of whom show a special aptitude and understanding of the logic of computer code. But if they are isolated from other children and spend too much time alone on screen it could lead to some loss of social development. If they have these excellent digital skills it may help to invite a student to show someone else how to do certain steps online. Students will need to use devices with filters and be monitored to ensure their online life is safe.

English as an additional language

Huge challenges face schools where pupils may speak any of at least 300 different languages. I have visited a London school where more than 100 languages were spoken. How can a school monitor or filter students communicating in their home language with people all over the world? On the other hand, ICT is a gateway to rich opportunities for students to stay in contact with their heritage and learn about others' backgrounds and history, music and food, costume and customs. It can help students learn English as English has become a global language.

Impress upon them the importance of Acceptable Use Policy (AUP), check with them as often as possible that they know how to report anything troubling, and adjust or translate the training materials where necessary.

If a student is newly arrived from another country, an early check on their e-safety knowledge is vital. They may have missed the lessons in your school and you will need to top them up.

Looked after children

When a child is placed in a children's home or in foster care, there is a scheme to provide them with access to modern technologies. But because there are many dangers for these children, the care system has understandably put in place a range of protective measures. Young people will often circumvent the filters and rules in the care setting by using a smartphone on wi-fi when out and about. They might be given a flash mobile phone by a 'friend'. This is an alarming sign. Girls are often groomed by so-called boyfriends who want to control them all day and night via this phone. They might tell them they love them, and give the phone as a 'gift' to prove this. But later, girls are misused within gangs or threatened and hurt in other ways.

Children in the care system may be searching online for former friends and relatives, unaware of the reason they were taken from the family of origin for their own safety.

The danger of them planning to meet up with someone they meet online is high. Many children in care have a history of suffering abuse; they are also reporting high levels of bullying and cyberbullying. Therefore this group needs the highest level of protection and awareness of the risks. They need enhanced e-safety education. Safeguarding young people in both the real and virtual world is part of the duty of care that applies to everyone working with young people. Safeguarding is everyone's business. It is therefore important that the school has identified looked after children and monitors the success of any interventions by careful follow-up work.

Young carers

Young carers are doing heroic work caring for family members with responsibilities way beyond their years. Yet because of this they may miss out on some of the socialising their friends are doing. This can lead them to go online and look for friendship, intimacy, affirmation and validation. Everyone wants someone to say, 'You look cool', 'I like you', and so on. At home, if a parent is very ill, he or she may not be able to have those conversations about staying safe online. Young carers are another group reporting high levels of bullying and cyberbullying and they also say their e-safety education is lacking.

Online terms to explain to the children

- A *blog* is like an online diary where the writer (blogger) writes often about their daily life or their thoughts on the news or what is happening.

- A *chat room* is an online space called a 'forum' where people can chat to others at the same time. Some focus on one thing like music or movies, and people meet to talk about these.

- A *file-sharing program* lets users share films, music and photos.

- A *geolocation service* or *GPS* can let other people know where you are when you send a message with a photo or want to see where your friends are. Facebook and other popular sites may use this to let people know where you are even if you do not want this to be shown to people you do not know. You can switch off this service.

- *Grooming* is when someone you usually do not know tries to become friends with you to force you into doing something that you do not want to do.

- *Instant messaging* is a service that lets people instantly share messages with their friends.

- *Malware* that may harm your computer includes viruses, spyware, adware and browser hijacking software.

- On a *social networking service* (SNS) you have a page about yourself – your profile – and you can send and receive messages from your 'friends'. People post messages about what they are doing and try to make it seem fun and interesting. You can set your SNS so that only your friends and family can see your page. But remember, your photos and messages stay online forever. Unless they are set up for children, many social networks are meant for over 13 years old and some are for adults.

- A *URL* is the real address of a website. URLs can be useful to check that you are not on a fake version of the site you want. Always check the address bar to see that the address is the same as on adverts, store receipts and letters. See more at: www. knowthenet.org.uk/knowledge-centre/spotting-fake-site#sthash.JV2psK7E.dpuf

4

What Do Schools Need to Have in Place?

Coherent practice relies on stepping back and taking an overview of all the policies and strategies your school has in place and somehow linking the pieces of the jigsaw into one picture. Even then the 'picture' needs to be refreshed and evaluated to stay alive. It also needs to be communicated. In this chapter we look at what schools need to have in place for effective e-safety. Schools should provide:

- leadership and management
- behaviour and safety
- staff training.

Schools should also consider how to address:

- policy and procedure
- e-safety training and infrastructure
- cross-policy links
- communications strategy
- serious incident management – safeguarding and child protection
- the law – is your school compliant?
- new ways of doing things with BYOD (bring your own device)
- general anti-bullying work
    - o recognising bullying of all types
    - o raising awareness
    - o prevention, including teaching e-safety
    - o response when incidents occur
    - o recording and monitoring
    - o staff training
    - o pupil peer support training
    - o engaging parents
    - o complaints procedure for parents.

A cycle of reflective practice

Keeping the strategy alive involves a cycle of prevention and review that is continuous – there is no end point! With each new term and intake, awareness-raising begins anew. Policy planning and strategy have to be responsive to what is happening among pupils and what your data tell you.

Mindlessly repeating what you did last year may be acceptable on the surface, but does not take into account new devices, apps and messaging services. It overlooks new behaviours that have popped up and national or international trends that have come to dominate since last year – witness the selfie craze! Who could have imagined in 2012 that the president of the most powerful country in the West would be in on the trend within twelve months? Who can forecast the next craze?

Reflective practice demands that we evaluate. The ongoing process of collecting data and the views of the 'clients' – your pupils and their parents – will lead you to tweak your strategy, update your information and re-think your communication plans.

At the same time everyone has one eye on best practice guidance and what the inspection process requires. The rise of rather militant parents who lay the blame for out-of-hours cyberbullying at the school's door, the 24/7 character of cyberbullying and the powers schools have to discipline pupils for behaviour that takes place off premises all combine to bring schools into the front line of intervention.

This chapter will look at what schools need to have in place and why. But first take a look at the cycle of reflective practice (Figure 4.1).

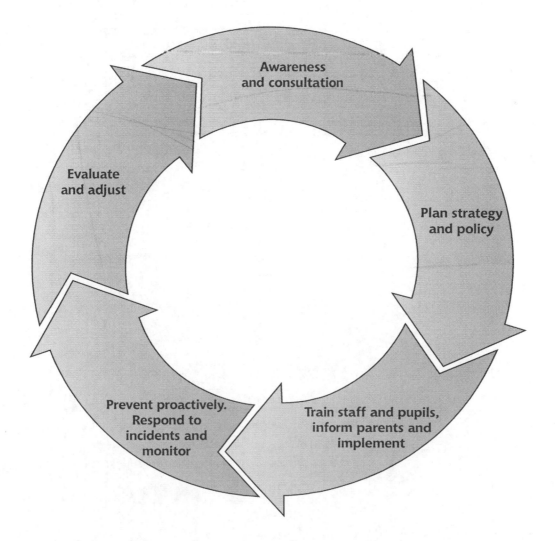

Figure 4.1 Cycle of reflective practice

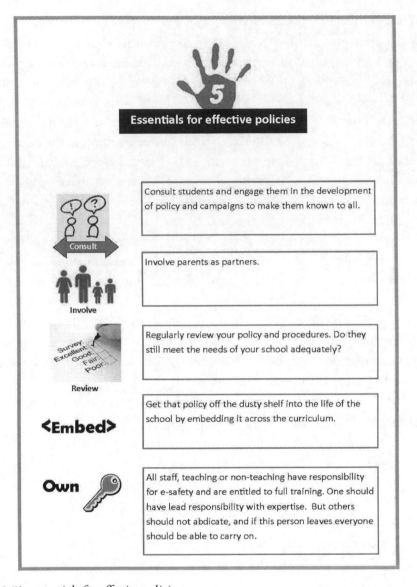

Figure 4.2 Five essentials for effective policies

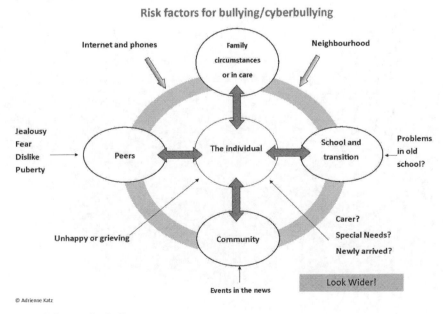

Figure 4.3 Risk factors for bullying

BYOD – using learners' own devices in the classroom

'BYOD' traditionally stands for 'bring your own device'; it can be used in a formal education programme in which a student learns at least partly through online delivery of content and instruction, with some element of student control over time, place, path or pace.

If it feels like a whirlwind of choices and responsibilities against a rapidly changing backdrop – it is! But others have done it with great success and it is clearly the way of the future.

In your planning you will want to explore and weigh up the advantages and disadvantages, then plan for the change. Here are a few points to consider.

What are the advantages?

- Budget impact is low

- Encourages and develops anywhere, anytime learning

- Students can access any web-based functions or learning platforms and network resources

- Empowers students with the choice of their own device when working together, alone or on homework

- Prepares students for the modern world of work

- Promotes independent learning as students can access and edit their own files

- Gives shy students opportunities to shine in a collaborative platform

- Slow students are helped by the collaborative platform

- Students develop self-discipline using devices in the allotted time

- Students find it easy to use devices they are already familiar with when they do their school work – it can therefore seem natural

- A broader range of functions are available to students in the classroom and out, such as video capture for field trips

- Dedicated apps can be downloaded onto all devices for specific purposes

- It can ease the pressure on shared resources in the classroom.

What challenges should be considered?

- Digital equity for all students

- High risk of distraction for students

- Teacher management of all the devices in the room

- Setting up the networking infrastructure for the new demands

- ICT manager issues – worries about security, firewalling sectors of the school system and having to problem solve on many devices

- Network safety – keeping your primary network safe

- There is the need to re-think your Acceptable Use Policy (AUP) – does it cover software licensing, virus protection and software updates, as well as turning off a phone's 3G capability while it is being used in the classroom?

- Training teachers and staff

- Obtaining the right new solutions – i.e. Windows and Mac computers can both run agents which would allow the teacher to view the student's desktop remotely, for example RM Tutor on CC4

- Mobile solutions vary in quality

- Parental agreements

- The risk of introducing viruses into the school's network.

Infrastructure and technology

Infrastructure describes the school ICT network and its related component parts and systems across the whole organisation (or venue if it is a service for children). Whenever an organisation provides services to children and young people and ICT is offered, they should:

- Undertake a full e-safety risk assessment on all the systems and devices in use. Maintain updated infrastructure that is responsive and appropriate.

- Some schools today are running ICT systems that are as complex as those in a small business but with added data security requirements more like those in a medical practice.

- These systems are often supplied by an external IT company and the commissioning conditions may govern the extent to which an individual school can request changes. Develop safe infrastructure including firewalls and encryption software to isolate the school's main site and protect data.

- Have distinct online areas that students and staff can access. Many schools now use software that creates a site especially designed for education, called a virtual learning environment (VLE). Programmes such as Moodle allow school staff to set assignments, tests and activities and to track their learners' progress. A VLE might only be available from the school network, or might be accessible from any Internet connection (i.e. from home or the student's own device).

Filtering tools should:

- subscribe to the Internet Watch Foundation (IWF) Child Abuse Images and Content (CAIC) URL list

- block 100 per cent of illegal material identified by the IWF

- be capable of blocking 90 per cent of inappropriate content in each of the following categories:

  o pornographic, adult, tasteless or offensive material

  o violence (including weapons and bombs)

  o racist, extremist and hate material

  o illegal drug taking and promotion.

BYOD: Ten things to address[15]

Schools may issue tablets to students or they may consider having them bring their own devices into class. If you are weighing up these options, here are some points to consider.

1. Think through why you need this option and list the benefits – what educational goals are being met by BYOD?

2. Prepare a thorough plan before you try to get approval from senior management and parents. Be ready to answer questions.

3. Decide on a list of devices to be allowed on site. Determine whether you will allow wi-fi connectivity or 3G/4G connectivity.

4. Review and update your AUP for ICT so that staff, pupils and parents are aware of the changes and how the new rules apply. Ensure buy-in from everyone.

5. You will need to limit the times when IT support will be offered, and outline what IT support will or won't do. (They won't fix personal devices.) Have people signed to show that they have understood this?

6. Train your teachers to deliver lessons across multiple platforms.

7. Make provision for those who do not have their own device and draw up terms and conditions for using devices that belong to the school. Work out how many supplementary devices you will need to purchase and store.

8. Prepare your network. Is your wireless infrastructure ready for the new demands that will be made on it?

9. Ensure your primary network is secure – divert personally owned devices onto a separate LAN and ensure filtered access through the LAN. Security walls can separate this area from your main system.

10. Provide a platform for this new 'anywhere, anytime learning' – it will need to be compatible with any device students and teachers can access for schoolwork or group discussions, assignments, resources and submissions.[16]

Be well prepared but remain flexible. Try to visit schools that have adopted this approach and learn about the challenges you might face while looking for bright ideas.

Percolate

Your e-safety education will need to become embedded in every part of the curriculum. This is a far more effective approach than single-event sessions with a guest speaker who leaves and then is not in school to provide any follow-up discussions or answer questions. So blended learning ideas need to percolate through the curriculum.[17]

Establishing a peer support programme

The participation of the pupils is a crucial element of a coherent approach. This piece of the jigsaw includes finding ways for them to 'own' the strategy. One visible and tangible method is to train peer mentors or buddies.

First decide on the aims and anticipated outcomes of the support scheme you plan to set up. There are many different forms:

- friendship schemes

- mediation between pupils or groups of pupils

- mentoring (academic and social)

- counselling.

All seek to provide children or young people with some form of support from their own peers. Many schools look for peer support schemes to reduce bullying and the time spent by teachers sorting out minor fall-outs. Others aim to improve reading grades or other academic success.

The BIG Award, a national award programme run by the Bullying Intervention Group (BIG) that rewards schools and services for children for excellence in bullying intervention, looks for a peer support scheme that helps with friendship and support, offers a route to report problems and trains pupils to recognise all forms of bullying. These peer supporters contribute to a school's Bullying Intervention Focus Group (in which the views of all pupils, staff and parents are brought together) and help set the school's approach and strategy.

Training peer supporters and staff

Can children really be trusted to counsel other children? What happens if bullies are amongst the peer supporters? What if they say the wrong thing and make things worse? What if they spread other people's secrets?

Providing children undergo good-quality training and that appropriate safety measures are put in place, these concerns generally prove unfounded. This does not mean you should not remain alert to the possibilities – but if good support is given to the team and careful debriefing is in place, it is safe to go ahead.

Key to success are three elements:

- careful selection of the peer supporters

- thorough training

- support from a teacher responsible for the scheme.

Selection

Peer supporters need to be carefully auditioned and selected. Avoid appointing a clique of powerful friends. Equally avoid choosing all the peer supporters from people who have been bullied themselves or who are seen as weak. You want the group to be seen as credible with a good mix of strong, sociable, popular people and those who have been bullied and have true empathy with potential victims. Ask people to give reasons why they would like to be a peer supporter and what they will bring to the role. Look to appoint people from different year groups.

They will be dealing with sensitive issues and a lot of emotion! They will need to be committed – no dropping out half way through the term – and discreet and level headed.

Training

The training should include effective listening, training on confidentiality matters and some scenarios in which they explore real-life cases and work out what to do in these circumstances. Some clear rules or protocols need to be in place. They cannot promise total confidentiality to those they help – in cases where the client is at risk the peer supporter must share this with the teacher in charge even if they are implored not to tell anyone. This can be very hard.

Mediation approaches do not tell the person what to do but explore possible options with them. They identify the harm they feel has been caused and work with the perpetrator to try to have them recognise the harm they have caused and make amends. Mediation is only suitable in some types of cases. In other situations a victim needs someone to walk with them at playtime, sit with them at lunch or simply be there for them to talk to for advice now and then. The presence of peer supporters in a school is known to make many pupils feel safer, even if they have never been personally bullied. Peer supporters tend to run awareness campaigns, design logos and wear a badge or uniform – a cap, sweatshirt or tabard. It is something that should be on their record as a contribution to the life of the school. Peer supporters can feed back to the teacher or the focus group any new trends they are spotting.

When someone tells a peer supporter something very upsetting it may affect their judgement. It can be hard to be objective. The problem presented to the peer supporter is very often not the real problem at all. Peer-support training will include teaching the children a series of questions to ask. Though these provide a framework for the supporters to work from, peer supporters cannot know what to expect and should be prepared and supported thoroughly. Training includes:

- active listening
- presentation skills
- conflict management
- facilitation
- problem-solving
- summarising
- building rapport
- assertiveness
- managing mediation.

Ownership

Peer supporters are likely to have greater ownership of the system if they help plan how it will be run on a daily basis. They will need to consider:

- a catchy name and logo
- how to advertise their service – mine enjoyed using an assembly involving plenty of role-play at the initial launch
- when and where it will run
- how they will be identifiable to other students
- how long they will serve and how they will integrate newly selected peer supporters – i.e. when Year 6 leaves.

Support

They need a lot of support when they are told something in confidence and are upset by it. They may feel very loyal to the person who disclosed this because they trusted the peer supporter. Training helps them know when to report cases to the teacher in charge. That is why debriefing sessions are vital. Never leave a young child worrying over a case he or she has heard that day. Record-keeping and action plans should all be regularly reviewed.

Providing children undergo good-quality training and that appropriate safety measures are put in place, the peer support scheme can turn out to be a very valuable contributor to the ethos of the school. It demonstrates that pupils can be responsible, take a lead and help one another.

Proper training matters

A full training package will incur costs, but when the benefits, both emotional and academic, are considered, these are minimal. Before a new peer support scheme is set up, staff must understand its purpose and limits. They need to designate someone who will give the time to it that is required, and all staff should enthusiastically help 'advertise' it to their classes. Moreover, the leading staff must be given the time and resources to implement and run the system effectively. Peer supporters have told us that when it is led by an individual who is also the headteacher they are often too busy to give the scheme the time it requires! It is therefore useful for the leading staff to undergo the same training as the peer supporters. This way, they will understand the rationale and methods of the system and how to ensure that it is effective in practice.

To develop a thorough training programme, advice and training is given by the BIG Award.

Netta Cartwright's book *Peer Support Works* is a user-friendly manual that is well worth reading.[18]

Getting the programme running

How do you select your peer supporters? Some schools like children to apply for the job; others prefer to hand-pick or choose those recommended by other teachers. However, bear in mind that if you only choose 'good role models' as your supporters, who will the more mischievous child identify with and feel comfortable talking to?

Whatever form of peer support chosen, there is little doubt that the presence of such a system benefits both the peer supporters and their clients. Furthermore, it is a good advert for the school, showing that it takes the wellbeing of its students seriously and promotes a positive ethos.

Top tips for sustainable peer support

- Don't rush it – set it up carefully and work to sustain it.
- Buy in good-quality training.
- Train staff as well as pupils.
- Select a range of personality types as peer supporters and keep the group credible.
- Give the peer supporters status and make sure that they are clearly identifiable.
- Ensure that there are sensible, easy-to-follow safeguarding procedures in place.
- Hold regular, effective meetings with the peer supporters.

- Top up their skills training occasionally via visits from peer supporters in other schools.

- Make sure that children know when and where they can receive help.

- Create a suitable and comfy space where the peer supporters will see clients without everyone knowing.

- Don't put the headteacher in charge of it! Pupils say that headteachers are too busy to have time for the support required and the pupils cannot access the headteacher as often as they need to in order to report concerns.

While adults are the intended readers of the majority of your policies, there are some that should have a child-friendly version that children know and understand. Anti-bullying and staying safe messages should be given in the clearest possible style. Figure 4.4 is an example of the work done by Holmer Lake Primary School as part of their comprehensive project on keeping children safe. As well as creating jingles for local radio, children from this primary school gave presentations in conferences and training events, were supported to develop a programme to share safeguarding messages with other local schools and increased their own confidence and competence in a remarkable way.

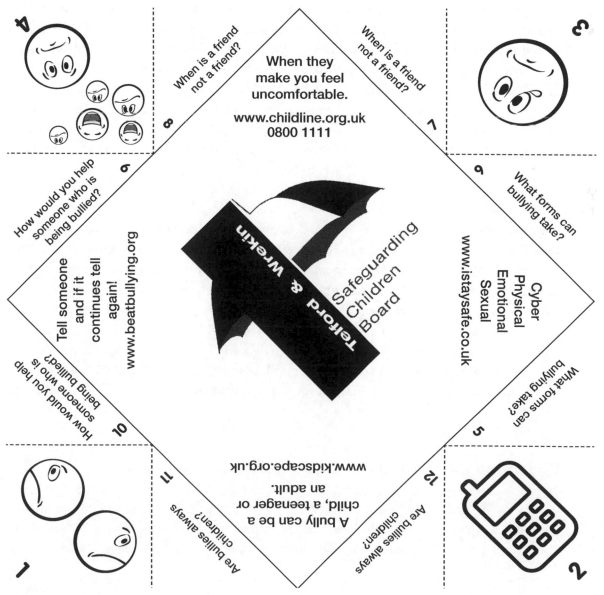

Figure 4.4 How to keep safe at Holmer Lake Primary School

What reduction in bullying is it realistic to expect?

If you implement a whole-school approach to reducing bullying and cyberbullying, what reduction in this behaviour could you reasonably expect? Bullying and aggression do not of course magically disappear. Bullying is a very complex and often secretive behaviour, but fewer incidents occur, conflict is considerably lessened and your students are better equipped to deal with it if it does happen. Your teachers and non-teaching staff are far more effective in their prevention and intervention actions, so there are fewer very distressed children who feel nobody is listening to them. Prejudice-driven behaviour or biased bullying is vigorously addressed, preparing children to learn to live in a diverse society like ours.

The pupils and their parents understand what is acceptable and that positive behaviour is the norm. Transgressors are quickly picked up and they are encouraged to change and rewarded for their prosocial behaviour as they 're-join the majority'.

High pupil involvement

The overt and very public style of the approach, with high pupil involvement, means that many children who have no incidents to report nevertheless see all the action to make everyone feel safe and respected, valued and understood – so they in turn feel able to relax and thrive in your school. The quietest child who has never articulated any problems is benefiting from what she sees around her. The boy who fears he might be bullied online by someone who has threatened him once in class now feels he has the tools to deal with it and that, if he ever needs to, he can come and tell someone he trusts. When children relax and are not living in a flight or fight mode, they can learn and thrive. But these benefits do not show up in crude data which only measure reported incidents! That is why we also ask children what they see around them – not only about what they experience personally.

Parents trust

Another benefit of the effective approach is that parents trust the school to keep their children safe. As time goes on, you are imposing a model on your school community – 'this is how it is at this school'. Anyone joining the school will soon learn that it is like a club where you play by the rules. But do not expect a sudden, enormous reduction if you start to implement a whole-school approach – in fact, when pupils trust that you will do something about their case, a higher number are initially more likely to come forward. This is a good sign! When more people come forward it signals a confidence in your approach. But this rate should subside and reduce, except for spikes such as during National Anti-Bullying Week when some children understand for the first time what cyberbullying is and come to report it.

Gradual small reductions

In many research programmes, anti-bullying approaches have been evaluated. It is quite common for small, incremental reductions to be seen. We have found this with our schools' programme too – however, we also note the influence of what is going on in the neighbourhood and media at the time as well as on the world stage. As I write, we are in the midst of a political battle about immigration here at home and Islamophobia brought on by shocking events in the Middle East, but equally there has been a rise in anti-Semitism after the recent events in Gaza and general anti-Eastern-European feeling. Five years ago this was considerably different. We have also noted periods when Travellers were in the news every day, making Traveller children vulnerable as the targets of school bullies. These background factors are not excuses for racist bullying but should be in your mind as you look at your data. When planning an intervention they might shape what you do to counter children's fears and worries and of course to challenge prejudice and stereotyping.

Every intervention has a cost in terms of staff input. This includes the time it takes to train staff, agree procedures and implement the scheme the first time. There is the communications strategy and effort needed in getting buy-in from children and parents. Then you will want to monitor how onerous it is for staff to fill out the incident forms and how sustainable your systems are. Very often it is more productive to introduce something less complex but flexible and sustainable, rather than start with a huge blitz and then see it fade away. A good test is to consider each incident and think about how effective your policies and systems were in this case. Did they work? Did they help you? Do they need a tweak? Do they cater for this type of case?

Monitoring is essential. Don't leave the data gathering dust on a shelf or in some long-forgotten computer file. Are there messages in your data about what is actually going on each Thursday afternoon in a particular part of your school? Is there one year group where the trouble is focused? Are any particular groups being singled out for discrimination? There is no point in persisting with a strategy that is not working well. But you may also want to consult staff, parents and pupils when your policies are due for review.

Considering the answers from among over 10,000 respondents in the Cybersurvey, I looked at those that said 'My school deals with bullying very well' and compared them with those saying 'My school does not deal with bullying at all well'.

In the effective schools where they had worked to develop a coherent, consistent approach, we see that prejudice-driven bullying was less likely:

Effective schools %		Ineffective schools %
12	Sexist bullying	30
14	Homophobia	35
29	Racist bullying	35
7	Bullying about a long-term illness	21

Note: Effective schools are those judged by pupils to be dealing with bullying 'very well', as against ineffective schools who are 'not working well at all'.

There was evidence of less staff time wasted with endless conflict. But we can see that with the national discourse focusing heavily on immigration, that racist bullying was less amenable to change than other types of prejudice-driven bullying. One year before, racist bullying was down. This might be an illustration of changing attitudes and public and media discussions.

A further finding was that there were also other reductions and cyberbullying halved in the effective schools:

Effective Schools		Ineffective Schools
7%	I have been bullied a lot	29%
12%	I've been bullied in cyberspace	24%
15%	I told nobody	22%
27%	I experienced rumour-spreading	35%

So what were the effective schools doing that the ineffective schools were not doing? Students said that effective schools:

- train pupils to be peer supporters/mentors and other pupils in how to help one another

- engage pupils in policy reviews (consult everyone)

- are twice as likely to teach pupils to 'respect people who are different'

- teach pupils to be safe online

- provide pupils with safe routes to report bullying

- are more than three times as likely to get bullying to stop if it occurs.

Teachers' support

Another element in the coherent approach is good e-safety support for teachers when using internal systems for staff. Both management and staff are involved in this process.

Encryption

If you carry around any important documents on a USB stick, these could so easily be lost. Should this material ever leave school premises? If yes, has this information been encrypted?

Archive it and retain access

You may need to have access to this data when working at home or at another site or campus. Would a dedicated cloud service be the answer? How secure this would be is a question that recent hacks have put in doubt. There are also services where you can securely store large files. You are advised to use these on Internet-connected drives that you own and control. Any cloud service or public wi-fi system is not secure. Using a private virtual private network (VPN) owned by the school is more secure.

Consider also how data is transmitted around the school. Where are the gaps and weaknesses in your system? How often are passwords changed, for example? This should take place every 90 days. To check the obligations (and the fines) on handling data, visit the data protection guidance on the website of the Information Commissioner's Office.[19] Remember that the headteacher is the data controller. If data is lost it must be reported to the academy chain or the local authority.

Long-term storage

Storage of data is always an issue as the data grows exponentially. Consider using a secure file archiving service.

Browsing

Every search is tracked and filtered to provide you with more adverts for 'blue toddler shorts' or 'man with van' ads after you have ever once searched for these. This targeted advertising is worth millions of pounds and becomes more sophisticated all the time. But this system also keeps throwing up suggestions to a vulnerable young person who has once searched for websites on self-harm, for example. It will keep offering them links to such sites as they search generally. As they begin to see more and more of these suggested sites, a young person can come to believe everyone is visiting these sites, or simply be tempted back to one. If you are worried about safeguarding a young person, suggest to their parents or carers that filters are adjusted at home and on their mobile device to block these sites being promoted.

As far as teachers and other professionals go, please remember that their search history or clickstream can be examined. The code of conduct should be actively enforced and reminders given that it is a sackable offence to contravene this code. They must act professionally at all times.

Hackers often use weaknesses in browser set-up to try to compromise a system. It is possible to configure your browser to be more secure. To find out more about this visit www.uscert.gov.uk/publications/security/securing-your-web-browser. Often, the browser is not set up in a secure default setting. This can allow spyware to be installed and create a number of computer problems. Check all new devices to see what has been pre-installed.

Don't simply click on a site you have searched for without checking it is not a fake site first.

Updates are important as they fix weaknesses that could have become apparent since the software was first developed or sold to you – you will not be able to get these updates if your software is not genuine or original. This is relevant to staff who may work from home with school data. How up to date is the software they are using?

When downloading software on your individual laptop, perhaps at home, beware of additional programs piggy-backing onto the download. These can be disabling or cause problems to your computer. It is all too easy to blindly click 'OK' or 'Allow' when installing a program you planned to download but in fact it may be asking you if you want a new browser or adding some search feature you did not ask for.

Get help from your school's ICT manager if you are not sure how to configure your browser settings at home and get advice on which settings can weaken your security. Attackers can use these vulnerabilities to take control of your computer, steal your information, destroy your files and attack other computers by using yours. Exploiting vulnerabilities in web browsers represents an easy, low-cost route for attackers to do this. An attacker can create a malicious web page that will install Trojan software or spyware that will steal your information.

Consider the security level for different sites. Settings can be customized and various filters put in place. If you have multiple browsers you could select one to be used for sensitive functions like banking or handling secure school data, which you wish to remain very secure. This can lessen the chance that your sensitive information is compromised.

Using Tools and Internet Options in Explorer you can adjust settings by visiting Microsoft's Setting Up Security Zones advice. Google similarly has online advice for using Chrome. Visit the website of the browser seller to learn more about your browser settings.

What is a cookie?

Are cookies benign with their cute name? Or are they an intrusive form of spying tracker? Cookies are files placed on your system to store data for websites. Cookies may contain information about the sites you visited, or details that enable access to the site. They help the site to recognise you when you return, perhaps as a member or account holder, and open your personal account.

Cookies are designed to be read only by the website that created them, so you will encounter them in many locations, usually when a pop-up warning flashes asking whether or not you accept the use of cookies as sites are obliged to do. They are not a program! Usually they contain the site name and your unique user ID. So, when you visit a site, a cookie is downloaded and at the next visit your computer checks out whether it has a cookie for this site. If it does, it then sends the information contained in the cookie back to the site, so that the latter recognises that you have visited before. Cookies can help show what items you have bought or what is on your wish list, for example. Cookies are a solution to online shopping and membership websites.

Are there risks to cookies?

Cookies can be used to uniquely identify visitors of a website, which some people consider a violation of privacy, so sites are obliged to tell you about the use of cookies. If a website uses cookies for authentication, then an attacker may be able to acquire unauthorised access to that site by obtaining the cookie. Persistent cookies pose a higher risk than session cookies because they remain on the computer longer. So the cookies have asked your permission to store and retrieve data about your browsing history. In most cases you check that the website is genuine and say yes and carry on as normal.

- You can change how cookies are stored on your computer by using the Tools menu in your browser.

- Session cookies carry less risk than persistent cookies.

- You can set your system to alert you to every cookie request so that you can decide whether to accept the cookie if it comes from a reliable website.

- You can also specify which websites are permitted to use cookies.

Ensure all IDNs (internationalised domain names) are displayed and check whether it is the actual address of the site you intended. This means you want any encoded address to be shown. There is a setting for this. BT.com may be the name of the site but a convincing fake could be set up on BT.co.uk and pose as the genuine site asking for your details. Stay alert.

5

What Does the Law Say?

Every school must have measures in place to prevent all forms of bullying. This includes academies and independent schools. Please note that while many of the governement documents mentioned in this chapter and elsewhere relate to England, the principles are broadly the same for the rest of the UK.

Education law
Education and Inspections Act 2006

Section 89 of the Education and Inspections Act 2006 provides that maintained schools must have measures to encourage good behaviour and prevent all forms of bullying amongst pupils. These measures should be part of the school's behaviour policy, which must be communicated to all pupils, school staff and parents. Headteachers, with the advice and guidance of governors and the assistance of school staff, must identify and implement measures to promote good behaviour, respect for others and self-discipline among learners, and to prevent all forms of bullying. This includes the prevention of cyberbullying.

The Act outlines some legal powers which relate quite directly to cyberbullying: headteachers have the power 'to such extent as is reasonable' to regulate the conduct of learners when they are off-site or not under the control or charge of a member of staff. This is of particular significance to cyberbullying, which is often likely to take place out of school but which can impact very strongly on the school life of the learners involved.

The Act also provides a defence for school staff in confiscating items from learners. This can include mobile phones when they are being used to cause a disturbance in class or otherwise contravene the school behaviour/anti-bullying policy. School staff may request a learner to reveal a message or show them other content on their phone for the purpose of establishing if bullying has occurred, and a refusal to comply might lead to the imposition of a disciplinary penalty for failure to follow a reasonable instruction. Where the text or image is visible on the phone, staff can act on this. Where the school's behaviour policy expressly provides, a member of staff may themselves search through the phone in an appropriate case where the learner is reasonably suspected of involvement. (Staff should not seek to view nude or pornographic/sexting images of under-18-year-olds where these cases have been reported to them, but should secure the evidence and contact the lead for safeguarding within the school.)

Independent School Standard Regulations 2010

The Independent School Standards Regulations 2010 provide that the proprietor of an academy or other independent school is required to ensure that an effective anti-bullying strategy is drawn up and implemented.

The Equality Act 2010

The Equality Act 2010 replaces previous anti-discrimination laws with a single Act. A key provision is a new public sector equality duty, which came into force on 5 April 2011. It replaces the three previous public sector equality duties for race, disability and gender, and covers age, disability, gender reassignment, pregnancy and maternity, race, religion or belief, sex and sexual orientation. The duty has three aims. It requires public bodies to have due regard to the need to:

- eliminate unlawful discrimination, harassment, victimisation and any other conduct prohibited by the Act

- advance equality of opportunity between people who share a protected characteristic and people who do not share it

- foster good relations between people who share a protected characteristic and people who do not share it.

Maintained schools and academies are required to comply with the new equality duty. Part 6 of the Act makes it unlawful for the responsible body of a school to discriminate against, harass or victimise a pupil or potential pupil in relation to admissions; the way it provides education for pupils; provision of pupil access to any benefit, facility or service; or by excluding a pupil or subjecting them to any other detriment. In England and Wales Part 6 of the Act applies to maintained schools and academies and to other independent schools.

Safeguarding children and young people

Under the Children Act 1989 a bullying incident should be addressed as a child protection concern when there is 'reasonable cause to suspect that a child is suffering, or is likely to suffer, significant harm'. Where this is the case, the school staff should report their concerns to their local authority children's social care. Even where safeguarding is not considered to be an issue, schools may need to draw on a range of external services to support the pupil who is experiencing bullying, or to tackle any underlying issue which has contributed to a child engaging in bullying.

Keeping Children Safe in Education guidance

All education establishments must comply with their safeguarding duties.

The DfE's *Keeping Children Safe in Education* guidance considers the key changes and their implications for LSCBs, LAs, schools (excluding maintained nursery schools) and colleges.[20]

The Equality Act 2010: Twelve key messages

The general duty
Have due regard for equalities

Specific duties

- publish information which shows compliance with the general duty
- publish at least one equality objective.

1
One Act of parliament replaces several earlier Acts on discrimination.

One overall duty – the Public Sector Equality Duty (PSED).

One requirement – schools and other public bodies should have due regard for equalities.

2
There are two kinds of duty:

- the general duty.
- the specific duties.

There are two specific duties.

3
Schools and other public bodies must have due regard to these three aims:

- eliminating discrimination
- advancing equality of opportunity
- fostering good relations.

4
Ofsted is bound by the PSED, and with the explicit approval of government it will inspect four kinds of personal development amongst pupils: spiritual, moral, social and cultural, in accordance with the PSED.

5
Good practice suggests objectives should be SMART:

- specific, measurable, achievable, relevant and time limited.

6
There are six principles established by case law underlying the concept of 'due regard':

- *Awareness*: All staff should know and understand what the law requires.
- *Timeliness*: The implications for equalities of new policies and practices should be considered before they are introduced.
- *Rigour*: There should be rigorous and open-minded analysis of statistical evidence and careful attention to the views of staff, pupils, parents and carers.
- *Non-delegation*: Compliance with the PSED cannot be delegated.
- *Continuous*: Due regard for equalities should be taking place all the time.
- *Record-keeping*: Keep bullying incident records and achievement analysis, including minutes of staff and governors' meetings.

7 The seven letters in 'operate' can be used to help memorise these important concepts. The seven points are derived from ministerial statements in the House of Commons.

- *Outcome-focused*: Closing gaps in attainment and other outcomes at school, in the use of sanctions and punishments and in fostering and maintaining good relations.

- *Proportionality and permissiveness*: Schools are permitted to interpret legislation according to their own context and circumstances, not a one-size-fits-all approach.

- *Evidence based*: There should be sound evidence for decisions made.

- *Reasonable and rigorous*: Not just box ticking but no more than good enough.

- *Accountability*: Schools must make themselves accountable for their progress on equalities to parents/carers and to local groups and organisations.

- *Transparency*: Information must be published which enables schools to be held to account. This should be easy to find and easy to understand.

- *Engagement*: It is good practice to consult and involve people with a legitimate interest.

8 The number 8 has played a part in the history of struggles to change the laws of the UK over many years. Milestones such as: 1928 saw women get the vote, and in 1948 the Universal Declaration of Human Rights set the global context on anti-discrimination legislation.

How many more milestones can you think of that carry the number 8?

9 The legislation sets out nine strands or aspects of human diversity known as the nine protected characteristics: age; disability; gender reassignment; marriage and civil partnership; pregnancy and maternity; race; religion or belief; sex; sexual orientation.

> Age and marriage or civil partnership are not applicable in the provision of services to children and young people. However, they may apply to parents or carers. They apply to teachers.

10 There are ten protected characteristics if you add the important aspect of social class.

11 In 2011 the duties under this Act came into effect.

12 By April 2012, schools were required to publish information showing compliance with the public sector equality duty, plus at least one equality objective.

This has been developed by Adrienne Katz from an initial piece of work by Robin Richardson of INSTED Consultancy.

Criminal and civil law
Cyberbullying

Although bullying in itself is not a specific criminal offence in England, it is important to bear in mind that some types of harassing or threatening behaviour or communications might be illegal under existing laws such as those below. At the time of writing, there is considerable discussion among MPs about whether to develop a specific law against cyberbullying and on making so-called 'revenge porn' illegal. This is when a former partner posts intimate and personal photos of their former partner in a bid to wreak revenge after a split.

The following indicates when cyber aggression could be a criminal offence.

Protection from Harassment Act 1997

This Act is relevant for incidents that have happened repeatedly (i.e. on more than two occasions).

- Section 1 prohibits behaviour amounting to harassment of another.

- Section 2 provides a criminal offence.

- Section 3 provides a civil remedy for breach of the prohibition on harassment in Section 1.

- Section 4 describes a more serious offence of someone causing another person to fear, on at least two occasions, that violence will be used against them.

A civil court may grant an injunction to restrain a person from conduct which amounts to harassment and, following conviction of an offence under Sections 2 or 4, restraining orders are available to protect the victim of the offence.

Communications Act 2003

Section 127 covers all forms of public communications. Subsection 1 defines an offence of sending a 'grossly offensive…obscene, indecent or menacing' communication. Subsection 2 defines a separate offence where, for the purposes of causing annoyance, inconvenience or needless anxiety, a person sends a message which that person knows to be false (or causes it to be sent) or persistently makes use of a public communications system.

Malicious Communications Act 1988

Section 1 makes it an offence to send an indecent, grossly offensive or threatening letter, electronic communication or other article to another person with the intention that it should cause them distress or anxiety.

Public Order Act 1986

Section 5 makes it an offence to use threatening, abusive or insulting words, behaviour, writing, signs or other visual representation within the sight or hearing of a person likely to be caused harassment, alarm or distress. This offence may apply where a mobile phone is used as a camera or video rather than where speech writing or images are transmitted.

Obscene Publications Act 1959

It is an offence under this Act to publish an obscene article. Publishing includes circulating, showing, playing or projecting the article or transmitting that data, for example over a school intranet. An obscene article is one whose effect is such as to tend to deprave and corrupt persons who are likely to read, see or hear the matter contained or embodied in it.

Computer Misuse Act 1990

When cyberbullying takes the form of hacking into someone else's account, then other criminal laws will come into play, such as the Computer Misuse Act 1990, in addition to civil laws on confidentiality and privacy.

Anti-Social Behaviour Crime and Policy Act 2014

In the Anti-Social Behaviour Crime and Policing Act 2014, ASBOS were replaced by an injunction, which is a civil order and is available against individuals aged 10 or over. The maximum term for under 18's is twelve months. It can be applied for by a wide range of agencies. Criminal Behaviour Orders were also introduced –for people convicted of a crime if the court thinks they will continue to cause anti-social behaviour. They can give a Criminal Behaviour Order to stop them carrying out more of this anti-social behaviour.

The Police, Local Authority, or other relevant agencies will try and stop a problem quickly when they can. They can use:

- verbal warnings
- written warnings
- mediation
- Acceptable Behaviour Contracts

Defamation

Defamation is a civil 'common law' tort. It applies to any published material that damages the reputation of an individual or an organisation, and it includes material published on the Internet. A civil action for defamation can be brought by an individual or a company, but not by a public authority. It is up to the claimant to prove that the material is defamatory. However, the claimant does not have to prove that the material is false – the burden of proof on that point lies with the author/publisher, who has to prove that what they have written is true.

This has been included here as we increasingly see cases where parents spread ugly rumours about a teacher or say defamatory things on a Facebook page for example, where they encourage other parents to add their negative views.

Where defamatory material is posted on a website, the person affected can inform the host of its contents and ask the host to remove it. Once the host knows that the material is there and that it may be defamatory, it can no longer rely on the defence of innocent dissemination in the Defamation Act 1996. This means that the person affected could (if the material has been published in the jurisdiction, i.e. in England and Wales) obtain a court order (an injunction) to require removal of the material, and could sue either the host or the person who posted the material for defamation. Teachers are advised to contact their union or the helpline for professionals for advice.[21]

Bullying outside school premises

Teachers have the power to discipline pupils for misbehaving outside the school premises 'to such an extent as is reasonable'. This can relate to any bullying incidents occurring anywhere off the school premises, such as on school or public transport, outside the local shops, or in a town or village centre.

Where bullying outside school is reported to school staff, it should be investigated and acted on. The headteacher should also consider whether it is appropriate to notify the police or antisocial behaviour coordinator in their local authority of the action taken against a pupil. If the misbehaviour could be criminal or poses a serious threat to a member of the public, the police should always be informed. More detailed advice on teachers' powers to discipline, including their power to punish pupils for misbehaviour that occurs outside school, is included in the DfE advice to headteachers and school staff on behaviour and discipline in schools.[22]

Parents' views and complaints

Schools are increasingly worried about parents' actions on social networks where they gather to criticise the school. The following case examples are some drastic steps that should not be necessary. However, it pays to make clear to all parents what the school complaints procedure is, encourage them to use it and also make clear in your anti-bullying policy that it addresses the bullying of pupils, staff and parents, in fact the whole school community, so that you pre-empt bullying of staff online by parents. You might also put something in a home–school agreement about this and explain that if parents are not satisfied they can escalate their case to the governors. It pays to avoid the problems outlined below.

In one case, parents who alleged the school had not done enough about bullying targeted at their primary-aged children created a page online to criticise the school and headteacher. They also complained to Ofsted. It appears they were receiving some support from a political party with a point to prove.

Sometimes it is parents being supported by a 'No win, no fee' law firm which takes to the airwaves on radio and TV, and in one case picketed the school for weeks.

To avoid this type of unnecessary treatment of your teaching staff, ensure that you make parents aware of how to bring their concerns and grievances to the school rather than complain outside and on the net. Treat their concerns with the greatest respect and keep notes of all action taken to help their child. Write back promptly if they write to you with their concerns. In one case I was presented with many letters parents had written to their child's school over a period of 18 months but there were no letters back from the school. The school insisted it had met with the parents and taken action to stop the bullying their child experienced, but they kept no record of the meetings, what was agreed, or what actions they had put in place. Nor were there any records monitoring the situation of the child.

Ofsted provides a route for parents to give their views about schools online via Parent View, and it is often only those with problems or complaints who take the trouble to visit this option. Parents are also asked their views in some inspections.

The BIG Award offers member schools free online parent surveys, alongside the anonymous pupil surveys. If you have data showing that parents and pupils are mostly satisfied with the way you safeguard or deal with bullying situations, this could be very helpful.

Safe recruitment

The *Keeping Children Safe in Education* guidance sets out the elements of safe recruitment, an important part of safeguarding and e-safety. In the light of several recent cases involving staff in schools who have been found to be abusing children or contacting them inappropriately, Deborah Steele, a consultant in safer recruitment, suggests schools should always keep in mind the phrase 'It could happen here' and examine their recruitment procedures in the light of this.

There is now greater emphasis on the role of the governing body to ensure compliance and on recommendations from the local authority and the local safeguarding children board (LSCB). Disclosure and Barring Service (DBS) checks have replaced the former Criminal Records Bureau (CRB) checks. Governors now have overriding responsibility for everything their school is doing and need to be able to show this. They must be able to evidence safe recruitment practice from the advert through to the application form and reasons for decisions, along with references followed up and any recommendations. Log the DBS checks and any other checks such as barred list or prohibition checks. Safe recruitment also extends to those who work in your school during an extended day.

The background to this concern about safe recruitment echoes back to the Soham murders in 2002 and the subsequent Bichard report in 2004. This led to the implementation of sections 157 and 175 of the Education Act 2002, which contained a statutory duty for all schools and local authorities to provide their services in a way that 'safeguards and promotes the welfare of children'.

In 2005 the first version of the guidance was issued setting out recommended guidance for safer recruitment. This was followed by regulations in 2009 on a requirement for maintained schools to have heads trained in safer recruitment and for every interview panel to include at least one person who had completed this training. In 2014 the DfE issued *Keeping Children Safe in Education*, which came into force with immediate effect.

Serious case reviews can provide vital learning on what went wrong in some cases. Mistakes tend to include appointing people known to the school and undertaking fewer checks than are necessary, not acknowledging that women can be abusers, taking shortcuts when following up references, and ignoring information that does not fit with what the panel wants to believe.

If there is a clear written policy and procedure for safer recruitment known to all and followed accurately with attention to detail, this is the safest route. We must acknowledge, however, that someone determined to work with children and hide their past may in fact get through even the best procedures. So simply having good recruitment procedures should not make anyone feel complacent or relax their vigilance. These should be balanced with excellent induction and staff training cycles, regular staff updates and training on e-safety and safeguarding and good whistle blower systems or ways for children to report anything worrying them.

Code of conduct

Every school should have a staff code of conduct which links to Acceptable Use of ICT policy. A Code of Conduct should include:

All teachers must follow the Teaching Standards 2012 Part Two:

Personal and professional conduct

A teacher is expected to exemplify consistently high standards of personal and professional conduct. The following statements define the behaviour and attitudes which set the required standard for conduct throughout a teacher's career.

Teachers uphold public trust in the profession and maintain high standards of ethics and behaviour, within and outside school, by:

- treating pupils with dignity, building relationships rooted in mutual respect

- observing proper boundaries appropriate to a teacher's professional position

- having regard for the need to safeguard pupils' well-being, in accordance with statutory provisions

- showing tolerance of and respect for the rights of others

- not undermining fundamental British values, including democracy, the rule of law, individual liberty and mutual respect, and tolerance of those with different faiths and beliefs ensuring that personal beliefs are not expressed in ways which exploit pupils' vulnerability or might lead them to break the law

- having proper and professional regard for the ethos, policies and practices of the school in which they teach, and maintain high standards in their own attendance and punctuality

- having an understanding of, and acting within, the statutory frameworks which set out their professional duties and responsibilities at all times.

These standards are also good practice for all support staff, Governors and volunteers.

6

Serious Incident Management

The dark side of the net

Child exploitation in all its guises is the horrific, ugly side of the net. While you may never come across such cases, all professionals working with children need to be alert to this possibility.

In 2013 the Internet Watch Foundation (IWF) saw a 31 per cent increase in reports processed compared to 2012. It identified 13,182 webpages containing child sexual abuse imagery from 51,186 reports.

Of the 13,182 webpages:

- Over half (51%) showed the rape or sexual torture of a child or children.

- Over 80 per cent were of victims aged 10 or under.

- The vast majority of the victims were girls (76%). Ten per cent were boys and 9 per cent showed both genders.

- Twenty-four per cent of the images and videos were being sold on a commercial basis.

Most of the images and videos were hosted in North America (54%) with 43 per cent hosted in Europe (including Russia).

The UK still leads the world at removing this criminal imagery; less than 1 per cent of all the child sexual abuse images and videos identified were hosted in the UK. However, due to a rise in the number of UK businesses' websites hacked to host folders of child sexual abuse images, the number of UK-hosted images increased [between 2012 and 2013].[23]

What should you do if you suspect that a child has been or is being sexually exploited online?

- Make the child safe.

- Save any evidence.

- Put the device out of use if relevant.

- Contact your safeguarding lead, who will contact CEOP and the local authority designated officer and children's social care if required.

- Notify the Internet Watch Foundation.

Staff may understandably be very upset by a case of this nature and will need support and debriefing. They should follow the school's serious incident protocols.

Local figures from the Cybersurvey in England

In 2014, there were 660 people aged 10–11 in the cyber survey:

- seventy-one per cent use a smartphone

- fifty-three per cent use social networking sites, mainly Facebook

- fifty-six per cent use a laptop or a netbook

- seventy-six per cent use tablets

- nineteen per cent have been cyberbullied.

Online risk

Around 20 per cent report issues of concern: One in five have been cyberbullied, seen websites urging you to be too thin, or seen sites urging people to hurt or kill yourself and been involved in sexting.

One in four have come across pictures of nudity or violence they did not search for and 14 per cent have been in touch with someone who pretended to be a young person interested in them but who subsequently turned out to be someone quite different.

Nearly a third say they have come across websites giving dangerous advice. 22 young people say they have been tricked into buying fake goods and 29 have been tricked into paying for something online that they did not want.

How to capture and preserve evidence

It is important to capture evidence of cyberbullying before the perpetrator alters or takes it down. Cyberbullying on social networks can be deleted by a pupil or member of staff when it gets out that you are investigating and then the evidence is lost. Or a perpetrator might use a live chat service where the dialogue is not saved or a self-destruct service where a message disappears after a few seconds. An offensive photo can be altered to look better or be taken down once the case is being investigated. In all cases of bullying, evidence is that vital component that proves what the victim alleges. Even to get something taken down or to report it to a website, the victim may have to produce the evidence. Bullying may intensify, in which case having evidence of how long it has gone on will be helpful. So how can this be achieved? Of course you can print out any emails, but few young people use email today. Here are some ideas.

Capture a screenshot or screengrab on a computer

A screenshot is essentially a photo of what you can see on your computer screen. It captures everything just as it looks in the original context such as a Facebook page or full email. This has more credibility than if only the message is copied and pasted.

Capturing a screenshot

Google screengrab instructions for your particular device or operating system. The following are useful links for how to take a screenshot: http://support.apple.com/en-gb/HT201361 (Mac), http://windows.microsoft.com/en-GB/windows-xp/help/setup/take-a-screen-shot (Windows) and www.youtube.com/watch?v=2r66JM5iL2M (iPad).

Storing the image

Once you have the screenshot on the screen in Paint, you need to save it as an image. To do this:

- Click on the 'File' button followed by the 'Save as' button. This will open a list of folders on your computer and there should be one named 'Pictures' or 'My Pictures'.

- Click on the folder to open it. The screen will ask you for a name to save the file as and will also ask for the file type. Choose JPEG. Type in a name for the image such as 'Cyberevidence1' and label subsequent ones as 'Cyberevidence2', 'Cyberevidence3' and so on.

- It might help to open a subfolder inside your My Pictures file called 'Evidence'. Do this by opening 'Pictures', right-clicking the mouse and clicking on 'New' and then 'Folder'. A folder icon will appear and you can type in the name you want to give it.

- Select 'JPEG' as the file format.

- You can also do this using Microsoft Publisher if you prefer – simply paste the screenshot into a Publisher blank page and go to 'Save as' – where you select a name and type as above.

Finding the stored screenshot

When you need your evidence, you will easily find it by looking in 'My Pictures' and then in the 'Evidence' folder. The images can then be printed, emailed or saved onto your camera's SD card.

It can help to create a timeline or diary, noting the date each time there is another incident.

Emailing the screenshot

You might be required to send your screenshots to the police, lawyers or other people who are involved in your case such as a designated safeguarding lead or the service provider.

- Open the saved 'Evidence' folder and decide which images you want to send by email.

- If your email goes through Outlook Express, select the images by holding down the 'Control' key and clicking on them. The computer will highlight them for you.

- Right-click on one of the pictures and a list of options will appear. Select 'Send to' and the computer will open a new email with the pictures attached. All you need to do is type in the email address you want to send them to.

- If using Outlook Express, Gmail or Hotmail, open a new email. Find the 'Attach' or 'Insert a file' command, then click on it. It will open a list of folders. Find your 'Pictures' folder and inside it will be your 'Evidence' folder. Once you open it you can select which pieces of evidence you want to attach to your email. Hold down the 'Control' key and click on the images you wish to send.

Note. In cases which involve nude or explicit images of young people under 18 it is not advisable to look at them nor to download any on to your own devices. Lock the device into a drawer until the designated person within your school or the police are able to look at it. Ask the victim to save the evidence first.

On mobiles and tablets

Capture the evidence

The victim can place the phone onto a photocopier or take a photo with another phone. Screenshots can be saved. You can also take a photo of a computer or tablet screen with a phone.

Preserve the evidence

It is advisable to keep a record of the abusive or aggressive incident. Note down the date and time, the content of the message(s) and, where possible, a sender's ID (e.g. username, email address, mobile phone number) or the web address of the SNS page or the content. Even better, keep an accurate copy of the whole web-page address, as this will help the service provider find the content you wish to complain about.

Keeping the evidence will help in any investigation into the cyberbullying by the service provider, but it can also be useful in showing what has happened to those who may need to know, including parents, teachers, pastoral care staff and the police.

How to preserve the evidence

It is always useful to keep a written record, but it is better to save evidence of bullying on the device itself:

- With mobiles, ask the young person being bullied to keep or save any messages, whether voice, image or text. Do not have them forward the message to your staff phone. This could cause vital information from the original message to be lost. The following are useful links for how to take a screenshot: http://electronics. howstuffworks.com/screen-capture-smartphone.htm (smartphone) and http:// support.apple.com/en-gb/HT200289 (iPhone). There are also apps available which can be used to take screenshots. See https://play.google.com/store/apps/ details?id=com.longxk.ascreenshot&hl=en.

- On instant messaging generally, some services allow the user to record all conversations. The user can also copy and paste, save and print these. If you think about it, it is obvious that if evidence is kept via a copy-and-paste method it might appear less genuine, as it could have been altered. This is why, when reporting a case to the service provider or the police, authentic evidence made from saved evidence is more convincing, so conversations recorded or archived by the instant messaging service are better for evidence here. Conversations can also be printed out in hard copy or sections can be saved as a screen grab.

- On SNS, video-hosting sites or other websites, copy and save the site link, print the page or take a screen grab of the page and save it. You can also take a photo of the entire screen using a mobile. Aim for a high-resolution image.

- Some versions of Messenger offer the option to archive conversations. Check your Messenger toolbar for your preferences and privacy options and switch on the archive setting.

- Where this option is not available, either copy and save the conversation or use one of the ideas above such as a photo or a screengrab.

- For chat rooms, print the page or produce a screen grab of the page.

- On email, ask the person being bullied to print it; forward the message to the staff member investigating the incident and encourage them to continue to forward and save any subsequent messages. Preserving the whole message, and not just the text, is more useful as this will contain 'headers' (information about where the message has come from). They can also print out the emails and keep a folder.

A note about images

If images are involved in cyberbullying, it is important to find out if they might be illegal or raise child protection concerns. Indecent or sexual images of children (people under the age of 18) are illegal to produce, circulate or possess in the UK. These include images that children have taken of themselves or their friends, using their mobile phone for example.

In cases which involve nude or explicit images of young people under 18 it is advisable not to look at or download them onto your own devices. Lock the device in a drawer until the designated safeguarding lead in your school or the police are able to look at it. Ask the victim to save the evidence first.

Contact the Internet Watch Foundation if the images are Internet content or the local police if illegal images have been taken of a child and circulated. Similarly, if the case involves an assault on another young person or some other crime, contact the local police. If it is a safeguarding matter, trigger your school's safeguarding procedures. If the case involves child sexual exploitation, contact CEOP.

Less serious situations

If the case involves images that are not illegal or taken of an illegal act, you may prefer to try to contain the incident within the school. Some cases benefit from the utmost discretion and it is not always necessary to tell the whole school about the case. However, cases should trigger useful work across a year group – for example, to counter any prejudice that has emerged or to teach them a new aspect of staying safe. Cases may trigger letters home to parents about particular sites or warnings about new behaviours that are coming to light.

Identifying the bully

In cases where you do not know the identity of the bully, we can often find out the IP address[24] of the device used, but it is wise to remember that someone else might have used that device, even using someone's identity or SNS account. Many young people do lots of social networking with friends who can memorise their password, or someone may know that their friend's phone is always linked to their Facebook page so they could use it when their friend goes out of the room for a moment. Siblings often know or can guess the password their brother or sister is using. Evidence of an IP address is just that; nothing more is proven.

But there may be witnesses who visited that page, school logs and service provider data. The police would have to request an action from a service provider if it involved someone else. If the bullying person withheld their number then the date and time of the call or message should help the provider identify the caller to the police.

Schools can often have a number identified because they have a list of students' mobile numbers or other pupils can recognise the number. But there are situations in which it is more difficult. When phones are using local wi-fi to communicate, the call is not processed by the provider's network. Texts sent from a website to a phone are also difficult to trace.

Where a crime has been committed and reported to the police, the police have protocols for working with service providers if they wish to request information.

Investigating allegations against staff

Allegations against staff are a safeguarding and possibly child protection matter. Devices should be put out of use and safely stored. All evidence should be saved.

Parents

We also see cases where parents or pupils attack staff members online. Parents should use the school's complaints procedure rather than go online and encourage other parents to comment on or defame a teacher. Staff can gain advice from their union or the professionals' helpline. The behaviour may involve defamation or damage to a teacher's professional reputation. Governing bodies should invite parent instigators to a meeting in the first instance, and written notes should be taken.

If pupils perpetrate inappropriate actions against staff

Follow the appropriate steps below:

1.   Screengrab the evidence.

2.   Identify who is involved.

3.   Discuss the incident with the pupil(s) and aim to get them to acknowledge the harm caused.

4.   Remind them of the school's acceptable use agreement signed by all students.

5.   Find out if they have shared the offensive material with others and try to get all versions of it removed if it was shared within the school.

6.   Ask the perpetrator to remove the offending material they have posted.

7.   If it is taking a long time to get the material removed, contact the Professionals' Helpline to get it taken down.

8.   If the perpetrator(s) are under the age of 13 years and the material is on a social network, contact the social network and have the account closed if they do not cooperate.

9.   If the insults contravene the Equality Act 2010, inform them and their parents that this is against the law.

10.   If the insults involve altered images or sexual content, refer to your serious incident protocol.

11.   Inform parents/carers if the incidents are serious and persistent.

12.   In serious cases, inform the police.

13.   Bear in mind some young people display aggressive behaviour because of problems in their own lives.

14.   If the students' behaviour suggests to you that they might be behaving this way because they are at risk, contact your school child protection lead who may decide to contact the LADO.

15.   Refer to a counsellor if required.

16.   Reinforce the Acceptable Use of ICT policy with all students.

17.   If the offensive material has been widely circulated among many students, write to all parents and insist all versions are withdrawn and removed. Remind them of the Acceptable Use of ICT policy and the Home–School Agreement.

Contact the Professionals' Helpline for advice or to have material removed faster 0844 381 4772

Unions can advise staff members

Reinforce your Acceptable Use of ICT policy among all students

Provide support to your staff member

Notify parents as needed

Figure 6.1 If pupils perpetrate inappropriate actions against staff

Serious incidents

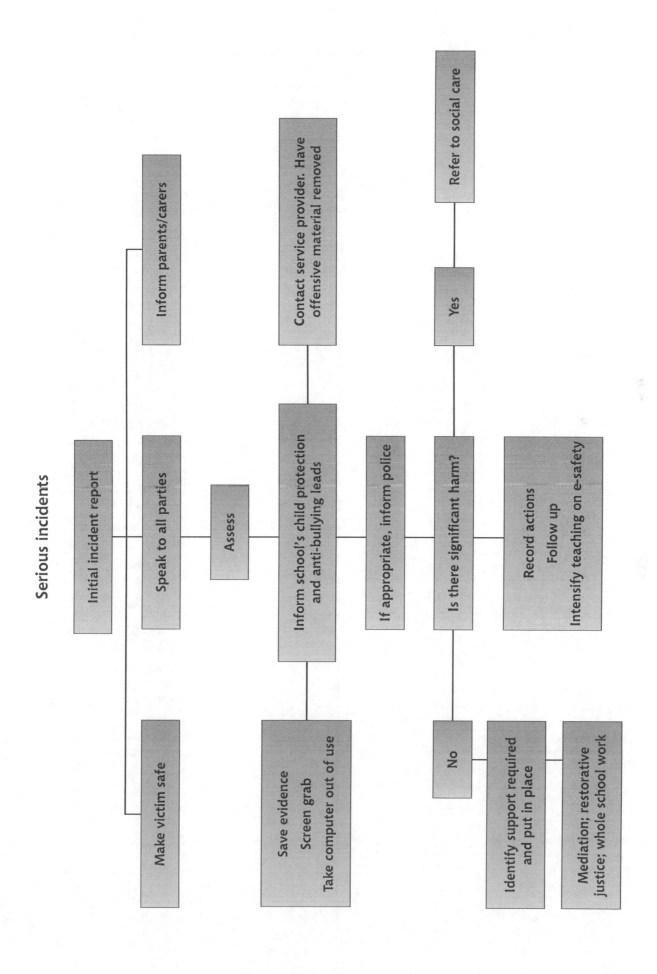

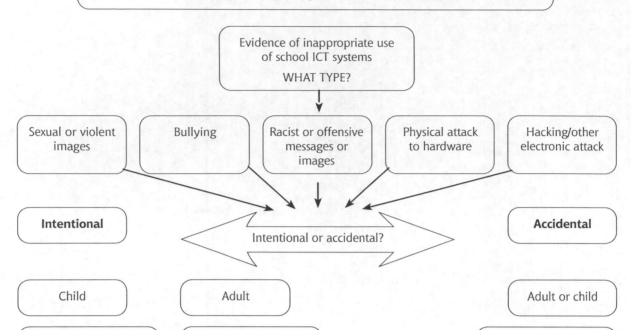

E-safety incident procedures for staff

Evidence of inappropriate use of school ICT systems

WHAT TYPE?

| Sexual or violent images | Bullying | Racist or offensive messages or images | Physical attack to hardware | Hacking/other electronic attack |

Intentional — Intentional or accidental? — **Accidental**

Child — Adult — Adult or child

Child

Quarantine computer or confiscate mobile device

Provide effective listening.

Is the child at risk? If yes, contact CP lead or safeguarding lead who will contact appropriate agencies and apply the CP procedures.

Is an adult involved? If yes, such as in cases of sexual images or CSE, contact police.

Is a child the perpetrator? If yes, contact the lead and assess the case, and take screengrabs of evidence unless it is of illegal images.

Identify victims and make them safe.

Plan approach to be used. Apply sanctions and check back with victims to ensure actions have stopped.

Adult

Quarantine computer/device

Contact the designated safeguarding lead for advice. If a child is involved, the safeguarding lead should contact the police.

Treat this case as confidential.

Retain detailed notes of report and actions taken, plus screengrabs, if available.

ICT manager should check school filters and e-safety settings used on devices by this staff member and re-visit good practice for staff.

Follow advice from police.

The designated safeguarding lead to take appropriate steps when investigation is complete.

Re-train staff.

Adult or child

Quarantine computer/device

Contact ICT manager and report URL if known. Inform the designated safeguarding lead.

Fill out incident record.

Carry out any technical steps or advice.

Inform parents of children who may be affected by witnessing the incident.

Advise all staff to update their systems and practice.

Remind staff to view all clips and searches in advance of using them in the classroom.

Group work with class to counter offensive messages and to discuss the Internet and risk.

Extra support for those with SEN or emotional difficulties, to ensure they understand.

Serious incidents that are or might be against the law.
What do we mean?

Downloading pornographic images of under-18s

Sharing/distributing child pornography images including 'sexting' where the young person in the image is under 18

'Sexting' where an adult is involved with a child

Hacking or otherwise attacking a system

Inciting hatred of a particular group of people

There is talk of making 'revenge porn' illegal, but if images of under-18s are shared this action is already illegal

Inappropriate communications between staff and a student

Promoting discrimination against the protected groups in the Equality Act 2010

Stalking or harassing someone

Malicious communication

Promoting illegal acts

Persistently downloading and sharing pirated content

Some things are offensive but not actually illegal. Remember the law will distinguish between these two.

CEOP works to prevent child sexual exploitation – do not use it for bullying cases!

In certain situations the police may give a young person a warning, but if repeated, this behaviour could land them with a caution on their record.

Internet Watch Foundation

Laws relating to the IWF's remit

The Internet Watch Foundation's remit covers three types of Internet content:

- Child sexual abuse content hosted anywhere in the world
- Criminally obscene adult content, including extreme pornography, hosted in the UK
- Non-photographic child sexual abuse images hosted in the UK

IWF
Internet
Watch
Foundation

STOP Child Sexual Abuse Imagery Online

DO the right thing ✓

Parents/carers as instigators of abusive, defamatory material aimed at staff

1. Contact parent(s) or lead instigator and invite them into school.

2. Explain that you are aware of some discussions between parents taking place online/on Facebook concerning the school/key teachers or governors.

3. Remind them that you have an open door policy/a parents' complaints procedure/a parents' survey, so you are disappointed that they did not contact the school in the first instance via one of these, as agreed in the Home–School Agreement.

4. This agreement also clearly states that parents will support the school to uphold standards of equality, openness and anti-bullying approaches.

5. If parents at your school sign a Home–School Agreement, remind them they have signed this.

6. Make clear that defamatory material targeted at a professional is damaging to their career and the person concerned may wish to take legal action.

7. If the remarks are sexual, racist or otherwise contravene the Equality Act 2010, it may be a matter for the police.

8. Request the offending material be removed.

If this does not solve the problem:

1. Report the case to the chair of governors. Use the screengrab you have saved.

2. Contact the Professional's Helpline to get it removed.

3. If, however, there is evidence of wrongdoing by a member of staff, do not hesitate to investigate. In such a case, inform the parent and set a date when you will report back to them. In the interim, offensive material must be taken down.

4. Note down what has been agreed with the parent(s). Write to them confirming the agreed actions at this meeting. Re-confirm what they are taking down. Include any steps you have agreed to take to look into what may lie behind this frustration.

5. Consider what support this member of staff might need with a difficult class?

Screengrab the evidence and save it

Contact the Professionals' Helpline for advice or to have material removed faster: 0844 381 4772

Unions can advise individual staff members

Home–School Agreements can be useful in these cases

Give parents several ways to report concerns

Write to all parents reminding them of complaints procedures and unacceptable actions

What should an Acceptable Use of ICT policy cover?

- *School name*: It also needs to state who is responsible for the policy – for example, a named staff member and a designated governor; and the date it was last reviewed and the next planned review date.

- *Who does this policy apply to?* Our policy applies to all students, staff, governors and volunteers associated with the school.

- *What does the policy relate to?* The use of ICT in all forms, current and emerging. It is part of the school development plan and relates to other policies including those for behaviour, anti-bullying, safeguarding and child protection. It has been written by the school and approved by staff and governors with pupils' participation. It works in conjunction with the school's e-safety policy.

- *Our vision*: We want every member of the school community to be using the opportunities offered by digital technology safely. Everyone has a right to be free of bullying and discrimination, exploitation and harassment.

- *Our objectives*: To inform every member of the school community about how they can be safe on the Internet and when using mobile phones and hand-held devices; to set up clear boundaries and agreement on the Acceptable Use of ICT, the school's systems and those used by every individual, both staff and pupils; and to make staff, pupils, parents and governors our partners in the delivery of an e-safe school.

- *The five main areas of the policy*: current digital technologies; teaching and learning; e-safety risks; strategies to minimise risks; and how complaints about e-safety will be handled. There are often two agreements: one for staff and another for pupils.

  o *Current digital technologies*: ICT in the 21st century has an enabling, creative and essential role in the lives of children and adults. New technologies are rapidly enhancing communication and the sharing of information, images, music and film. We want our students and staff to benefit from the opportunities this represents but we acknowledge there are risks. Current and emerging technologies used in school and outside school include: the Internet accessed by a wide and growing range of devices; intranets and virtual learning environments (VLEs – e.g. Moodle); mobile phone texts, messaging, email, apps, cameras and video; instant messaging services; social networking sites; video-sharing sites; chat rooms, webcams, blogs and podcasting; Twitter; gaming; image-sharing sites; virtual worlds; and music and film downloading sites.

  o *Teaching and learning*: The Internet is an essential tool for learning in 21st century life and is integral to education, work and social life; the school has a duty to provide pupils with quality Internet access as part of their learning experience; Internet use is part of the statutory curriculum and a necessary tool for staff and students; the school infrastructure will be designed specifically for pupils' use and will include safety features and filters that are up to date and well monitored; pupils will be given clear guidance on acceptable behaviour, use of ICT and how to stay safe; pupils will be taught how to search for information safely and effectively and to cross check information to ensure accuracy; pupils will be taught how to publish and present information to a wide audience; pupils will be shown how to evaluate content and respect other people's ownership rights; pupils will be taught to be responsible digital citizens and respect others; and pupils will be taught how to report abusive or offensive content.

Our pupils will be partners in carrying out this policy and they will be consulted regularly on its use. They are asked to sign up to our agreement on Acceptable Use of ICT as a condition of use.

o *E-safety risks include*: content – exposure to inappropriate material for their age and stage, inaccurate and misleading information, socially unacceptable material such as inciting violence or hatred or urging unsafe behaviour, and coercive websites such as those promoting anorexia or self-harm; contact – grooming, harassment or stalking, or unwanted contact of any kind; e-commerce – spam and phishing emails, exposure to advertising that is not suitable for children, e.g. online gambling, and pressurised and hidden selling such as free apps or games that have hidden costs; conduct – cyberbullying, cyber-aggression or abuse, child sexual exploitation, rumour spreading, unwanted image sharing, illegal downloading of music and films, and plagiarism.

o *General strategies to minimise e-safety risks*: all students and parents will sign the Acceptable Use Policy (AUP) for ICT; staff will receive training in effective strategies and how to respond to incidents; parents and pupils will be asked for consent before photographs are used on school websites; parents will be sent regular briefings on e-safety; pupils will receive e-safety education embedded in the curriculum; e-safety advice will be displayed throughout the school; all pupils will log in through a screen which asks for acceptance of this policy; filtering systems will be in place and will be regularly updated, although smartphones, games consoles and other devices can bypass the school's system and access the Internet directly – this represents a risk for the management of content; good infrastructure will be in place and regularly reviewed; staff will use safe searches and vet video clips before showing them to pupils; and mobile phone use within school is limited to certain times and lessons.

As we develop the use of devices such as tablets for learning, we reserve the right to amend this policy and we will undertake regular pupil surveys to consult with them.

All staff sign to show they have read and accepted the terms of this policy.

o *E-safety concerns*: child protection concerns should be reported to the designated safeguarding lead. The school will take steps to protect data and keep personal information about pupils private and securely encrypted; no data will be permitted to leave the school site unless encrypted; pupils' names will not be used with any photograph on the school's websites; pictures and work will only be shown where consent has been given by parents; parents will be clearly informed of the policy on taking and posting photographs; the use of social networking sites in school or for school use will not be allowed unless by agreement with all parties; pupils will be taught never to give personal details online, and will be encouraged to use moderated SNS sites and to use avatars or nicknames on SNS; no member of staff will contact any pupil on matters of a personal nature, using mobile phone, messaging or any other form of direct contact, unless it is expressly agreed by senior management or the pupil is a member of their direct family; webcams will not be used unless specific reasons demand it and consent is sought; and sending abusive or aggressive messages, jokes, images or videos is unacceptable, and any incidents must be reported to staff who are trained to support students.

o *Liability*: Due to the global scale and linked nature of Internet content, the wide availability of mobile and digital technologies and speed of change, it is not possible to guarantee that no unsuitable material will ever appear on a school computer or mobile device. Neither the school nor the Local Authority can accept liability for material accessed, or any consequences of Internet access. The school is not responsible for students under the age of 13 who access Social Networking Sites against their advice.

o *Staff School Computer and Internet Acceptable Use Policy*: All staff having access to the networks must sign a copy of this Computer and Internet Acceptable Use Policy and return it to the Senior Administrator.

o *Checklists*: Teachers and children must complete these to show that they have understood the terms of the policy.

o *User signature*: This acts as confirmation that the user has agreed to the terms of the policy.

Harmful or inappropriate sexual behaviours

Harmful sexual behaviour includes children:

- using sexually explicit words and phrases
- using inappropriate touching
- using sexual violence or threats
- having full or attempted penetrative sex with other children or adults.

Children and young people who develop harmful sexual behaviour harm themselves and others.[25]

Child sexual behaviour can range from normal to inappropriate, problematic, abusive and violent.[26]

Young people with learning difficulties who exhibit harmful sexual behaviours are a particularly vulnerable and neglected group. They may require intensive and targeted intervention responses accompanied by extra e-safety education and support that is tailored to their learning ability. Research shows that they experience high rates of victimisation and trauma and are typically described as having a number of social skills deficits, a lack of sexual knowledge and understanding of relationships and high levels of social anxiety. Their family background may be violent, interrupted, unstable or problematic. This combination can lead them to problems in establishing appropriate intimate relationships and sometimes to attempt abusive sexual interactions with children. Below are some of the factors to be taken into consideration when assessing them for external support you may need to seek:

- early onset of concerning behaviour
- behaviour that is potentially or actually harmful to others

- behaviour that is potentially or actually harmful to self

- learning difficulties

- has suffered victimisation

- other behavioural difficulties

- personality characteristics that make friendships/relationships difficult

- family support

- e-safety concerns

- consideration of whether this behaviour is part of a generally antisocial set of behaviours/aggression.

The victims of harmful sexual behaviour should be supported and made safe according to the safeguarding or child protection policy of your school.

AIM

AIM is:

a UK-derived initial assessment tool for young people with harmful sexual behaviours that can be used across professional systems and between local and regional safeguarding bodies. AIM, and its more recent AIM2 iteration, offer a clinically adjusted actuarial model of assessment, which takes empirically supported factors and adds in those factors which are clinically supported by practitioners. Combining static and dynamic factors, the model builds in the use of guided clinical judgement across four key domains:

- sexual and non-sexual harmful behaviours

- developmental factors

- family

- environment.

In each of the key domains, both strengths and concerns are addressed.[27]

7

Staff Training

What should staff training cover?

The following are key:

- signs a child might be being bullied/cyberbullied
- effective approaches to counter bullying and cyberbullying
- what the law says
- how to handle incidents
- preserving evidence (see Chapter 4)
- positive reinforcement as practised at John Keble School.

Signs a child might be experiencing bullying or cyberbullying

- Loss of usual friends
- Seems lonely and isolated
- Unwilling to go to school
- Unexplained bruises or injuries
- Belongings damaged
- Complains of tummy or headache before school
- Schoolwork results are below usual standard
- Over-use of computer or phone, obsessively checking
- Stops gaming suddenly
- Drops websites down on computers if you enter the room
- Reluctance to answer mobile calls
- Fearful and edgy
- Not sleeping well
- Depressed
- Lunch money 'lost' or child is asking for more
- Loss of appetite
- Nervous and startles easily
- Tearful

- Irritable
- Stammering
- Sudden angry or violent outbursts
- Sleep problems and nightmares
- Bedwetting
- Avoidance behaviours
- Nervousness, anxiety
- Thinks everything is 'unfair'
- Does not want to walk the usual route to school.

Ten points for e-safety educators

They should:

1. model positive and exciting use of technology
2. involve students as co-researchers
3. involve students as peer-teachers
4. chunk the information into digestible bites
5. consider the age and gender of their audience
6. ask for feedback on what they have learned
7. poll students to keep up with trends and their view of risk
8. monitor the effectiveness of what they do
9. engage with parents and ensure they are up to date
10. update themselves regularly on safety advice from hand-held devices, SNS sites and all other available safety advice, which often changes.

Professional conduct

In 2009 DCSF issued guidance on appropriate and safe behaviours to all adults working with children. On page 16 of 'Guidance for safer working practice for adults who work with children and young people' it advises on safe communication:

Communication between pupils and adults, by whatever method, should take place within clear and explicit professional boundaries. This includes the wider use of technology such as mobile phones, text messaging, e-mails, digital cameras, videos, web-cams, websites and blogs. Adults should not share any personal information with a child or young person. They should not request, or respond to, any personal information from the child/young person, other than that which might be appropriate as part of their professional role. Adults should ensure that all communications are transparent and open to scrutiny.[28]

Effective strategies to counter bullying and cyberbullying

Before deciding on which of the many effective approaches you might use, it is important to have some structure in place across the whole school community. There are several structural components to effective practice. Putting these in place can be described in these five steps:

1. raise awareness and consult to find out the extent of the issue

2. develop policy and strategy

3. incorporate communication, training and implementation – staff, pupils, parents and governors should know about your policy, values and approach and be trained where required

4. implement – prevention, responses, recording and monitoring all in place

5. evaluate and adjust as necessary.

See Figure 4.1 in Chapter 4 for the cycle of reflective practice.

Reflective and continuous

Effective practice is not creating a good strong policy and simply imposing it. To be truly effective your practice now enters a continuous cycle, which keeps the work alive, flexible and up to date. Reflective practice alerts you when an approach is not working well. It gives your school scope to be flexible and change with the times, for example as the technology changes. After a serious incident, always consider whether your policy and systems were suitable for this case and make the necessary changes.

Monitoring and review

Ask:

- How effective is your strategy?

- How do you know?

- Could it be improved?

- Do some approaches work better in some circumstances?

- Are some good ideas not working well because of one small change needed?

- Is bullying regularly occurring in one area of the school or on certain days and times?

- Do staff complain it is too time consuming?

Consult your community to achieve 'ownership' and increase effectiveness.

Sustainability

The most effective interventions are 'sustained over the long term, and developed with staff, pupils, parents, carers and partners in the community. They are monitored and evaluated as circumstances change, and supported by a school ethos that inhibits bullying and promotes empathy and respect for diversity.'[29] But if staff find the systems too onerous, they may gradually drop aspects of it. This can weaken implementation.

Policy and systems underpin any strategies but they have to be communicated. Think of this as a public relations drive – to get everyone on board. Where this is a good policy that is 'live' and well communicated, everyone will know what the school's approach is, all staff will know what is expected of them, and parents and pupils will be clear on what approach the school takes. You will find that administration of the systems runs more smoothly and takes less time. Recording and monitoring is vital to understand trends and patterns, but above all should lead to review and evaluation.

Train all staff, teaching and non-teaching. Train pupils to support others via a peer support programme, and make clear to pupils and parents alike how they can report any concerns.

A menu of intervention tools

Menu

Peer support
Nurture group
Mediation
Restorative approach
Befriending
Circle time
Drama
Group work
Shared concern
Resilience development
Challenging prejudice

Figure 7.1 Menu

At this age, cyber incidents tend to originate from other pupils, or migrate to cyberspace from in-school bullying or friendship fallouts. That is why we link bullying intervention strategies to e-safety work. No single strategy provides a complete solution, but choose one from a menu of tools to suit each incident.

Why have a whole-school approach?

A whole-school approach has been found to be more successful than a piecemeal approach, even where there is one brilliant teacher leading the anti-bullying work. This person might be ill one day or leave the school. Other staff members will tend to leave it to this person, thinking that they do not have to deal with bullying because there is this excellent individual who always does it.

- It needs to be sustainable rather than a single, high profile 'blitz'.

- It needs to be owned by everyone – teaching and non-teaching staff.

- It needs to be supported by the senior management team.

- Parents and pupils need to be engaged.

- Governors have responsibilities to oversee this.

- It should not be so onerous that busy staff members do not want to follow it – so too much paperwork or too controlling a style will not necessarily get staff on board.

Rights of the child

Anti-bullying work is based on a foundation of equality and rights, outlined in the United Nations Convention on the Rights of the Child (UNCRC).[30] A 'rights-based approach' develops shared values, beliefs and attitudes that inhibit bullying. This approach recognises that every pupil has a right to be safe and respected and has a right to education, which is of course interrupted or thwarted if they are victimised or experience discrimination. They have a right to have their views heard. Their family and culture deserve respect.

Reward positive behaviour and reinforce rights

A safe environment is underpinned by these values and promotes and rewards positive behaviour.

Have you ever stopped to think about the fact that the majority of pupils do *not* bully others? Your aim is to make this behaviour the norm. Give it more profile than the negative behaviour by modelling and rewarding prosocial behaviour. The bullying intervention approach should aim to become part of an embedded curricular approach to bullying whether on- or offline.[31]

Parents

Inform parents of the school's strategy and make the policy available to them. Include them in the review process annually. Parents should agree at the outset to support the school's efforts to prevent bullying. (Prejudice is often fostered at home.) Your approach should include how parents can report any concerns, how they will be supported and how the school will report back to them when putting in place an action plan to change bullying behaviour whether their child is a target or a perpetrator.

A few effective approaches

You cannot bully people to stop bullying

Just because an approach works well in some schools and services does not mean it is ideal for your setting. You will need to choose approaches that you think are appropriate and then monitor how well they work for you. Don't be afraid to try a different strategy if you see that the way you are handling a case is not working after giving it a fair amount of time.

Curricular approaches

One-off lessons on e-safety and cyberbullying, or short 'blitz'-type activities, are less likely to succeed than work embedded in the curriculum which progressively addresses relationships, positive behaviour and resilience. E-safety should not be a separate 'subject' but be embedded across the curriculum and particularly referred to when relationships are discussed.

Work within circle time, English, drama, maths, ICT, art, SPHE (social, personal and health education), RE and history builds a supportive school culture and shared values. It can enable and empower pupils to acquire and maintain the social skills that will allow them to constructively manage their relationships with others and equip them to respond to bullying in an appropriate and, if necessary, assertive way.

> This approach to bullying has the advantage of ensuring that the issue is introduced progressively in an age, gender and culturally appropriate way and not treated as a 'one-off' lesson. It allows pupils to make use of preferred and appropriate learning styles and can include the use of: literature, audio visual material, drama, music, debates and outside visitors.[32]

The BIG Award has found that this is often more effective than the approach often described as the 'legal approach', that is, a complaint and investigation, a punishment route which can put the target of the aggression in a position of greater risk of retaliation, more social isolation, contempt from some peers for being a 'grass' and encouraging a sense of helplessness in some individuals. Targets of bullying often want to be accepted in the social group more than anything. While some sanctions or consequences should follow if a pupil bullies others, a heavy-handed, punitive approach is not likely to achieve this social acceptance for the targeted pupil.

Embedding the work in the curriculum enhances the likelihood of peers taking steps to intervene if fellow pupils with special educational needs are targeted, and enables onlookers to report it and get help. Furthermore, anti-bullying work succeeds fully only if there is supportive work in the curriculum. For example, if sex and relationships education addresses relationships and negotiating consent, this will have an impact on online behaviour, sexting, cyberbullying and bullying linked to jealousy and relationships.

Peer support

Peer support covers a range of planned and structured approaches to bullying that aim to make use of the knowledge, skills and experience of children and young people to understand, support, inform and help develop the skills, self-esteem and confidence of their peers. Evidence confirms that peer support makes a significant contribution to the reduction of bullying.[33] Used to support an anti-bullying policy in schools, it allows children to reject bullying behaviour, to take responsibility for themselves and others within the school community, to develop their capacity to empathise and connect with others and to contribute to the safety and wellbeing of their peers.

A high level of school and teacher commitment is required to ensure its effectiveness as pupil volunteers must be trained and their work monitored, with staff available to deal with issues that require referral. Peer support should not be seen as a replacement for adult involvement in anti-bullying strategies and should be used as one approach among others.[34]

Different terms have been adopted to describe different peer support approaches more accurately.

- *Peer education* involves one pupil sharing their knowledge, skills and experience individually and in groups. Used to promote understanding and knowledge of life skills, it can be used to help support a pupil who has been bullied. The process also positively benefits peer educators in terms of their own personal development.

- *Peer listening* gives pupils access to a friendly and empathetic ear and allows problems to be shared. It can be particularly effective in bullying situations where there is reluctance to share concerns with an adult because of fears of not being taken seriously, or of adult involvement making things worse.

- *Peer befriending* involves children and young people building on the helping skills they have already acquired through everyday interaction with friends and family. It can involve informal chats (when the approach overlaps with peer listening), but can extend to the use of 'buddy' systems and circle of friends schemes, when the bullied pupil is befriended by another pupil of the same age with the aim of increasing their sense of belonging and of ending their feelings of isolation and loneliness.

- *Peer mentoring* involves a supportive relationship between two pupils: the mentee and the mentor. It is commonly used as a preventative rather than reactive strategy and allows the mentor to take an active, personal interest in their mentee, which combines friendship with guidance, advice and encouragement. It is used to support a pupil during a challenging time, such as when they join a new school or after a bereavement, but can also be used to support a pupil who may have been identified as vulnerable to bullying. Peer mentoring is a more developed, structured version of peer befriending and is usually cross-age.

- In *peer mediation* trained peer mediators solve problems between pupils by encouraging them to: define the problem, identify and agree key issues, discuss and arrive at a solution and negotiate a written agreement signed by all participants. They then follow up the outcome. This approach usually adopts a 'no blame' view of the situation and emphasises the importance of recognising bullying behaviour, apologising for it, putting it in the past and agreeing a way forward. Everyone involved should come away feeling that the outcome is fair to all sides.

- *Peer advocacy* involves getting children and young people to identify the views and concerns of others (which may include bullying) and speaking on their behalf. In schools, this can be done through the school council.[35]

Work with bystanders

Increasingly there is more understanding of the importance of an 'audience' for bullying behaviour and the power of the majority. Work to allow the group to express their dislike of bullying behaviour in group work or circles or via drama can empower children to stand up to bullying or report it where necessary. This may be unnecessary, however, for frequently when the bystanders are alert and prepared, they challenge bullying behaviour when they first see it and the perpetrators can come to realise that popularity and power will not be gained through bullying.[36]

Circle time

Circle time is used in many schools, with different age groups, to address constructive discussions and issues of concern. Over 20–30 minutes, with some clear ground rules, the teacher facilitates a safe and positive environment for pupils to take turns (if they want to) to talk about an issue, such as bullying. Participants are encouraged to listen to each other with respect and to discuss issues in a problem-solving way. Names are not mentioned. A very useful opening question might be 'I don't like it when…'.

Circle time can be used to help young children become aware of bullying in a supportive environment and discuss ways of dealing with it without scaring them. The approach improves listening and communication skills, teaches pupils to take turns and to consider the feelings of others, allows them to explore their own and others' feelings about difficult issues and increases their confidence and self-esteem as they find their own solutions. Members of the circle can put forward suggestions on how they might help someone who has described a situation they do not like. It is then up to them to decide whether or not they think these ideas are helpful. An idea might be the following: 'We will walk with Joey when we go into lunch so he is not alone when those bigger boys try and bully him.'[37]

Circle of friends

Also known as 'circle of support', the approach provides emotional support to vulnerable pupils who may feel isolated and rejected by their peers. Pupils are trained to befriend and support another pupil identified as vulnerable to bullying. One of the strengths of the approach is that it also supports those who bully as a result of feeling isolated and rejected themselves.

With the agreement of the child who is being bullied, the class meets to discuss the situation. The supervising teacher encourages the class to speak about the targeted child positively and to say how they would feel if they were isolated or excluded themselves. The target is not present. A small group of pupils volunteer to be in the circle of friends and agree ways to help the other child.

The technique teaches children and young people to empathise with peers who are feeling socially excluded and to look at how this might have been linked to their own behaviour. As well as benefiting the person for whom the circle of friends was set up, it provides all participants with a creative way of forming positive relationships with their peers. This is important, as there is evidence that children find that having friends is one of the best ways to prevent or deal with bullying.[38]

Mediation

Both students need to agree to this approach. It works best when there is not a great imbalance of power. It is necessary for staff to be trained in this method. Learning to deal successfully with conflict through mediation can deliver skills for later in life. However, in certain cases of cyberbullying, this approach is not always appropriate due to an imbalance of power and fear, or the unwillingness or impossibility of the perpetrator and target coming face to face. When used, it is best after a period of time has elapsed since the incident and if it involved former friends.

Restorative approaches

Restorative approaches are designed to restore damaged relationships and make good the harm caused. Large numbers of children in bullying situations long 'for things to be like they were before'. This approach can be helpful in such situations. However, when the cyberbullying children (and their parents) are in total denial, it is too early to embark on this approach. The aggressor will need to acknowledge the harm or wrongdoing and then act restoratively via a compensatory action or apology.

Strengthening the victim

- Rehearse possible responses

- Practise purposeful body language

- Fogging; learning verbal ways to contend with the remarks

- Explore a web of support (who have you got around you?)

- Detach from the power of the bully – you are not defined by this person

- School and parents work in partnership to strengthen the child's self-esteem

- Building on the strengths of the child; engineer opportunities for the child to succeed at things or help others.

Some young children need to learn prosocial behaviour such as taking turns or losing in some games without making a fuss. Your help can make them less of a target. Practise *Snakes and Ladders*. Help them if they are never selected into teams by other children by simply organising the teams.

Classroom dynamics are important– rearrange where people sit, re-partner people and control the room.[39]

The support group approach

The support group approach was formerly known as the 'No Blame' approach. Developed by Barbara Maines and George Robinson this approach challenged the 'investigate, interrogate and punish' approach which often resulted in a hostile perpetrator and drove the bullying underground.

This approach focuses strongly on how the victim is feeling, and it draws the focus and energy away from finding someone to blame. The bully and henchmen are encouraged to change their behaviour and make amends. A wider group involving bystanders and other students are drawn in to finding a solution, relying on group dynamics and appealing to empathy and understanding. This approach has at times been misunderstood as 'letting the perpetrator off the hook' but is very demanding as it requires a lot of people to look at their behaviour and change. It can have a lasting impact. Considerable staff time is wasted in traditional interrogative methods when everyone denies being involved and children are sent to the headteacher over and over again accusing one another. This approach should be used accurately and not in any way diluted. When used well it can bring about change rapidly. There are seven clear steps to the approach and no specialist skills are needed.

- *Step one*: Interview with the victim: talk to victim about their feelings, but do not question them about the incident directly.

- *Step two*: Organise a meeting with the people involved (minus the victim).

- *Step three*: Explain the problem: teacher tells them about the way the victim is feeling.

- *Step four*: Share responsibility: the teacher does not attribute blame but states that they know the group is responsible and they can do something about it.

- *Step five*: Ask the group for their ideas: each member of the group is encouraged to suggest a way in which the victim could be helped to feel happier. This singles out each person rather than treating them as a group.

- *Step six*: Leave it up to them: end the meeting by passing on the responsibility to the group to solve the problem.

- *Step seven*: Meet them again: about a week later to hear from each student, including the victim, how things have been going.

This approach has been controversial where parents have falsely believed that the bully 'gets away with it'. However, when correctly used, the bully is helped to see the impact of their behaviour and supported to change. This approach, often known as the 'no blame approach', has been widely used in several countries, but it is important that, if using it, to do so correctly and not in some diluted form which might have been a cause of the controversy. People who use it correctly are very positive about the outcomes. I recommend you attend training or read the information below.[40]

Shared concern (Pikas approach)

Often compared to the no blame approach, this is another non-punitive approach based on counselling. It focuses on those doing the bullying as well as those who are bullied and is designed for situations where a group of pupils has been bullying one or more pupils for some time. It does not try to identify all the events of the bullying situation and aims to allow the pupils to coexist rather than to create friendships. This is the opposite of a forensic investigative approach, which seeks to get all the evidence in place and then apportion punishment, possibly leaving resentment in its wake and the way open for retaliation and ostracism.

A teacher uses a structured script to talk to each of the pupils who is doing the bullying, with the aim of reaching an agreement that the bullied pupil is unhappy and concluding by each pupil agreeing to try to help improve the situation. These meetings are followed by a supportive talk between the teacher and the bullied pupil. In cases where the bullied pupil's behaviour may have been seen as provocative (about 20%) – by irritating other pupils, or by being unable to handle disagreement or conflict – the teacher encourages the bullied pupil to understand that their behaviour should also change. Individual follow-up meetings are held to review progress and finally a meeting of all pupils is held, with the aim of reaching a public agreement about reasonable behaviour by everyone over the long term. The approach aims to help young people reflect on and change their behaviour and learn from the incident. It is not a quick fix that drives bullying underground.[41]

Quality circles

The approach is borrowed from industry where quality circles are used to introduce employees to participative management. In short, it involves setting up a group of pupils to identify, prioritise and discuss problems such as bullying and to develop solutions. The process involves five stages:

- *identifying and prioritising the problem*: members identify all the problems they have encountered and decide which to tackle first

- *analysing the problem*: pupils talk about the possible causes of the problem and collect information to establish its extent – for example, through a survey, interviewing pupils who have been bullied and observing playground behaviour

- *developing the solution*: pupils break down a solution into its smallest parts, identifying a starting point for action and formulating a plan to implement it

- *presenting the solution to school management*: teachers, headteacher and governors

- *reviewing the solution*: if it is agreed to implement the solution, its effectiveness is evaluated by school management and results fed back to the quality circle; if agreement cannot be reached to implement the quality circle solution, school management discuss their reasons for refusal with the quality circle, which then reviews the solution in the light of these reasons.

In order to be effective in a school setting, it is essential that this approach has the backing and commitment of the adult school community, who must be prepared to share power and decision-making with pupils.[42]

Roots of Empathy

Roots of Empathy is an evidence-based primary classroom programme that has shown significant effect in reducing levels of aggression among school children while raising social/emotional competence and increasing empathy. Founded in 1996, this is a well-tried programme for emotional competence and is used with very young children to break cycles of violence. Children connect to a baby on a deep level to discover their emotions and the feelings of others.[43]

Assertiveness training groups

This approach aims to change the behaviour of the pupils who are bullied and to help them use verbal and body language in a way that discourages bullying. Working individually or sitting informally in a group (which should not contain those being bullied *and* those doing the bullying), pupils learn how to respond to bullying in a calm, controlled, assertive and safe way. This can include learning how to:

- make assertive statements
- avoid the use of threats or manipulative behaviour
- deal with name-calling
- escape from physical restraint
- get help from bystanders
- increase self-esteem
- stay calm.[44]

Bully boxes

Pupils write down their concerns about bullying and post them in a post box known as a 'bully box' or 'worry box'. The approach creates opportunities for anonymous, confidential communication, but is open to abuse if pupils post malicious or frivolous comments. To be effective, there must be a quick response to issues raised by the bully box and it should not be located where everyone can see who is using it. Many pupils prefer to text a number set up by the school for confidential reporting. Nevertheless, there will always be some for whom writing on a piece of paper is easiest. A number of routes to report bullying should be available.

KiVa

This is a research-based anti-bullying programme that has been developed in the University of Turku, Finland. It is funded by the Ministry of Education and Culture. The effectiveness of the programme has been shown in a large randomised controlled trial. In Finland, it is much sought after: 90 per cent of all comprehensive schools in the country are registered KiVa schools. It is intended to be a permanent part of school life, to be universally applied, with key actions used for incidents. Evaluations show excellent outcomes.[45] KiVa has begun to work in the UK.

Dolls and puppets

The use of dolls and puppets has proved useful to address a range of issues including bullying, in early years settings and for children with special needs. Very often the fact that you are talking about what has happened to the doll and how she feels can free up the child to explain what is going on.[46]

Tougher measures

These are measures that include sanctions such as the following:

- removal from class

- detention

- withholding participation in non-curricular activities such as school trips and sports events

- a fixed period of exclusion – 'Where serious violence is involved, the headteacher can and should normally permanently exclude a pupil. Appeal panels have been told that they should not seek to overrule such a decision on appeal.'[47]

- where there has been a serious assault, warnings can be given by community safety police officers

- where cyber-abuse or aggression is involved, it may be necessary to have material removed from websites after evidence has been saved. The right of the school to confiscate a mobile phone or hand-held device to investigate where necessary has to be clarified.

General approaches

The following are important:

- *working with parents/carers* to promote good behaviour, encourage involvement in promoting the school ethos, and to consult over the school's approach to bullying

- *a playground policy* for pupils, teachers and lunch-time supervisors, which should set out clear guidelines for managing pupil behaviour during break and lunch times, including the use of mobiles

- *training supervisors* so that they can better identify and help vulnerable children who may be more at risk of bullying/cyberbullying and providing supervisors with routes to report their concerns

- *improving the school grounds* so that they provide a safe, secure and more easily supervised environment in which children can play and educational, social and physical activities thrive, reducing the opportunity and likelihood of bullying

- *developing transport schemes to and from school* as a way of addressing bullying incidents off school premises, perhaps with the help of outside agencies or pupil bus monitors. Cyberbullying often breaks out on the bus after school. When the unfortunate victim gets home he finds a blizzard of messages on his social network page or a flurry of messages showing they are talking about him. Some schools use a negotiated agreement with pupils on behaviour on transport

- *group work* to teach social and communication skills to help in the development of positive relationships so that children can make and keep friends, for example R Time – a programme to develop positive relationships in primary schools[48]

- *questionnaires* for use with children, parents/carers and school staff to gain an indication of the extent and nature of problems related to bullying

- *school assemblies, flashmobs, group tweets, poster campaigns, screensaver campaigns and internal plasma screens* can be used to raise awareness of bullying/cyberbullying and e-safety issues

- *Art work, song competitions, What is a friend?* See Activities, page 158.

School example: Positive behaviour reinforcement used by John Keble Primary School

This programme of behaviour management heavily rewards prosocial behaviour in all aspects of school life, and the bullying intervention work sits comfortably within the school's vision and overall behaviour work. Their playground citizen awards and other nominations are very democratic.

The school aims to give positive reinforcement and praise as frequently as possible, and to avoid the build-up of poor behaviour. They acknowledge good behaviour by:

- approval by non-verbal and verbal means

- a thank you

- stamps, stickers and certificates

- house points

- class DoJos

- sending children to the Head, Deputy or Assistant Head

- talking positively to parents/carers in front of their child, or phoning home

- awards and prizes at assemblies, for behaviour, attendance, effort, etc.

- showing good work to another teacher by prior arrangement with that teacher

- a visit to the class by a member of the leadership team.

To ensure continuity in the school's expectations of the children, they have a range of incentive systems in place, which are followed by every class. Nursery and Reception teachers have their own methods of reward in their class. Formal school incentive reward systems include:

- stay on green

- star of the week

- lining up points

- house points

- stickers or stamps

- playground citizen awards

- class attendance awards.

Stay on green

This is the behaviour management system used throughout the school from Years 1–6 with Reception joining in the summer term. Each class has a 'Stay on green' chart which has 30 pockets and 30 green cards – one for each child.

- Each day begins with children on green. Children should aim to stay on green the whole day by behaving well.

- The stay on green record goes home at the end of the week and is returned on Monday mornings, signed by the parent/carer. Children who have stayed on green all week and return their signed card receive five house points.

- Children who stay on green each half term get a certificate and a treat.

- Children who stay on green for a whole term get a special certificate and a special mention in the end-of-term assembly.

- Children who stay on green for a year get a medal and a special mention.

Class DoJos

DoJos are electronic icons which can be personalised for children. They prove highly motivating for most children and can be used as instant rewards for general classroom behaviours. A free app can be found at www.classdojo.com/resources/.

Special award

Two children from each class are chosen each week for a special award for demonstrating one or more of the Christian values of the school. These children are congratulated in Achievement Assembly on Mondays. An example might be 'Well done to X for showing endurance by persevering with a challenging task in Maths'. The school's Christian values are on display in the main hall and include: compassion, endurance, thankfulness, creation, forgiveness, reverence, peace, justice, humility, hope, friendship, wisdom, trust, service and koinonia (teamwork).

House points

All children and staff across the school belong to one of four houses – St Matthew, St Mark, St Luke or St John. Children are awarded house points for positive social behaviour, citizenship and academic excellence. The points for each house group are collected at the end of the week and announced weekly at Achievement Assemblies. The winning house has a ribbon in their house colour tied to the cup, and a special celebration is held for the winning house at the end of each half-term.

Playground citizen awards

Children nominate each other for positive social behaviour in the playground. This includes acts of kindness, being friendly towards each other, helping and buddying each other and being good role models or showing one of the Christian values. Children fill in a nomination slip and put it in the playground citizen box. These are counted at the end of the week and a certificate and playground rosette are awarded to a KS1 child and a KS2 child with the most nominations in Achievement Assembly.

Lining up points and class attendance awards are also given.

Other schools such as Coln House have suggested a positive behaviour and reward programme based on the format of the Premier League, Championship, Division 1 and Division 2.

Steps to compliance: Schools should have in place -

Clear and updated e-safety policies	How recently was your e-safety policy updated.? (This is often called an acceptable use of ICT policy). Is it easily understood by all staff, pupils and parents? Is it known to all staff, teaching and non-teaching?
An action plan to become Ofsted compliant	Check for Ofsted updates. Look at the Framework for Inspection Check any new Safeguarding documents. The former Section 5 Briefing on e-safety inspection is useful
Staff training	All staff should be trained and kept up to date on cyberbullying and e-safety practice and procedures in your school. This is vital on induction and in any professional code of conduct.
Pupils' AUP interacts with anti-bullying policy	No more silos! Bullying cannot be separated from acceptable use of ICT, digital citizenship and behaving respectfully online. Cyberbullying is often an extension of face-to-face in-school bullying. Victims may need extra e-safety support.
Easy and secure ways for pupils to report incidents	Pupils do not want to be seen reporting a problem . They may be seen as a grass. Provide safe routes and privacy. Ensure reporting is easy for young children and parents
Recording/monitoring system	Does the recording of incidents feed into review of policy or approach? Do the records get monitored in order to take action to prevent future e-safety incidents? Does the information indicate how you can proactively prevent discrimination and challenge prejudice?

What makes a child a 'bully magnet'?

If we understood the dynamics of the behaviour, could we be more proactive and respond more sensitively if cases occur? That is the challenging question behind this brief exploration of what makes a child more likely to be bullied.

There are extensive studies on this subject from psychologists, sociologists and educators, and while I don't have the opportunity to go into great depth here, I want to raise the question so that in your own practice you might become more aware of the whole child.

Some argue that, deep down, fear of abandonment is what makes victims often do all they can to please a group who are not accepting them. In his book on ostracism, Kipling Williams[49] talks about the ways victims feel they must change in order to be accepted. This can mean getting extra thin or running errands for their torturers. The urge to be accepted is so strong that their efforts can become ever more desperate until they almost lose sight of who they really are. Yet the more they show this vulnerable eagerness to be accepted, the more the bullies toy with their emotions.

Author Robert Evans Wilson Jnr goes further, arguing that parents 'groom' children to be bullied by providing unstable homes or by being 'absent' in various ways. In *Psychology Today* he wrote that he experienced this himself: 'Until I was about ten years old, I was fearful. Nearly afraid of everything. And, this made me a bully magnet.' He continues by saying that children who lack confidence cannot shrug it off; they cry or get upset or run away, giving the very signals to the bullies that they seek:

> Those behaviours almost guarantee that you'll be bullied again. And once you see yourself as a victim, the bullies seem to come out of the woodwork.
>
> I wasn't visibly different. It was my fear that made me a victim. I grew up in an unstable household with a narcissistic mother. She always needed to be the centre of attention. When things didn't go her way, everyone suffered. She was verbally abusive and occasionally physically abusive. And, my father never defended me; he was too busy trying to please her.
>
> Parents who create unstable homes are fostering victimhood in their children. They are setting them up to be targets of bullies. Narcissism, alcoholism, neglect, abuse, divorce, and heated arguments can lead to an unsound environment for a kid. These situations stimulate a fear of abandonment and the child does not feel safe. A child in these conditions cannot develop the self-esteem and self-confidence necessary to protect himself.

Evans Wilson suggests that the bully is often experiencing a similar 'volatile environment', so the victim is easy prey, exactly what the bully is seeking.

> They don't attack the strong and confident because the bully himself feels weak and insecure. It is the attacking of someone weak and defenceless that makes the bully feel powerful.[50]

In research at the University of Oxford, in which I was an associate, the team found some significant differences in the lives of both bullies and victims when their responses were compared to those from children who were not involved in bullying. The project received over 11,000 responses from across the UK. We explored the answers of those who were severely/persistently bullied, leaving out those who were bullied once or twice or very mildly.

We found that bullies and victims were significantly more likely than other children to describe a home life with a negative punitive parenting style. They were also significantly more likely to be smacked or beaten. Family 'togetherness' and 'father involvement' were both measured using a number of different factors, resulting in a score we created. These two family measures turned out to be enormously important even when the father did not live in the household. Depression was significantly more likely among the bullies and bullied compared to other children.

Table 7.1 shows where significant differences were found. The use of the word 'significant' in this context refers to a statistical test which shows that the young people who were bullied or bullies gave responses that differed markedly and unpredictably from those of their peers who were not involved in bullying. This is indicated by the symbol +; NS = not significant and ND = no data.

Table 7.1 Significant factors in the lives of bullies and bullied young people compared to their peers

	The bullied		The bullies	
	Boys	Girls	Boys	Girls
Violence in their lives				
Smacked or beaten a lot	+	+	+	+
Prepared to use violence to defend self	−	+	+	+
Parenting style				
Negative, punitive parenting style	+	+	+	+
Low family togetherness score	+	+	+	+
Low father involvement score	+	+	+	+
Personal profiles				
Negative antisocial coping strategies	+	+	+	+
Depression/suicidal thoughts and attempts	+	+	+	+
Think boys/girls 'must be tough to survive'	+	+	+	+
School				
Think 'school is a waste of time'	+	+	+	+
An anti-bullying policy does not work	+	+	+	+
Right and wrong				
Views about right and wrong same as parents	NS	+	+	+
Views about right and wrong different from friends	+	+	NS	NS
Pressured to use drugs	+	+	+	+
In trouble with the police	NS	ND	+	ND
Believes there is no equality in the home	+	NS	NS	+

Other findings included the following:

- A similar proportion of bullied and bullies were anxious about their parents.

- Severely bullied children were three times more likely than those who were not bullied to say they would not use a helpline to get help because 'people would think I was useless'.

- More than a quarter of bullies and victims said they would not seek help from a helpline because 'they can't do anything about my life'.

- Males who bully are twice as likely as their peers to say that when distressed they drink alcohol.

- Forty-three per cent of male bullies believe boys are expected to deal with problems on their own rather than report them, in a tightly policed 'script' pushed by other boys and many fathers of what being male means – i.e. 'Stand on your own two feet.'

- Bullied boys were less likely to say their parents were loving: 76 per cent vs 92 per cent of their peers.

- Seventy-five per cent of boys and over 80 per cent of girls who were NOT bullied come from families who do things together.

- Parents of victims were also described as over-controlling.

- Bullied girls were twice as likely to say that bullying was their number one cause of stress.[51]

Steps that have helped in real cases

When supporting a child who has been bullied, it is vital to engage with the parents and try to encourage them to work with the school where possible. This can be very sensitive work, but by gaining their trust we have seen some very successful cases resolved. Serious cases may involve a counsellor. You should also explain that new approaches may take a little time to show success if a situation has been embedded for a long time. Parents should also expect progress with some intermittent setbacks! This is more realistic, so help them manage expectations and get regular feedback from them and their child on how they think the new approach is going. If the approach chosen is simply not working, do not persist beyond half a term. Select another tool in your armoury. Reflective practice is never afraid to say something could be working better.

The boy who could not lose at games

In one case the parents were asked to play games like *Snakes and Ladders* with a Year 6 boy who simply threw a tantrum if he lost at anything – football, playground games, school work that was not perfect – leading others to bully him and easily 'press his buttons'. They were to laugh it off when they lost and play the game again. They were asked not to be too exacting or demanding with him at home. This would eventually help him learn to cope better with losing. Gradually he coped in football too. His fear of failure had been making him so anxious and wired up he blew a fuse every time anything did not go right for him. School accompanied this with strenuous efforts to show him that making a mistake or losing was a learning opportunity. Over a number of weeks with some setbacks as expected, he began to cope with losing, and the other pupils stopped targeting him.

The boy who modelled his behaviour on his father

Regarding children who bully others, there is no point in prescribing more of the same – those very punitive behaviours discussed above that may have contributed to the bullying behaviour in the first place. In any case, you cannot bully someone out of bullying! So model the behaviour you want. Try to address this with parents if it is safe to do so – one headteacher I know tried to talk to the parents of a boy who was bullying others in a visit to their home, but before she could say anything the father took off his belt and began to beat the boy. There in front of her was an illustration of why he bullied other children – he was not prepared to be a victim in the school setting as he was at home and he had internalised the idea that you have to assert yourself as the powerful person to avoid being the victim. He modelled his father's behaviour and had an iron grip on the other boys.

The girl who believed what the bullies said

This girl believed that she deserved to be bullied. In some way she had internalised the attacks on her and felt she was not worthy of respect. She said that they criticised her online and called her awful words and that must be because she was, or looked like, 'a fat slut'. Work on her view of herself was a vital component of the support package. Getting to the bottom of how she came to have this view of herself was sensitive, lengthy work. But she could not go forward without it. This uncovered many concerns at home, and family counselling was added to her package of support, while work with the girls who tormented her continued in parallel. She was not strong enough for a restorative justice approach.

More advice

Home is where you make a contribution as part of a team

Parents can be encouraged to let their child contribute to family decisions or do tasks that help the family and get rewarded with high regard by all members. Often they have not noticed that this child is never the leader or decision-maker in a busy household with many other people.

Identifying the child's support network

Help the young person to draw a web of support to identify who they can count on for help (see page 89).

Help them be a success

Devise activities in which they can shine or succeed and encourage parents to do the same at home. Offer them opportunities to help others – either younger pupils or as an anti-bullying focus group member. These activities must not make it seem as though they are a teacher's pet. Encourage self-reflection: 'I was small and mouthy I suppose, so I got bullied.' While bullying should never be viewed as inevitable – nobody deserves to be bullied – it is a good thing to be self-aware.

> We made her stop talking about how rich she was cos we bullied her every time she did it, you know, lording it over us.

Control what is in your power!

Change the classroom dynamics with a new seating plan; keep the warring factions well managed. Pair them with people yourself when asking students to work together so that victims are not isolated or shunned.

Reading body language

Work with the victim to help them change their body language by using drama scenarios, cartoons or jokey demonstrations. Practise confident body language.

Rehearse the retort

Help them think of responses they might use in advance, preferably assertive and witty. Help them change their thought pattern so that they do not see every little pinprick as a slur or a bullying incident, by giving them tools to laugh about it. Also, check their friends list on SNS and clean.

Be aware of remarks teachers make without thinking

> I heard him say, 'These girls are so bitchy.' He doesn't understand.

> My teacher said she hates teaching in a single-sex school. You wouldn't go to her with your situation, would you?

Be aware of local gangs and neighbourhood territorial wars

I think bullying is getting more dangerous. They've got knives now and they threaten me on my mobile.

I was a member of a gang. In a way it was comforting. It was an all-boy gang. Some would help you if you were in trouble. There were older and youngers in it. They controlled us all by mobiles and told us what to do and where to be.

Our school is next door to two others. There were loads of hostilities between them. People punched at the bus stop for no reason and that. Then they made hate pages about us online and posted photos of the fights.

Quick quiz for teachers

Online jargon is the specialised language, chat acronyms, text message shorthand and technical lingo that is used while communicating in the online world. Be sure to check out the list of funny new online jargon in the twitterverse! The blogosphere has its own lingo, some very shocking. Don't worry if you cannot remember all the terms but know where you can conveniently look them up, for example www.netlingo.com. In some cases you will need to look up terms to know what is being said.

How many of these do you know?

netlingo, a.k.a. blargon	
electronic language	
hybrid shorthand	
slang	
cyberslang	
email style	
interactive written discourse	
slanguage	
cyberterms	
geekspeak	
net lingo	
textese	
e-lingo	
hi-tech lingo	
netspeak	
textspeak.txt lingo	

Preparation before starting activities
Creating a safe space

When you are planning to start a group discussion on sensitive topics such as cyberbullying, it is good practice to create a safe space with agreed rules and codes of behaviour before you begin. This pre-planning can help create a safe, supportive atmosphere, but more importantly the ground rules can protect children. They also protect staff, as you can adequately prepare and if necessary take advice in advance. Think about the seating arrangement. Are people sitting around comfortably as a group or stiffly in rows? Is the environment friendly and calm? Of course there will be times when a child tells you something at the most inopportune moment – and you will have to take immediate decisions on how to handle this. But for group work it is possible to plan ahead.

Ground rules and preparation

Any staff members involved should be well prepared for disclosures. Discussions that involve explorations of how we treat one another, of what is and is not acceptable behaviour, will occasionally reveal domestic violence or some other difficult or sensitive issue as the children begin to think about this.

Ensure staff know how to report any concerns and how to support a young person if it should be required. All staff members should know and understand the school's anti-bullying policy and its safeguarding and child protection systems as well as the Acceptable Use of ICT policy and e-safety policy if they are separate. They should be able to call on a colleague to take over if they need to take a child out of the group for one-to-one support.

Take care not to single out any pupils in the class or group – if you are aware someone is vulnerable or a little different – those who are an asylum seeker, gay, badly bullied or in care, for example – do not single out this child too often in the discussion asking for their insights, or focus too much on someone who is a newcomer from another country when discussing racism. Your eagerness to involve this pupil may bring unwelcome attention to someone who only wants to fit in. As adults leading group discussions we always have to be aware of our own prejudices and attitudes – could something a child says unfairly affect our attitude towards him? Professional behaviour is required now more than ever. We like the child, but we do not like an attitude, a view expressed or a behaviour.

The group should agree some ground rules. These include the following:

- respect the views of others

- start with and keep an open mind

- use no names – talk about behaviour you do not like, not a person

- no question is too unimportant or wrong

- no answer is 'wrong'

- accept that some people have different views and opinions, and learn

- let others speak

- what is discussed here today remains here.

Discussing bullying or cyberbullying based on prejudice or stereotypes

It can help to take a 'rights-based approach'. If we start from the idea that we all have certain rights, it is easy to take the discussion into areas that look at stereotypes and prejudice. You might find the UNCRC a useful starting point, or the Equality Act 2010. Another advantage of a rights-based approach is that it underlines our common humanity at the start and again at the finish if it is used in this way.

Agree on what universal rights we think we have:

- a right to be safe

- a right to education

- a right to a family life

- a right not to be discriminated against.

What will be discussed are situations in which these rights are overridden. Everyone agrees that nobody should be bullied or cyberbullied.

- Expect some views to be uncomfortable.

- Learning that prejudice-based bullying is unacceptable may take quite some time for some individuals. But it is vital to air the arguments and demonstrate that it is unacceptable and will be challenged within the school and in future workplaces. It is against our law to discriminate and to incite hatred.

- If people express offensive views, challenge the discriminatory attitudes and behaviour, not the person.

- Don't ignore racist, disablist or homophobic insults, jokes or name-calling because they are difficult to challenge or because staff feel nervous. This would give the impression that you and your school support such views. Language matters.

- Just like the pupils, staff members will have their own attitudes, stereotypes and expectations. It is best not to trivialise or deny other people's concerns and feelings, but to model an inclusive style of teaching and behaviour.

- Challenge incorrect assumptions or rumours with accurate information.

- If you tell a child to 'ignore it' they might feel you are denying their pain. You want to fully support them in various ways, even if you are suggesting they do not feed the trolls or bullies. Rather, say: 'Do not reply, save evidence, and let's take the following steps…'

Responding to disclosures

- If a student makes a disclosure which suggests that he or she is at risk of harm, from other people or him- or herself, action must be taken. Staff cannot promise confidentiality in this situation. A calm response and effective, compassionate listening will need to be followed by the next steps in your safeguarding or child protection policy.

- First, thank the student for coming forward with this matter and assure them you and the school will do all you can to support them.

- Never underestimate the enormous step it represents for a young person to have chosen you as the person they trust! This child may have agonised for weeks about what to do; they may have been lying awake at night racked with worry. You might have come to represent a solution in their mind.

- They may feel desperate, anxious or relieved – and usually there are a multitude of problems piling up upon them at once. Once they have settled on you as the person to tell, they may be expecting more from you than you are actually able to deliver. You will need to support them into the next steps.

- It is not uncommon for someone to present at first with only one of these multiple problems. It is likely they will be in a fragile state. Your demeanour is vital. Looking shocked or panicky is not helpful. Offer warm, non-judgemental support. Ask gentle questions. Gradually the situation will be revealed.

- You will need to refer the case to the designated safeguarding lead in your school. You should try to get the student to agree to this, even though you will be obliged to do it anyway. Then offer to consult the student on next steps and work together to try to resolve the situation wherever possible. In less serious cyberbullying cases that do not involve the designated safeguarding lead, there may be a possibility of handling the case discreetly without talking to the class about it.

- Listen carefully and write down what the pupil has told you and check back with him/her that you have got this right. Make any evidence safe (screengrabs, texts saved). Do not download evidence onto your own phone or laptop.

- It would be useful to explain that things may take a while to resolve. It can take a little time to get the support from a range of agencies into place, for example.

- Report wrongdoing to a website to get material removed if necessary or report to the police.

- Check whether the parents know, and offer to support the student when they are to be informed.

Why don't they tell anyone?

Large numbers of children never tell any adult that they are being cyberbullied or have other problems in life or online. The discussions below reveal some of the reasons children do not tell an adult. Thinking about what they say can help us to come up with ideas to enable more people to report if they need to.

How do you feel about getting help from an adult?
Fine, but some people are scared because bullies threaten them.

What do people do about it?
Not much; people are scared that the teachers will tell them off and people will then bully them more.
I like to keep it to myself cos he says if I tell someone he will do worse. (Female who said she had been 'strangled' the previous day)

Mum doesn't know… I didn't want them to get worried about me being teased at school. (Female, 9)

When a person gets bullied the person doesn't tell.

Why not?

The person will be watching them all day so they don't tell cos they're scared. (Female, 10)

They keep going on and on and the people don't tell the teacher or their mum and dad cos they're too scared. (Female, 10)

I never told anyone cos he told me it was secret and if I told he would hurt my mum. I didn't want to say anything cos my mum has so many troubles already. There is no point, nobody can do nothing. (Male, 11)

Solutions to being too scared to tell

Young people called for other people to be responsible for finding out and reporting bullying rather than solely relying on the victim. They wanted teachers to watch out for signs and suggested that turning to friends to tell a teacher on your behalf was a good idea.

You could have systems, you could write something anonymously and then put an announcement out about punishment. You could set a patrol of people to help, like older pupils to patrol school. (Male, 13)

People could look and see, look out for people, or the teachers could tell you to look out for people. (Female, 13)

Peer support schemes not only help those who actually do come forward but they reassure others that, if they needed to, there would be someone they could talk to.

Effective responses which actually help the situation will in turn encourage others to come forward, but if children see that telling is not successful, then they will not do so when they need to. That is why it is so vital that staff training looks at effective interventions and that monitoring should measure the outcomes of cases. Did the problem actually cease? Was the reporting child successfully reintegrated into friendship groups? Was online behaviour subsequently safer? If a school has a high rate of reports this does not necessarily mean that they are ineffective, but it does suggest a level of pupil trust in the school. If cases are not successfully resolved in most situations, then the school's anti-bullying strategy may be ineffective.

If a case needs to be referred to the police or an outside agency this is done by the designated safeguarding lead. Cases of grooming, sexual exploitation and coercion are matters for the police. Report these either via your local police service or direct to CEOP. Provide support for the pupil concerned and their family where this is required.

Summary

- Preparation
- Ground rules
- Recap (or rewind)
- Support if someone wants to talk about anything after the session
- Good procedures on what to do if a child does make a disclosure.

Always conclude an e-safety lesson with a short recap and end by saying that, if anyone is worried about anything or would like to talk to someone about this, here is how to do so.

- What did we learn today? Recap and wrap up.

- What is e-safety all about? Tell your partner three things.

- What kind of things can you do now to stay safe? Start with the words: 'I learned how to...'

Let's recap and think about what we did in this lesson.

1. Name three messages you will take away from it.

2. What kinds of things will you now do to stay safe?

3. Quiz time with some games...

Text to this school number if you have any questions you'd like answered next time (or use Moodle).

Contact peer supporters or report anything you are worried about to the worry box text number.

Reviewing procedures

Always review your procedures in the light of a case. How well are your systems serving you? Figure 7.2 is a self-review tool that may help you do this.

Strengths, Weaknesses, Threats and Opportunities - the SWOT DIAGRAM

Could this diagram help trigger regular reviews of your systems and training?

Could you develop this concept further? Will it help you keep on top of things?

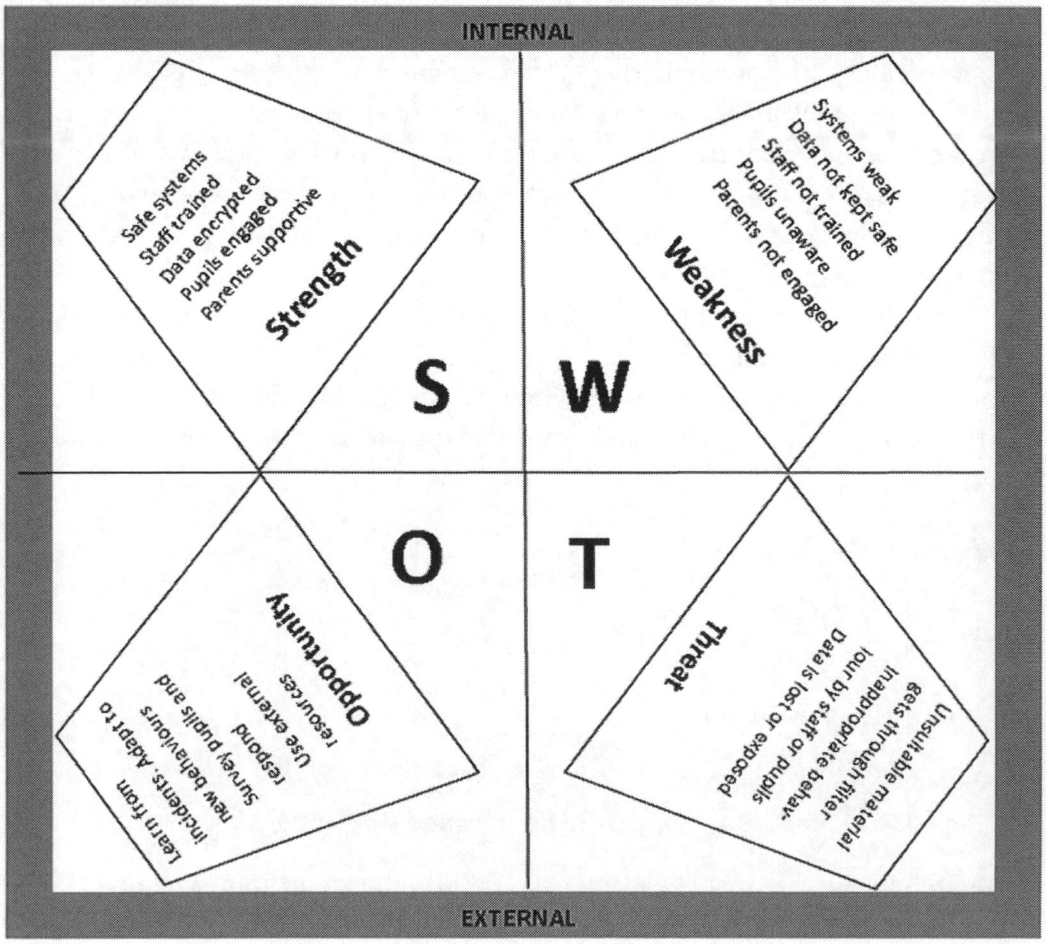

Figure 7.2 SWOT diagram

8

Policy, Practice and Inspection

Considering best practice

Is best practice for the benefit of your school, your governors, your pupils or for inspection? So often inspectors say the last thing they want to see is generic policies being used, or a lack of data so that a school does not really know how effective they are, or data present but not used to improve practice. So in this section, policy practice and inspection are brought together as they serve one purpose – to improve outcomes in your school.

Step back from the busy day-to-day rush and take a moment to reflect on what you have in place and what is working well. This is a reflective activity for the senior leadership team and governors to consider whether the school has the right strategies, education and training, and policy and procedures in place on e-safety.

First: Google your school. Consider that, before coming to your school, Ofsted inspectors (or parents considering sending a child to your school) would do a search. How often do you search for anything associated with your school online? Is a group of students from your school bringing the school into disrepute? Is a group of parents defaming a teacher online? Are former students saying things about the school? Check that your website contains all the required elements, including policies and a clear statement about child protection. It can deter applicants for staff posts from picking your school if they fear being found out for being interested in children for the wrong reasons. While it is a very mild protection, this has been recommended by safe recruitment trainers. It states your intent and focus. In a recent case, sixth form students were found to be engaging with 'extremists' in an online forum they had created.

Second: ask your staff to search on themselves periodically to be sure that no wild snapshot taken of them at a party has surfaced linking them to your school next to a photo-shopped distortion of them that some prankster has thought up.

What will Ofsted look for?
What are the e-safety goals?

E-safety is concerned with ensuring students use electronic resources safely and legally. The aims are to:

- protect and educate pupils and staff in their use of technology
- have appropriate mechanisms to intervene and support any incident where appropriate

- help students understand and manage risk

- train staff to improve their knowledge and expertise in the safe and appropriate use of technology.

E-safety encompasses a wide array of concepts and issues including the following.

Copyright awareness

Many students and staff show little consideration for intellectual property and ownership, which includes film, music and images. Many will happily download music without thinking of the need of the musician to sell it. The concept of plagiarism needs to be taught to children. See page 181.

Cyberbullying

This includes:

- bullying using technology such as computers and mobile phones

- identity theft

- hijacking control of social network profile pages or accounts in games

- misuse or malicious sharing of images.

Privacy

This includes:

- disclosure of personal information

- digital footprint

- online reputation

- safe social networking and digital communication.

Risks of harm for children and young people include:

- inappropriate content

- online pornography

- ignoring age ratings in games

- exposure to violence

- racist language

- pro-anorexia websites

- self-harm websites

- suicide websites

- hate sites.

What would Ofsted consider inadequate/outstanding in e-safety practice?[52]

The items below would indicate that your school is inadequate.

What does inadequate look like?

Personal data is often unsecured

Security of passwords is ineffective

Policies are generic and not updated

There is no progressive, planned e-safety education across the curriculum but only an annual assembly

There is no Internet filtering or monitoring

There is no evidence of good staff training

Children are not aware of how to report a problem

The items below would indicate that your school is outstanding

---

What does outstanding look like?

A whole-school consistent approach

Robust, integrated reporting routines are in place

Staff training regular and updated

Staff responsibilities well understood

Policies are rigorous and integrated

E-safety education is age appropriate and flexible

Infrastructure is excellent

Monitoring and evaluation taking place

Safe management of personal data

How would your school answer these questions?

Security Describe how personal data is secured. Describe rules or protocols for situations in which data leaves the school site – e.g. on teachers' laptops or USB sticks or in emails. How often are passwords changed? How is traffic filtered and monitored in your school?	
Acceptable Use Policy for ICT When was your AUP last reviewed and updated? Was it created specifically in and for your school or setting? Is it available for students in child-friendly language? How well does the entire school community understand this policy and how do you know this? (Surveys, quizzes, lesson assessments, staff training needs assessed, etc.) How well does it perform when you have incidents?	
Training How often are staff trained on the AUP and school protocols for e-safety? Who attends? Is this teaching and non-teaching staff? Is it only the senior leadership team or the ICT manager? What training has the staff had in understanding and addressing cyberbullying and safeguarding students from risks linked to the Internet or mobile phones?	

E-safety education Do you have a planned e-safety teaching programme that becomes more sophisticated as students move up the school? How do you educate students with special needs or other vulnerabilities in e-safety in your school? If outside guests come in to deliver e-safety sessions, what support is in place after they leave? What follow-up is planned?	
Reporting systems Do students and parents/carers know how they can report any concerns? What is the internal system for a member of staff who wishes to report a concern?	

Questions for staff	Red	Amber	Green
Have you had any training that shows the risks to your safety and that of pupils?			
Are there policies in place that clearly demonstrate good and safe Internet practice for staff and pupils?			
Are there sanctions in place to enforce the above policies?			
Do all staff understand what is meant by the term cyber-bullying and the effect it can have on them and on pupils?			
Are there clear reporting mechanisms with a set of actions in place for staff or pupils who feel they are being bullied online?			
Does the school have any plans for an event on Safer Internet Day?			

Who leads on e-safety?

Your school should appoint an e-safety coordinator to lead on embedding e-safety practice across the school. This is not a technical role such as ICT manager. E-safety should be managed as a safeguarding issue; it is therefore helpful if the designated governor for safeguarding plays a role in overseeing the e-safety practices of the school. While the headteacher carries responsibility for e-safety, and in academies and free schools this can be a legal responsibility for all trust members, the coordinator implements the work day to day. The e-safety coordinator might be the designated safeguarding lead or a member of the senior management team with a pastoral lead responsibility. In very large schools there might be two people appointed to this role.

It is helpful to remember that responsibility for e-safety cannot be delegated. What this means is that if a school employs a company to manage their e-safety and there is a major breach, the responsibility remains with the headteacher and the academy trust or the local authority, whichever has responsibility for the school.

How to integrate your policy

The BIG Award assesses a very large number of policies each year. The most successful school approaches integrate their policies so that they interlink and work together rather than alone. These policies should interact and align with your anti-bullying policy (Figure 8.3).

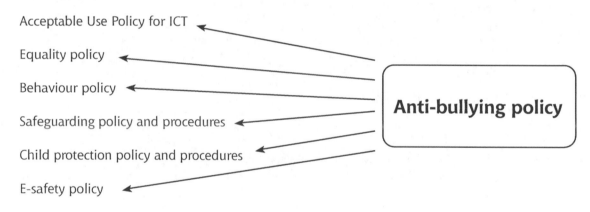

Acceptable Use Policy for ICT

Equality policy

Behaviour policy

Safeguarding policy and procedures

Child protection policy and procedures

E-safety policy

Anti-bullying policy

Figure 8.3 Policies that interact with the anti-bullying policy

A communincations plan (Figure 8.4) is important.

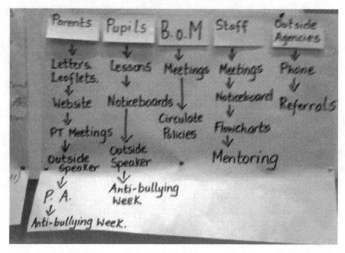

Figure 8.4 Communications plan

Run a workshop on your communications plan. How will you make your anti-bullying policy and e-safety strategy known? Who are your different audiences? What do they need? How can you reach them? Which policies should interact?

All the policies below should interact with the school's safeguarding and child protection policies. Show where these would apply and indicate when a serious incident would require assessment according to safeguarding or child protection procedures. Be consistent and avoid 'silos' – go instead for a joined-up policy approach so that all your policies are clear and consistent.

- *E-safety* is concerned with the relevant educational, management and technical issues. Who is responsible for e-safety in your school? What infrastructure is in place? Who can alter filters? How will disclosures or allegations be addressed? How will e-safety be taught in your school? What will the curriculum cover? How will reports to governors be made?

- *Acceptable Use Policies* (AUPs) mean that the whole school community must agree to use the Internet and mobiles in a responsible manner. Appropriate AUPs can be developed for all ages and settings. This includes versions signed by students and their parents or carers, and a version signed by staff with a code of conduct included.

- *Behaviour policies* set out the vision and ethos of the school and disciplinary measures around behaviour: how staff will model positive behaviour, how parents can bring a concern to the attention of the school and how parents will be informed by the school of any problems concerning their child. Include what is expected of pupils and what staff will do to help them change their behaviour where necessary.

- *Anti-bullying policies* are sometimes incorporated into the behaviour policy or work as stand-alone policies. They should be written in a consistent way – for example, schools may have one person leading the day-to-day anti-bullying work and another – perhaps a deputy head – writing the policy. One might favour punitive sanctions and the other a restorative approach. The anti-bullying policy should include cyberbullying and allude to e-safety education – as part of the prevention of bullying and an essential component of good bullying intervention practice. There should be internal staff guidance, a child-friendly version, and a public version on the website. Serious incidents do occur, and it is not uncommon for a child who is bullying others to disclose domestic violence at home, for example. In cases such as these it is the interaction with safeguarding and child protection that can clarify the action you want your staff to take.

- The *equality policy* addresses as a basic right the freedom to learn without being discriminated against, and your school is more likely to achieve this if the equality policy is not seen as some sort of add-on to the main policies of the school, but is instead an integral principle of the school environment. It should interact with the other policies, and the school should monitor whether any group or groups of students are discriminated against, are bullied or are otherwise not having their needs met. It should explain what will be done if inequality is evident. It would ensure, for example, that if BYOD is practised, then provision is made for any child who does not have their own device. It will also ensure that children with special needs are given the support they need to access the Internet safely, with reasonable adjustments made to help them understand and access learning on e-safety.

All of these should feature strongly in the staff induction handbook and training.

Additional points

- *Ofsted*: Understand how Ofsted will inspect e-safety and safeguarding within your organisation, and explain to staff how this will be evidenced.

- *Infrastructure and safe systems*: Ensure these are up to date and effective. The responsibility for safeguarding cannot be delegated – academy owners and boards are responsible, not the company or consultant supplying the internal system.

- *Mobile devices*: Know your legal rights to confiscate, search and delete evidence on mobile devices to help tackle cases of cyberbullying and sexting in your school.

- *Staff conduct*: Implement robust policies and procedures to ensure staff conduct themselves professionally online and offline.

- *Outside the school gates*: Clarify your responsibilities for safeguarding students outside of the school gates (Education Act 2006) so you can be sure of when you should intervene, and be clear about the powers to discipline students in these situations.

- *Allegations*: Make clear how you should appropriately handle and manage allegations against staff to protect both the child and adult.

- *Other relevant policies*: Bring these into a consistent framework so that they interact successfully with e-safety and safeguarding/child protection policies.

- *Consent forms – digital and video images*: To comply with the Data Protection Act 1998, permission must be given by both parents/carers before using photographs or video recordings of children and young people under the age of 18 for any purposes beyond the activity of the school/organisation – for example, by giving them to a local newspaper or website. There are many situations where a parent or carer would not want a child to be identifiable in a photograph or to have that image online at all. It is essential to abide by their wishes. In some schools, to assist privacy, only first names are used in newsletters and online photos. Staff members are never allowed to take photographs or videos on their personal equipment.

Communications plan

To draw up a communications plan to ensure your policies are known and understood by all, first consider your different audiences and then decide the media to be used. These are the elements to consider:

External		
Website		
Parents and new pupils		
All pupils in child-friendly format and language		
Prospective parents		
Promote reporting systems		
Promote peer supporters' service		
Prizes/awards for anti-bullying work		
Internal		
Staff induction process		
All staff and training updates		
Processes and incident-reporting systems		
Monitoring and review systems, data, survey		
Action plans		
Reporting to governors and senior leadership team		
Policy and strategy review consultation		

Prejudice-driven behaviour

Old prejudices die hard. Children have always targeted anyone who is weaker or more vulnerable, unless taught other ways to behave. And now they have new tools for communication which even allow anonymity! This is a gift for those who want to bully, threaten or otherwise intimidate someone else. Cyberbullying and all forms of online or mobile phone aggression can be directed at someone deemed weaker or more vulnerable for no reason at all other than the perpetrator wanting to look big in front of an audience. But it is common for bullying to be focused on difference. This difference could be because one person likes different types of music or wears different clothing. It can be based on any form of prejudice or stereotypes, but too often it is linked to:

- race, religion or culture
- special needs and disabilities
- sexual orientation
- gender
- aspects of family life, such as being in care or a young carer
- a perceived difference that may or may not be true.

It may also be directed at pupils who join the school in mid-year, those who are newly arrived and those who have changed school many times. But every pupil has the right to be safe and respected. Our laws and our work in schools should ensure this. The Equality Act 2010 puts general and specific duties on schools and public services (see page 58).

Interrogate your data – don't simply hoard it!

Monitoring bullying and cyberbullying data will reveal the most vulnerable children and the extent to which they are bullied. In a 2014 sample of young people aged 10–16, we looked at the proportion who reported that they were badly bullied. Out of a sample of 6747 students, 11 per cent were badly bullied. But for some students the likelihood of being badly bullied is far higher. In order to be able to help them we looked at who featured in the badly bullied group. This showed that certain vulnerable students are disproportionately more likely to be badly bullied than their peers. Those in care and those who need help with English were twice as likely to be badly bullied and disabled students and those with special needs as well as young carers, were three times more likely to be badly bullied. Students with long term illnesses such as diabetes or asthma were almost three times as likely to be badly bullied when compared to their peers with no difficulties.[53]

An analysis of ethnic background can reveal patterns of discrimination in your area, and the levels of homophobic, sexist and other prejudice-driven behaviour.

All these people require extra e-safety education to protect them when online. Children who are severely bullied are often at greater risk than their peers when they go online. If lonely and isolated, they may accept offers of friendship, and be vulnerable to grooming, coercion or threats. Pupils with special needs may need help understanding or remembering advice. Information may also need to be offered in other languages or in a story-board format.

Bullying of children with SEN

For pupils with special needs, bullying can take all the same forms as for their peers, but additional forms are often seen:

- *Manipulative bullying* makes the target child do something the bullying person wants them to do.

- *Conditional friendship* allows the victim to think they are in a friendship group but in fact they are only tolerated as a runner or to be humiliated and give the group someone to laugh at.

- In *exploitative relationships* the person doing the bullying understands exactly what the weaknesses of the target child are and exploits their sensitivities or reactions to get them to explode or goads them into getting into trouble for fun. We often call this 'pressing their buttons deliberately'.

Tips for dealing with bullying of children with special needs

Set up support

- A *nurture group*, or support from buddies or peer supporters, is a first step. Volunteers can create a circle of friends or agree that they will always walk to lunch around this child so that the bigger kids from another class will not bully the child.

- *Emotions charts* enable pupils to show how they are feeling at various times of the school day.

- Agree a small, discreet *signal* for the pupil to show a teacher if they need help or feel that stress is building up on a scale of 1 to 10.

- *Exit cards* can be used if the pupil is stressed and needs to leave the classroom or be 'sent on a pre-arranged errand to the office'.

- Set up a *safe* or *quiet place* as a retreat at breaks.

Educate

- Work to develop the understanding of special needs within the whole group or class and their appreciation and celebration of difference. Avoid any sense of 'tolerating' difference.

- Highlight the strengths of the child and spend less time focusing on their weaknesses in front of others; instead make a plan with the child to address these.

- Ensure children with special needs are carefully and repeatedly taught about e-safety basics. They need patient, practical demonstrations and should not simply be told what to do. To aid memory, connect the messages in ways that work for them – for example, colour coding, images or drawings, sing-song repetition or numbered lists. Try social stories made to fit the e-safety message. Use online videos that teach how to do things.

- Remind parents that games have age ratings. Our evidence is that children with special needs spend even more hours playing computer games than their peers. This may be because they are really happy doing this, but it may be an adult way of having them occupied and quiet – a digital babysitter. Organisations such as ChildLine, the Anti-Bullying Alliance and Childnet International offer resources for e-safety intended for use with children who have special needs.

- Encourage other pupils to report any bullying they see.

- Influence the group's dynamics and reward positive, kind and caring behaviour.

- Educate parents to understand that prejudice can be challenged at home and that the school expects parents to support its efforts to have every pupil feel safe and respected.

- Use books and stories to widen understanding – for example, *Wonder* and *Maggot Moon*.[54]

Liaise with professionals and external agencies

- Many charities, such as Mencap, the National Autistic Society and the Council for Disabled Children, provide specific advice and support or materials. Young Minds runs a professional helpline for parents.

- Parent support workers can help the family.

- School counsellors, if available, can be involved.

- Invite guests into school to share specialist knowledge.

Deal with bullying pupils constructively

- Ensure they understand the harm they have caused.

- Help them to change their behaviour.

- Monitor whether their behaviour changes towards children with SEN and, if so, reward this.

- Move pupils within the class seating plan or even into other classes if appropriate.

- Consider visits to special units or schools to improve understanding.

- Work with the pupil to enable them to make amends to the victim.

- Punish only as a last resort. Punishment often increases the chance of retaliation or even more secretive bullying. It can make children resent the bullied child even more. Appeal instead to their better nature, and only punish if they ignore all warnings and if efforts to change behaviour have failed.

All barriers in place?

©Adrienne Katz

Figure 8.5 Barriers

Manage the risks!

Prevention and proactive steps

1. Secure communications

2. Encrypt personal data

3. Rules about personal data leaving the site

4. Strong passwords that are often refreshed

5. Apply best practice standards

6. Trained staff

7. Raise awareness among all parts of your school community

8. Incident protocols ready in case they are needed

Staff activity – how are these working for you?

Rank or group the following in order of importance and impact.	
Assemblies about cyberbullying and e-safety	
Talk about bullying/cyberbullying in circle time	
Sanctions or punishments for perpetrators	
Reward prosocial or positive behaviour	
Teach pupils to be safe online	
Break e-safety information into chunks	
Anonymous pupil surveys	
Consult everyone about the anti-bullying policy and strategy	
Whole-school approach	
Group activities and workshops to explore relationships and behaviour	
Drama or telling stories to show people what to do if they are bullied or cyberbullied or experience problems online	
Picture and story books used to explore friendship and relationships	
Posters, artwork and graphics	
Peer support schemes (e.g. buddies, playground pals)	
Teach pupils to make friends with and respect people who are different from them	
Successfully stop bullying and cyberbullying if they occur	
Make sure pupils all know how to tell someone if they are bullied or cyberbullied	
Model the behaviour you want	
Restorative approaches	
Make sure nobody is left out	
Manage classroom dynamics (seating plan, partners, teams)	
Show how to keep safe by demonstrating on computers	
Treat everyone fairly	
A calm room	
A march around the playground against bullying of any kind on- or offline	
Make a video	
National activities, such as Anti-Bullying Week or Safer Internet Day	

Pupils rated the following the most effective:

- Successfully get bullying to stop if it happens

- Teach people to respect people who are different

- Treat everyone fairly

- Practical demonstrations of e-safety on computers

- Break the e-safety information into chunks

- Repeat it often

- Drama and video-making, graphics and large-scale activities like flashmobs.

A safer workforce

A safer workforce cycle would include safe recruitment, induction procedures, a cycle of training, regular updates, corridors of communication and safe follow-up systems.

Staff should be clear on the school's code of conduct. Data should be safely encrypted where necessary and staff need to be absolutely clear on the use of school-owned devices and laptops. When data containing information about staff or pupils leaves the premises for any reason, it should be safely encrypted or alternatively placed on a virtual private network (VPN) to be accessed using strong, two-stage security passwords. If based in a cloud, your data could be vulnerable to hacking.

No member of staff should communicate with a student as a 'friend' on social networks or using a personal mobile or device. It should be absolutely clear that no photos of pupils can be used without formal permission being obtained, whether that is in a school newsletter or on the website. Students should know this and would therefore regard any request for their photo as unusual and something they would refuse or report. If communications between staff and students are necessary, they should take place via a school system that is monitored.

Safeguarding
Key documents

- *Keeping Children Safe in Education: Statutory Guidance for Schools and Colleges* (2015) [55, 56]

- *Keeping Children Safe in Education: Information for All School and College Staff (part one)* (2015) [57]

- *Working Together to Safeguard Children: A Guide to Inter-agency Working to Safeguard and Promote the Welfare of Children* (2015). [58]

Definition of safeguarding

Ofsted adopts the definition used in the Children Act 2004 and in *Working Together to Safeguard Children*. This can be summarised as:

- protecting children from maltreatment

- preventing impairment of children's health or development

- ensuring that children are growing up in circumstances consistent with the provision of safe and effective care

- taking action to enable all children to have the best outcomes.

Safeguarding is not just about protecting children from deliberate harm. It relates to aspects of school life including:

- pupils' health and safety

- the use of reasonable force

- meeting the needs of pupils with medical conditions

- providing first aid

- educational visits

- intimate care

- appropriate arrangements to ensure school security, taking into account the local context.

Safeguarding can involve a range of potential issues such as:

- bullying, including cyberbullying (by text message, on social networking sites, and so on) and prejudice-based bullying

- racist, disability and homophobic or transphobic abuse

- radicalisation and extremist behaviour

- child sexual exploitation

- sexting

- substance misuse

- issues that may be specific to a local area or population, for example gang activity and youth violence

- particular issues affecting children including domestic violence, sexual exploitation, female genital mutilation and forced marriage.

Inspection

When evaluating the effectiveness of safeguarding arrangements, inspectors will consider the following:

The extent to which children are safe and feel safe

- Your pupil anonymous surveys are relevant here. There are a number of ways to find out how safe children feel in school even when they are not yet reading and writing. They can look at photos of different areas of the school and comment on how safe they feel in these places or state whether there are any areas of the school where they do not feel safe. Stickers are useful for this, green for safe, red for unsafe and orange for 'safe sometimes'. Small children can take an adult on a tour of the school and explain where they feel safest or least safe. Large google maps photos of the school can be useful in exploring the school with children.

- Children will be asked if they know how to tell someone if they have a problem and whether they can identify a trusted adult. Inspectors will want to check that adults listen and take children's concerns seriously, then respond robustly and responsively if children disclose problems. Staff should be proactively taking actions that reduce the risk of harm or actual harm to children. Inspectors will want to see that adults know how to recognise any indicators that suggest a child is, or is likely to suffer harm and that they take the appropriate action in line with local authority or academy chain procedures and statutory guidance.

Procedures and written records and plans

- A school may have procedures in place but inspectors will want to ensure that staff and other adults working within the setting are all fully trained in these procedures so that they know how to act in cases where they are concerned about the safety of a child. There must be a named and designated lead person who effectively pursues concerns and whose role is to protect children.

- Written records should be made in a timely way and stored securely. These records should be shared appropriately when required and with the necessary consent/s. Records of all referrals to local authority leads should be retained with evidence of the follow up to that referral.

- Your school should be able to demonstrate how children are supported, protected and informed appropriately about the action the adult is taking to share their concerns. Parents should be made aware of concerns and their consent sought in accordance with local procedures, unless seeking this consent would increase the risk of or actual harm to a child.

- A case should have a written plan in place with the agreed procedures on how to protect the child. In cases where a child is the subject of a child protection plan this should also set out the help the child should receive and actions to be taken if a professional working with the child has further concerns.

Working with other agencies

- Responses when a child goes missing from school should be well co-ordinated and these responses should reduce the harm or risk of harm to the child. Inspectors will want to know whether the risks are well understood and steps have been taken to minimise these risks. The school should be implementing the statutory guidance for children and young people who are missing from home or from education.

- There are further checks on how well local procedures for notifying the local authority are understood and followed, the records held and shared between relevant agencies and any risks such as children offending, misusing drugs or alcohol or self-harming are correctly notified and acted upon. (When discussing e-safety, I cannot overstate the need to be vigilant in relation to self-harm and the type of sites the child or young person is visiting. It is often necessary to explore the child's online history if effective help is to be provided.)

- If a child is going missing or being sexually exploited this should be immediately shared with the local authority children's social care service. There should be plans to reduce the harm and any risk of harm, to reduce the impact of risk and regular reviews and liaison with other agencies.

- As serious bullying can be a safeguarding or even a child protection matter in certain instances, inspections will check that children are protected and helped to keep themselves safe from bullying, homophobic behaviour, racism, sexism and other forms of discrimination. Any discriminatory behaviours are challenged and help and support is given to children about how to treat others with respect.

Online

- Adults are expected to understand the risks posed by adults or young people who use the Internet to bully, groom or abuse children and have well-developed strategies in place to both keep children safe and to support them in learning how to keep themselves safe. (More recently there has been considerable concern over violent extremism and the attempted recruitment of young people online to causes that are violent or send people to war zones. This is seen by some as a form of grooming.)

- School leaders must oversee the safe use of electronic and social media when the children are on site and take action immediately if they are concerned about bullying or risky behaviours.

- An important aspect of keeping children safe online is to enable them to 'take age-appropriate and reasonable risks as part of their growth and development'. This requires risk assessments and a consistent response by staff. Attempting a locked down approach with no age progression is not encouraged.

- Risk assessments can include these five steps:
  - identifying the hazards;
  - deciding who might be harmed;
  - deciding the risks (high, low or medium) and checking whether existing arrangements or precautions are adequate or more needs to be done;
  - recording the assessment and any action to be taken;
  - review and revise your assessment.

Behaviour

- Experience positive support from all staff, who respond with clear boundaries about what is safe and acceptable. Staff seek to understand the triggers for children's behaviour, develop effective responses as a team and review those responses to assess their impact, taking into account the views and experiences of the child.'

- There are sections on promoting positive behaviour and de-escalation techniques along with alternative strategies that are tailored for the individual and their needs. Force and restraint are only used in strict accordance with the legislative framework to protect the child and those around them. Children do not have their liberty restricted. Any use of restraint is reduced over time.

Recruitment

- Safeguarding also includes how workers and staff are selected and vetted and how unsuitable people are prevented from having the opportunity to harm children.

- Staff training and development in the protection and care of children is a vital element and regular supervision and support should be in place for those working directly with children where there are concerns about their safety and welfare. Staff may be carrying a distressing burden of knowledge and concern about a child or children. Professional debriefing is necessary.

Physical environment

- Safeguarding also includes the physical environment which should be safe and secure. The school should have a good understanding of any local risks and secure entry systems.

Whistleblowing

- Whistleblowing describes a situation when a staff member or volunteer raises a concern about potential danger or bad practice they witnessed at work. In schools it is likely to be in relation to child protection, but it may be another matter. An effective policy should protect both the whistleblower and the organisation by outlining a simple process for raising concerns. All staff and carers have a copy of and understand the written procedures for managing allegations of harm to a child. They know how to make a complaint and how to manage whistleblowing or other concerns about the practice of adults in respect of the safety and protection of children.

Leadership and management

- Governing bodies and proprietors must ensure that they comply with their safeguarding duties under legislation. This includes all policies, procedures and training.

- Among governors' responsibilities is their contribution to inter-agency working, in terms of which, they are expected to provide a coordinated

- Offer of early help when additional needs of children are identified.

- Governors must ensure that an effective child protection policy is in place, alongside a staff behaviour policy appointing a designated safeguarding lead. This person should undergo child regular and updated protection training every two years.

- Governors have responsibilities for prioritising the welfare of children and young people and creating a culture where staff are confident to challenge senior leaders over any safeguarding concerns

- Governors have responsibilities for making sure that children are taught how to keep themselves safe.

Recruitment

- Governing bodies and proprietors should prevent people who pose a risk of harm from working with children by complying with statutory responsibilities to check staff who work with children even asking for checks beyond those required when proportionate and ensuring that volunteers are always appropriately supervised.

- They should ensure that at least one person on any appointment panel has undertaken safer recruitment training.[59]

Allegations

Governors should

- have procedures in place to handle allegations against members of staff and volunteers

- put procedures in place to handle allegations against other children

- put appropriate safeguarding responses in place for cases of missing children, especially if this occurs repeatedly.

Governing bodies and proprietors should ensure that allegations against members of staff and volunteers are referred to the Local Authority Designated Officer (LADO). There must be procedures in place to make a referral to the Disclosure and Barring Service (DBS) if a person in regulated activity has been dismissed or removed due to safeguarding concerns or would have been had they not resigned. This is a legal duty, and failure to refer when the criteria are met is a criminal offence.

Absence analysed?

Absence and truanting data offer crucial information in safeguarding. Why is this child missing school so often? The Ofsted *School Inspection Handbook* puts an emphasis on the rigour with which absence is followed up and the decision-making process involved when taking pupils off roll.[60] Stories of children placed on the roll and then disappearing have raised fears that a child has been trafficked – into the UK, for example.

Absenteeism can also sometimes be attributed to bullying or online threats. Requests to transfer to another school should be investigated to ascertain the reasons behind the request – often bullying of some kind is implicated.

Evidence your safeguarding and e-safety work for Ofsted

- Write up a case study that is recent, and show a timeline, action plan, action taken and outcome. Collate evidence of working with other agencies, building relationships and co-working.

- Show your child protection record form with a chronology. Is this information now on little bits of paper? Odd emails? Keep a track record and give confidence that you are on top of current cases and have analysed earlier cases in order to learn from them.

- Ensure that you are tracking your vulnerable pupils – some schools use a pastoral tracker and compare that with the child's learning achievement record.

- Although the first duty of the school is to keep children safe, it also needs to teach children how to stay safe. Include a scheme of work and activities that show that staying safe and e-safe is explicit in the curriculum. Inspectors will ask children how they keep safe.

- Outline the staff induction and training cycle, and have available evidence that staff have signed to show they have received this training. They should also sign to show they have read and understood the AUP in ICT.

- Ensure the designated person has had training in safeguarding and child protection regularly and from an authoritative source. It is advisable that the governor who leads on safeguarding receives it too. Governors must feel that they can have confidence in the lead and the lead governor. Are there certificates to show for this training?

- Evidence your safer recruitment systems and procedures. An example of an advert, application form and decision-making process are needed, along with how references are followed up.

- Your safeguarding annual audit forms part of this evidence and it could also include your data on bullying (including cyberbullying) such as pupil surveys, strategies, case studies and outcomes.

- Always consider how you are monitoring for your goals set out in the Equality Act 2010.

Safeguarding procedure explained

Safeguarding related to internet safety, bullying and risky behaviour.

What inspectors expect to see. Check you have everything in place.

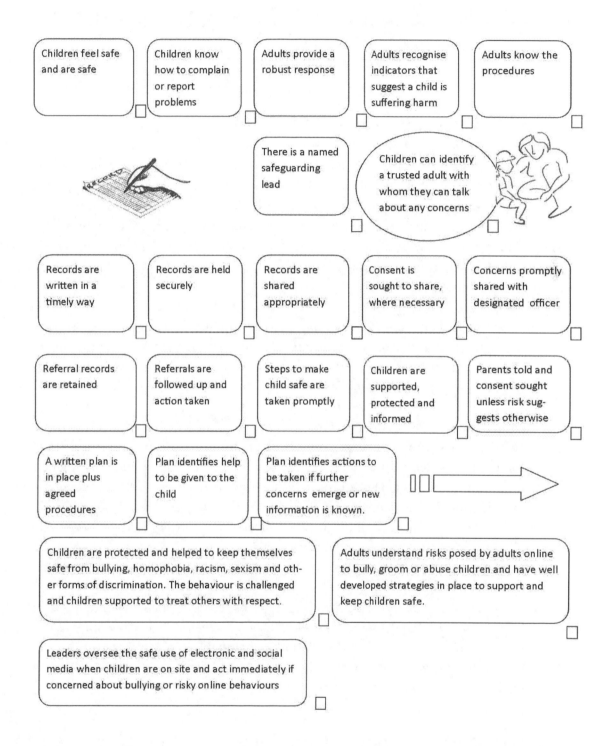

Children feel safe and are safe ☐

Children know how to complain or report problems ☐

Adults provide a robust response ☐

Adults recognise indicators that suggest a child is suffering harm ☐

Adults know the procedures ☐

There is a named safeguarding lead ☐

Children can identify a trusted adult with whom they can talk about any concerns ☐

Records are written in a timely way ☐

Records are held securely ☐

Records are shared appropriately ☐

Consent is sought to share, where necessary ☐

Concerns promptly shared with designated officer ☐

Referral records are retained ☐

Referrals are followed up and action taken ☐

Steps to make child safe are taken promptly ☐

Children are supported, protected and informed ☐

Parents told and consent sought unless risk suggests otherwise ☐

A written plan is in place plus agreed procedures ☐

Plan identifies help to be given to the child ☐

Plan identifies actions to be taken if further concerns emerge or new information is known. ☐

Children are protected and helped to keep themselves safe from bullying, homophobia, racism, sexism and other forms of discrimination. The behaviour is challenged and children supported to treat others with respect. ☐

Adults understand risks posed by adults online to bully, groom or abuse children and have well developed strategies in place to support and keep children safe. ☐

Leaders oversee the safe use of electronic and social media when children are on site and act immediately if concerned about bullying or risky online behaviours ☐

9

Activities to Do in the Classroom

Take a new approach to teaching e-safety

I know that 10- and 11-year-olds are the most likely of all age groups to adhere to the e-safety guidelines they have been taught.[61] However, even in this 'obedient' age group, as many as 42 per cent do not always follow what they have been taught about e-safety. So it is by listening to them that I have come to believe that we have to go about this in new ways, no longer simply delivering warnings about what scary things might happen and handing down rules, but moving towards a dialogue and exploration strategy which engages them, makes them critical thinkers, gives them skills and prepares them for any new developments in the future.

Our goal should be empowerment, not slavish obedience to a set of rules many of them grow to discard as they see them cramping their style or simply being irrelevant. The first rule is so often 'Do not give out your personal details', but even young children shop with their parents online and see them enter names and credit card details into forms – indeed the child often helps the parent to sign in to something. Once they decide that 'rule 1 is rubbish' it is easy for them to disregard all other rules.

Then there are those children who only learn by doing. They need to be shown *how* to change their password or settings. They need practical demonstrations, not assemblies or one-off sessions when a guest gives a talk. Some need constant reminding. Others hear what you say but only actually need this advice two years later when they have forgotten it, or say they thought they understood but now see that they don't really get it.

With high-speed changes in software, apps, devices and convergence, we have to think about preparing children to be capable and resilient, skilled and curious to learn more. They need to problem-solve and know how to find out when they do not know what to do.

Age-appropriate e-safety education needs to build skills incrementally, constantly recapping and building on the foundations that have gone before – like any other teaching. But above all it needs to engage the child and explain why it is necessary. Then perhaps there will be fewer groans when we ask if they have been taught about e-safety. The activities described in this chapter are created with this in mind.

Activities that look at how technology has changed our world
Why teach them about the pace of change?

Young children are of course born into this digital age. For them, the very idea of old-style phones or cameras is amusing, a curiosity. Two-year-olds understand that they can watch favourite characters on a tablet or their mum's smartphone. Videos of toddlers and even babies have been seen on YouTube, swiping any screen they see, even an oven door, in the expectation that the image will change.

So why teach them about a time before smartphones and tablets? I believe it is valuable to explore with children at Key Stage 2 how fast the pace of change has been and to prepare them for the changes that will undoubtedly come in the next few years. This is because this rapid change in the devices or apps we use and what they enable us to do has led to significant changes in our behaviour and how we conduct our friendships and relationships or protect our privacy and dignity.

You could say that the device is merely a tool and the behaviour is all ours alone, but it can also be argued that the devices and the Internet enable some of us to behave in ways we would not do face to face with someone. Exploring this question with the children helps lead into discussions about how we behave online and on our mobiles, as well as how we might think about what is good or worrying about any new device that is launched. It can act to engage their attention and explain why we need to learn to stay safe online in the first place.

There are two other reasons why this is a good starting point:

1. Approaching e-safety from this angle will inform any child who has not had access to the Internet or the latest devices at home, without exposing their lack of knowledge to the others.

2. This approach also lends itself to wonderful classroom displays and activities in which children can participate, suggesting their own ideas on how each new device might have changed how people relate to each other, and suggestions about how to stay safe. Most parents have a few discarded old handsets lurking about at home; phones in which there is no camera are useful for your display. Children might also design devices of the future and think about what would be needed to stay safe using them.

How things have changed in the last few years

Start by thinking about the rapid change that has occurred in the past few years. Mobile phones are fairly recent inventions, and smartphones even more recent. This is why we need to work together to find safe ways of using them for good things. The activity below is intended to put some perspective on this and help children to become partners in understanding how phones have changed and brought remarkable new possibilities into our lives, but there are some features of these phones that can be used negatively.

E-safety to many children is seen as a boring subject. These activities are linked into a narrative or some fresh ways of looking at e-safety in an effort to capture their imagination. I feel that saying to a class of nine-year-olds that we are going to research the history of the mobile phone might capture their interest rather more than if we said we are going to do more e-safety. When I talk to children of this age, they moan that they know it already and some see themselves as more knowledgeable than their teacher. So try coming at the subject obliquely through an interesting aspect of the technology perhaps – something they can get their teeth into and do some research for homework. You could have a classroom display simply by asking everyone to look for old mobiles lying around in desk drawers at home!

Activity: Happy birthday, Internet

Aims

- To involve and engage pupils in setting mutually agreed rules on online behaviour

- To pre-empt cyberbullying

Use the following to engage with the pupils.

Introduction

Who knows what the 'www' stands for in an online address? Did you know that the World Wide Web has not been around for all that long? Can you guess how old it is? It turned 25 years old in 2014. This birthday, its inventor Sir Tim Berners Lee suggested we have a new discussion about the next 25 years and talk about 'the Web We Want'.

You are the people who will be using the web in the next 25 years, so we can have some discussions today about this.

- Who can tell me some really good things that the Internet has made possible?

- Who can tell me about some not-so-good things that people have brought to the Internet?

- Who can tell me about some really harmful things that people have brought to the Internet?

So if we were looking ahead, what kind of web would we want?

Discussion

Although we cannot make the whole world put our ideas into action, we could make some agreements amongst ourselves about how we will behave on the web.

Today we will plan our web rules

Make three groups. Each group takes one of these topics and draws up five ideas.

1. How we treat one another

2. How we treat other people's work

3. How we can keep ourselves and our friends safe.

Benefits of the World Wide Web – examples

- It enables us to connect to people all over the world.

- We can keep in touch with friends and family.

- We can use the Internet to share science.

- Doctors can see patients thousands of miles away and help them.

- We can use the Internet to send news very fast all round the world.

- We can use the Internet when there is a disaster to tell people and collect money and organise help.

- We can learn about so many things, and people who do not have schools or universities can learn.

- We can play games.

- We can find out about plane and train times or events and book a ticket.

- Someone who cannot get to shops can order online.

- Disabled people are helped through new technology.

Not so good or harmful – a few examples

Conduct

- People can be nasty to one another.

- People can copy your work and pretend it is theirs.

Contact

- People can contact you even if they do not know you.

Content

- You can come across material that is nasty or upsetting.

- Your mistakes or silly photos stay out there forever.

Extension

If you had to explain to an extra-terrestrial what the Internet is, how would you draw it? This could be a diagram or a picture.

Activity: Happy birthday, mobile phones

Rationale

This is an approach to engage the pupils through the story of mobile phones in order to lead into the need to use them safely.

Aims

- To learn about the history of mobile phones

- To explore opportunities and risks with new technology

- To learn how to take steps to be safe

Use the following to engage with the pupils.

Group work on risks

You will need copies of the handout below, a scale and 1kg of items to weigh.

Opening warm-up – eight facts about phones

Did you know?

- The first public mobile phone call was made on 3 April 1973 by Martin Cooper, an inventor for Motorola.

- The phone used in the call had a battery life of 35 minutes and weighed 1kg.

- Ten years later, Motorola put a portable phone on sale at a selling price of $4000. This was very expensive indeed. The cost of that phone was so high that in today's money it would buy you a small car. The weight of this phone had been reduced to 749g, that is 0.75 of a kilo! (Weigh out something to test how heavy this is.)

- The first UK public mobile phone call was made in 1985 by Ernie Wise, an English comedian.

- Global mobile connections passed the 7 billion mark in April 2014; there could soon be more phones than people on the planet.[62]

- The first cameraphone was created by Frenchman Philippe Khan in 1997.

- The first smartphone was given a name. It was IBM's 'Simon', shown at the Wireless World Conference in 1993.

- Seventy-one per cent of 10–11-year-olds used a smartphone and 76 per cent were using a tablet in England in the autumn of 2014.[63]

What are the next steps in the development of mobile technology?

'Wearable tech' describes tiny computers built into glasses or items we might wear around our wrist or ankle. Soon we might have mobile phones made of gel so that they do not smash when dropped and can be moulded around your wrist when jogging. As with many new inventions, there are great opportunities and also some risks – let's think about this further.

Using the handout, write down all the products you or your family use and set out their good points and also any risks there are when we use them.

Each group also selects three important items of new technology and discusses the advantages and risks. They note these in the table provided and feed back to the whole group in turns.

Happy birthday, mobile phones

Product	Good things and opportunities	What could go wrong?

Once all the risks are identified the discussion turns to: What steps can you take to minimise risk of harm when you use these items?

What is the risk?	What can I do to reduce the chance of this happening?

Clunky 'brick' to 'wearable tech'?

Future proof advice?

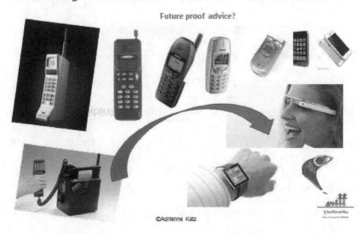

©Adrienne Katz

How many of these phones or devices can you identify? What is coming next?

Activity: How are cameras different today and what does that mean for us?

The rationale behind this activity is similar to the discussion on the history of the mobile phone but it can be done with 10- and 11-year-olds to explore the implications of cameras in phones and also the use of webcams. Children of this age are on the threshold of social networking, and requests for photographs may already be in the message inbox of a few of them. Instead of simply telling them not to post personal photos, this is an opportunity to explore our use of cameras, how different it is these days, what 'instant upload' means and how to keep safe. It is hoped that the historical element will engage them and they will find it a fascinating journey to look at the history of the camera – something that impacts on their lives every day. There are museums of photography around the country.

Invite children to bring in any old cameras from home for show-and-tell sessions and display. Set up a display using the Living Image Camera Museum illustrations in the handout that follows.[64]

Aims

- To prompt pupils to consider the opportunities and risks of using digital photography
- To reduce bullying using humiliating or hurtful images
- To lead pupils to an agreement on the acceptable use of digital images among pupils in line with the AUP of the school

Learning outcomes

After this lesson, pupils should have an understanding of:

- how to keep their own photos private
- the risks of putting images into cyberspace
- the hurt photo misuse can cause to others.

They will also be aware that:

- some behaviour is against website terms of service, and possibly against the law
- the school has an anti-bullying policy that we all agree to abide by and an AUP that governs how we use ICT within school.

Pupils will have drawn up a clear agreement in their own words.

Curriculum links

- Recognising issues of risk, safety and responsibility surrounding the use of ICT
- Citizenship 1.2a: Exploring rights and obligations and how these affect the individual and communities
- PSHE 1.4a: Understanding that relationships affect everything we do and that relationship skills can be practised.

Key points to convey

- Digital photography has changed our relationship with photos.

- Some people use photos to bully or humiliate/embarrass others.

- Some people generate photos of themselves which could cause them distress in the future.

- Copyright law protects people's work.

- The law prevents malicious communications.

Introduction: How new/old is digital photography?

Everyone sits around the display. Use the following to engage with the pupils.

- Who knows what the first use of digital photography was? (In the 1960s NASA started to use digital signals in space probes to map the surface of the moon by sending digital images to earth. Computers were developing and they used computer technology to enhance the images sent by space probes. Digital imaging was also used for spy satellites. The first filmless electronic camera was patented in 1972.)

- Who can tell us some ways of taking or getting a photo today? (Cameras, digital and non-digital, mobile phones, tablets, webcams, screen grabs, copying a photo that someone else has uploaded.)

- Why was it different when your parents were growing up? (You could only take the number of photos that your film could handle. These came in 12-, 24- and 36-shot sizes. Then you had to wait until the film in your camera was used up before you could take it to the chemist and hand it in to be developed. This might take a few days. When you came back to pick them up you got the photos and the negatives (the film from which more photos could be printed). You looked at them closely and chose which ones you would need more than one copy – say, to send one to your gran. Then you ordered the copies. Each time you had to pay for the develop and print process. So this made people very careful about their photos – they cost so much and it took a while. Taking a bad shot was a real waste. Sharing a photo with someone was something you thought a lot about and planned.)

- How is it different today? (Elicit: No wait to finish your film; no wait to have photos developed; no wait to have copies made; sharing is instant; but this brings risks.)

- What do you think the risks might be? (Elicit: Sharing too fast without thinking; uploading a photo that you don't think others should see; being embarrassed by a photo someone else has shared online; being bullied because of a photo someone else has shared online; people seeing your photo when you would rather it was private; people putting pressure on you because of a photo shared online.)

- How can we make sure our photos are kept private? (Elicit: Privacy settings on social networks and strong passwords on photo sites and storage sites. Think twice before uploading any photo.)

- Could we agree that in our school we are going to handle our photos with care?

- What would you like to see in our agreement on how to behave with cameras?

Some old and historic cameras

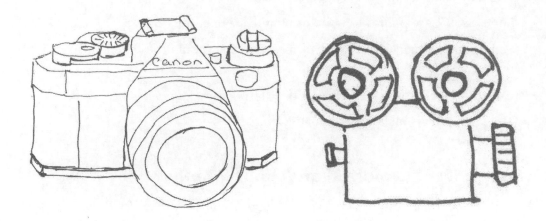

Activities that teach basic e-safety rules
Colour code e-safety messages

Figure 9.1 can be used with the children to agree on a common set of colours to represent different aspects of e-safety. Once agreed, you will always deliver the e-safety messages in this colour-coded way and the displays around the classroom will be coloured accordingly (or glued onto coloured backing sheets).

Colour coding the e-safety messages

To:

- separate them out into strands of activity
- help students remember where to find the advice they seek
- assist students with special needs.

Displays should be clear, uncluttered and in the same colours you have used in the table.

This figure allows for five top tips for each section; adjust yours as you choose. Add or change questions. Use the colour codes to get students to fill in a matrix or create colour-themed displays of advice.

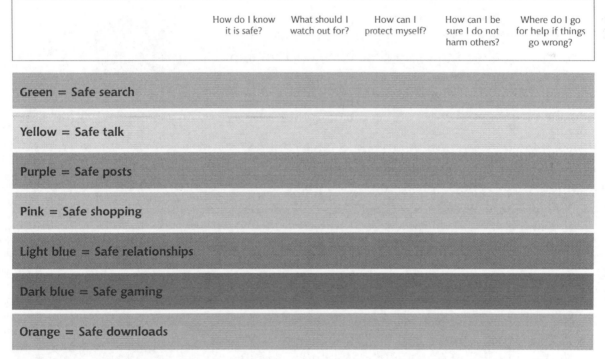

Figure 9.1 Colour-coding e-safety messages

The SMART rules

The following handout outlines the basics of staying safe online for young children.

SMART rules!

1. *Safe*: Keep safe by being careful not to give out personal information when you're chatting or posting online. Personal information includes your email address, phone number and password.

2. *Meet*: Meeting someone you have only been in touch with online can be dangerous. Only do so with your parents' or carers' permission and even then only when they can be present. Remember, online friends are still strangers even if you have been talking to them for a long time.

3. *Accepting*: Accepting emails or messages, or opening files, images or texts from people you don't know or trust, can lead to problems – they may contain viruses or nasty messages!

4. *Reliable*: Someone online might lie about who they are, and information on the Internet may not be true. Always check information by looking at other websites, in books, or with someone who knows. If you like chatting online it's best only to chat to your real-world friends and family.

5. *Tell*: Tell a parent, carer or a trusted adult if someone, or something, makes you feel uncomfortable or worried, or if you or someone you know is being bullied online.

These rules are the basics of staying safe online for young children.

Design cards to carry around in a pocket

This is for children at Key Stage 2. Introduce the idea of five key things to remember about staying safe online. Ask the class to divide into five groups. Each group should agree a brief message to go onto their card. Then they can design a few examples and colour or paint their cards. If they are doing this on computers they can use a graphic design programme to create and print professional-looking cards.

Some key things to remember

These cards should be easy to read. Messages should be short and clear. Colours should be bright so that the cards can easily be found. If you want to include more information than the cards can hold, consider a link to a page on your school's system where people can find out more.

The steps cards

These are steps to take if pupils are cyberbullied or experience any unpleasant, upsetting experience online.

Stay safe

Tell someone

Early

Prevent it getting worse

Solutions to try

Figure 9.2 Steps

Activity: Lesson basics – some special computer musts

This is for children at Key Stage 1 – to reinforce some basic advice. Use the following to address the pupils.

Introduction

Like brushing our teeth or crossing the road, there are some rules about using computers, tablets and mobile phones that go online. We all have to make sure our computer is protected and safe to use online. You need to know about what we call cybersecurity, because you could end up losing all your fun stuff and the pictures or music that you really love. Besides, viruses can get in and they can bring problems to your computer. You need to keep yourself safe and choose strong usernames and passwords that you keep carefully. These are like the keys grown-ups use to get into the house or the car.

When you finish playing a game or using an online club, always log out, as this closes your account, like closing a door so someone else cannot get in and play the game in your account and mess up your scores.

We can think about creating strong usernames and passwords.

Do you think this is a strong password?

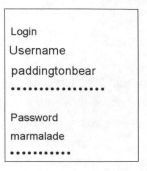

Login
Username
paddingtonbear
················

Password
marmalade
··········

Figure 9.3 Username Paddington

The work we are going to do next will help you to think about how to make your passwords strong and safe.

Activities to make e-safety fun and familiar for young children

Use characters the children know well. Explore situations through the medium of well-known characters from children's stories and TV programmes. This makes it easier to capture their interest and explore situations in which they can give advice to much-loved characters. It is more engaging than a set of rules. It allows you to explore various angles and add in anything you know has been going on in your class, such as some nasty comments or bullying. Here are a few examples of stories you can use with pupils, but you will have many ideas of your own, based on stories you have recently read to your class.

Paddington has a mobile at Paddington Station

What if Paddington Bear got a message on his mobile from a stranger wanting to meet him at the station when he arrived? He was not expecting this. What would you tell Paddington to do? Could this be from someone Paddington has never met before? How did they know he was at the station? What could the risks be? What should Paddington do now?

Charlie and Lola are playing at home on their tablet

Charlie logs into his account on [a popular game] and plays until he reaches a high score and is on an advanced level. All the way through, Lola is dying to play but he does not let her. Finally, he is tired and puts down the tablet when his friend calls and they go out to play. Lola picks up the tablet and she wants to play. She uses Charlie's account but she is not as good as he is and she slips back to a lower level in the game. Now she is very worried that when Charlie comes back he will be angry with her. What would you tell Charlie? What would you tell Lola?

Goldilocks and the bears

The bears had gone out into the wood for a walk to find some honey while their porridge cooled in three bowls on the table. They hoped to put the honey into the porridge and eat it all up when they got home.

Goldilocks was a little girl who lived with her mum on the edge of the wood. Goldilocks was often told by her mum not to go into the wood on her own, but she did not listen. Off she skipped along the path. Soon she saw the little house where the bear family lived. The door was open. Goldilocks went into the bears' house and ate up baby bear's porridge. Then she saw someone had left the computer on, logged onto his social network page. She sent a few prank messages. She thought this was fun! Then she got a bit nastier and sent some cruel, horrid messages. She rocked for a while on the smallest chair, faster and faster until it broke. She had a little doze on baby bear's bed. Then she skipped off down the path.

When the bears returned they were so upset to find the chair broken and the porridge in baby bear's bowl all gone – so they shared their porridge and the honey with baby bear. Soon they got messages from lots of angry parents saying their child had received a horrid message from baby bear. They looked at his social network account and saw that the messages had been sent at the exact time they were out on their walk.

They asked the woodcutter if he had seen anyone come or go from their house and he said: 'As a matter of fact I did. I saw that girl, what's her name? Oh yes, Goldilocks.' The bear family went down to the school to speak to the headteacher.

What would you tell Goldilocks? What would you tell baby bear? Write a postcard to Goldilocks giving her advice on staying safe.

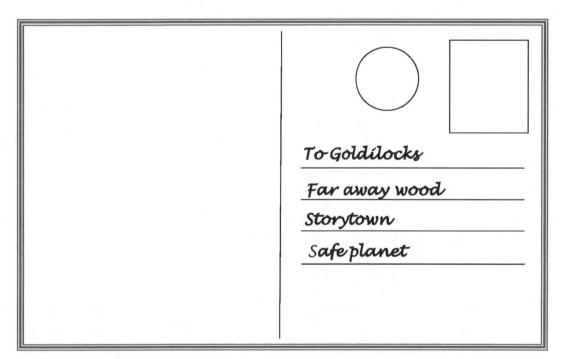

To Goldilocks

Far away wood

Storytown

Safe planet

Figure 9.4 Postcard to Goldilocks

Activity: A new kind of I-spy game for primaries

This is for children at Key Stage 1. It can be played in odd moments with a different focus such as:

- what I spy in cyberspace
- what can I do in cyberspace? (search, watch, listen, talk)
- what gets sent to me in cyberspace
- what I can send to other people in cyberspace (messages, emails, photos, videos).

The purpose is simply to make young children familiar with key words in computing using short sessions of a few minutes in frequent bursts. The following is an example you can use with the children.

I spy with my little eye something beginning with...

- a – the address or URL of the page (this stands for uniform resource locator but you hardly ever have to know this)
- i – icons help us find pages, games and programs
- l – links are code we can click on to get to another page
- w – www stands for World Wide Web and you see it in the address of a web page
- b – a browser is the program that navigates around the Web and helps you find the information you are looking for
- c – CBeebies
- m – the mouse
- s – screen
- k – keyboard
- s – the SMART rules.

Activities to teach about usernames and passwords
Oh hello, it's you!

This is for children at Key Stage 2. Use the following to engage with the pupils.

Introduction

- To play some games or visit some sites or clubs, we have to 'log in' and we get asked for two bits of information. Do you know why? Some games will store your scores and always remember you when you come back to play again. You might join an online club and you will be asked to enter a name and password to get into your club again.

- Some of you may have a nickname that your family use that is loving or funny. Well, when we are online we can have another name too, only this is a name we choose for ourselves. Does anyone know what a username is? Why do we need them?

- Is one enough? Why might we need a few of them? (If we always use the same username people could guess our username and pretend to be us.)

- Why is it a good idea to make up a new username and not use our real nicknames? (It is best to keep our real names safe and private.)

- Let's visit some safe sites where you need to make up a username. For example:

  ◦ SecretBuilders: Click 'New Player', select an age, and then select 'I'm a Girl' or 'I'm a Boy'.

  ◦ Scholastic's The Stacks: Click on 'Log In Now'.

  ◦ LEGO: Click on 'Sign Up'.

- Make up usernames for some well-known characters from stories you are reading in class.

- Remember the password Paddington had chosen? (See page 142.) Do you think you could do better? What would a good username be for Paddington? ('Station1'.) Think of a username for Katie Morag. ('Kamag3'.)

- It is a good idea to ask a grown-up at home or at school if your idea of a username is a good one. Sometimes we choose a word by mistake that is not a good one.

- Please don't use your real name, how old you are or the date of your birthday or any of your special private information that we've talked about in other lessons.

- Make it one word that you can remember and maybe add a number to the end of it.

- Sometimes you might find that someone else has already thought of this username and you will get a message to say it is already taken. You can either think of another username or add some numbers to your first choice.

- Now think of a password. This is not a name but could be any set of numbers and letters. You will be asked for your username and your password whenever you want to go back to a game, a website or a club where you are registered and you will be recognised.

- Write down your username (and password) and keep it in a safe place where you can find it if you forget it. Tell your mum, dad or carer.

- On the Government of Australia website https://budd-e.staysmartonline.gov.au/primary/main.php# there is a game you can play to test which usernames are good ones and which are weak.

Working in pairs:

- Use what you know about Findlay, Kayla and Sarvendra on page 148; try to make up some usernames for them.

- Compare the names you have listed and see if anyone else has guessed the same usernames for them.

- If this happens, how safe is that username? Would it be better to choose a different one that people can't so easily guess?

Passwords – keep them secret!

This is for children in Years 5 and 6. It takes 40 minutes.

Aim

- To explore how to make a password secure

Use the following to engage with the pupils.

Introduction: Four things to guess or name

1. Can you guess how many eight to nine-year-olds have shared their online passwords with someone else?

2. Can you name two things that make a password stronger?

3. Can you guess how many people use the same password for everything?

4. Splashdata told us, the public, the ten most popular passwords[65] – can you guess what the most popular one was based on? Do you have any ideas about which words were in the top ten?

Have you ever made a secret language or a secret code? Passwords should be like that. Watch *How to Pick a Proper Password*,[66] a video produced by Sophos, to find out how to make a strong password like a secret code. Then write a note to a friend in a secret code you two have agreed.

Answers

1. Seventy-five per cent of eight to nine-year-olds have shared their password. Why is this a risky thing to do?

2. You can make a password stronger by using a mix of numbers and letters, some upper case and some lower case, with no dictionary words.

3. Fifty-five per cent (more than half) of people use the same password for everything.

4. Pets' names were the most popular for passwords, while others were date of birth, child's name and favourite holiday. Did you guess that in the top most common passwords we even find the word 'password'?

   The top ten weak and common passwords are:

   - pets' names
   - a family member's birthday
   - another family member's name
   - a favourite holiday
   - the name of a girlfriend/boyfriend, husband/wife or mum or dad
   - a notable date, such as a wedding anniversary
   - child's name
   - birthplace

- something related to favourite sports team
- the word 'Password'.

Passwords for Pirates – a story

Use the following story for children aged 6–8.

Imagine the Pirates of Pennyrich are sailing away with the treasure they got when they fought the Pirates of Penury. They rig up their sails and get going as fast as they can with the treasure loaded onto their ship. They contact a few friends on various islands to check where the safest place might be to land and bury the treasure. A storm is coming and they want to be in a sheltered port as soon as they can. They do worry that the Pirates of Penury have very good computing on their ship and they might be trying to trap them into giving away where they are going with the treasure.

In fact, that is just what is happening. The Pirates of Penury go onto Facebook and Instagram, they go onto Snapchat and Vine, they look everywhere to try to find accounts belonging to any of the men on the Pennyrich ship. They hope to pick up some clues about where they are going. They give themselves new fake names and start chatting – trying to find anyone on the Pennyrich ship who might be posting a photo of himself on an island or any chat about a safe island. They look for anyone who is trying to order a lot of digging equipment. They also look for anyone online who likes the sea. They talk to lots of people about ports they have visited and chat about hurricanes and storms. They find lots of people who like talking about things like that. But do they find the Pirates of Pennyrich, I wonder?

The sea is rough and the winds are blowing hard. But the Pirates of Pennyrich are keen to hang on to their treasure.

- Do they give away which ship they are sailing on?
- Do they give away which island they plan to bury the treasure on?
- They would not want the horrid pirates to know their mobile numbers or their social network names.
- What personal information could a pirate give away by mistake that would lead to their enemies finding them?

Make a list of what they need to keep private.

Activities that explore what we mean by personal information

These three lessons are for children nine years and under.

Lesson 1: Privacy

Rationale

Rather than frighten young children with scare stories of what might happen to them, I think it best to try to create fictional stories with characters teachers can use in different ways to give the children a sense of competence. Most of all, the aims of these three short lessons are to give children the feeling that they are skilful detectives or skilful users of new technology and they know what the characters in the stories are doing wrong. Let them be the all-knowing ones, while the characters in the stories could be silly or make mistakes that the children can spot. We want to avoid making young children afraid of using the Internet.

What alerted me to the urgent need for this were the answers of ten-year-olds to the Cybersurvey – of girls especially – in which we can see a real 'fear of something happening to me' coming through. This fear could taint their experience of the Internet and I want to change that! Roads are scary and dangerous too, but we don't make children so fearful that they do not go out of the front door! They are taught to cross roads safely and in some situations to hold an adult's hand. So these sessions should be approached with a sense of discovery and enjoyment but a clear message that there are steps you can take to stay safe. These sessions contribute to a classroom display.

Aims

For children to:

- explore their understanding of personal information
- explore situations in which personal information should be withheld
- make the situations meaningful in relation to real life
- consider when they might have to give personal information

Learning objective

- To keep personal information private – online and on mobiles

Use the following to engage with the pupils.

What is personal information?

Findlay goes to St Joseph's Primary School. He loves football and supports Newcastle. He plays football near his home at a club down the road where he is in the under-11s team. The latest football strip is really smart and he has lots of photos of himself wearing it. He has this huge dog called Bailey and he enjoys his Playstation games. He is eight years old and his birthday is on 30 April. He lives at 7 Oak Avenue, Cramlington.

Kayla is eight years old and was born on 1 January. She is a real New Year baby and is often jokingly called that. She lives with her mum but she has her dad's surname. She is a fan of *X Factor* and she often sends friends pictures of herself singing or dancing. She posts these on her Facebook page too. She and her friend Bethany go to a dance class once a week and they also belong to a sports club where Kayla is a star at running. She has lots of photos of herself winning a race or receiving a cup for her team. Her club is called the Lightning Runners and she lives at 44 Castle Street in Brighton.

Sarvendra lives with his mum and dad and three sisters. His sisters are older than him and they use Facebook, Whatsapp and Instagram, so he knows a lot about ways to keep in touch with his friends. He is really good at using computers and plays a lot of games too. He beats his sisters most of the time and likes to brag about this to his mates. He was born in London on 3 March and is nine years old. He goes to New London Academy up the road from his parents' house at 133 New Road, Neasden. He walks to school. On the walk he uses his phone a lot to talk to friends and to send texts. He likes to meet up with friends before arriving at school, so he has worked out how to use GPS or Bluetooth to find out where they are. He loves Google maps too and is a good navigator.

Thinking about these characters:

- What information is personal information in these stories?

- Imagine the passwords they might have chosen. Would it be easy for someone who knows Findlay to guess what his password might be? How could he keep his personal details private?

Ask:

- What are the personal details about these children that they could accidentally give away?

- If you were a detective, how much could you work out about these three young people? What would you look for?

Elicit the following in the children's answers:

- school uniform in photos or mentioned in messages

- birth dates could give away identity and suggest passwords

- pets' names are often used as passwords

- names and surnames

- home address or local details

- names of brothers or sisters or parents

- sports clubs or team kit can give away a lot about where you spend time

- current location can be hidden in your camera setting so someone can work out from a photo where it was taken unless this is switched off

- Bluetooth reveals all the devices that are enabled within range

- some apps use GPS to track your location.

Follow-up:

- How could these three children stay safer?

- Write a postcard to Findlay, Kayla and Sarvendra with your suggestions and advice. Try to do this in a way which you think will get them to do what you suggest. (Display the postcards in the classroom with a big display of what personal information is.)

Lesson 2: E-safety

Use the following to address the pupils.

Personal information

In the last lesson we met Findlay, Kayla and Sarvendra. We thought a lot about how they might give away information about themselves online or on mobiles without really thinking. You all helped to imagine how a detective could find out a few things about them from the trail they had left. Today we are going to think about another story:

Red Riding Hood is nine, and she lives in the Faraway Wood with her mum. She always wears red. She often runs along the path to her gran's cottage with her basket of goodies. She really would like her gran to use a mobile phone more, because she, Red, is crazy about hers. She puts photos on Tumblr and Facebook all the time, of almost everything she does and where she goes. She likes to share her life with her friends. She knows her gran would enjoy it. She reads a lot of Jacqueline Wilson books and her best friend is Charlie's sister Lola. Red's password is 'RRHwood' and she has used it over and over again because she thinks it is brilliant and it is easy to remember. Just sometimes she uses her own birthday as her password, but all her friends know when her birthday is because she had a big teddy bears' picnic in the wood that day and she put lots of photos of everyone at the party online when she got home.

But the wolf is trying everything he can to catch her because she looks so red and juicy, so he pretends to be her gran one day.

- How did he know where she would be and when?

- What could he have found out about Red from looking at what she put online?

- If you were giving advice to Red, what would you suggest?

Lesson 3: Personal information and photos

When could it be OK to use or give personal details and photos?

Everyone stands up. Create an agree/disagree line across the classroom. Standing at one end of this imaginary line represents 'I agree'; the other represents 'I disagree'; and the middle represents 'In some circumstances'. Read out the scenarios and ask the pupils to take up a position on the line that represents their view of each scenario. Then ask them the reasons for their choice. After they have listened to the arguments, ask if anyone would like to change their position on the line. Clarify and repeat what the group has agreed.

- It is safe to upload photos.

- It is safe to use the same password for different accounts so that you don't forget it.

- It is safe to put your name and address into a form on a shopping website when you buy something.

- It is safe to give your name and phone number to someone who asks for it online.

- It is safe to agree to meet someone you only know through playing games online.

- It is safe to share your password with your best friend.

- It is safe to log in using your password when there is someone else nearby who is watching.

Complete the classroom display by adding these messages to your class display. Emphasise that the children have agreed these messages. Invite other classes to come and view your display. You might accompany this with messages the children deliver, such as reading out their postcards from Lesson 1.

Activity: Security word search

The following handout should be used for children at Key Stage 2.

Activity: Digital footprint

This handout should be used to explore pupils' digital footprint.

Security word search

Can you spot 12 words to do with security online? Can you explain what they mean?

P	V	E	R	I	F	Y	M	Y
Z	A	U	P	D	A	T	E	D
X	U	S	E	R	N	A	M	E
S	E	L	S	G	V	U	R	L
U	P	O	M	W	B	U	G	E
R	C	G	B	L	O	C	K	T
I	F	I	L	T	E	R	F	E
V	W	N	S	C	A	N	D	O

password, username, login, block, filter, delete, URL, verify, virus, scan, update, bug

DIGITAL FOOTPRINT

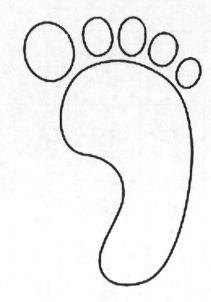

Do you know you are leaving a digital trail or footprint?

Will you be embarrassed by any of it one day?

Would a future employer see things about you that you would rather keep private?

In a new relationship? What can your partner find out about you by a quick search?

Search for yourself online

Check all privacy settings and photos

Look at your messages and tweets—what do they say about you?

Write down three steps you have taken to protect your digital footprint

Activities for bullying prevention
Reward badges

This is for children at Key Stages 1 and 2.

The BIG Award believes that rewarding prosocial behaviour should feature strongly in anti-bullying work – positive behaviour reinforcement can help children aspire to behave in the way the group has identified as heroic, a good friend or a kindly, trusted person. This behaviour can become the norm. On the other hand, a constant focus on 'anti-bullying' can become rather negative. Some schools have created positive systems such as a 'relationship charter' that puts the emphasis on good relationships. It is in this spirit that reward badges are suggested. But here, as in so many other activities, the pupil participation aspect is very important. No shortcut with teachers handing out badges they have made themselves will have as much impact, although it is obviously better than simply punishing people for negative behaviour.

Aims

- To create reward badges that pupils want to be awarded
- To set a goal of positive behaviour that pupils agree upon, both online and offline
- To involve pupils and create a sense of ownership
- To teach some graphic skills using Publisher or other software

Equipment

- Slips of paper and a ballot box
- Badge-making sets, crayons and felt-tip pens or a graphic software program like Publisher, or stickers

Use the following to engage with the pupils.

Discussion: What kind of behaviour do we like in our friends?

- When you think about other people, what do you admire about them?
- Write down three things you like in someone you admire, each on a separate slip of paper. Put your slips into the box.

The group looks at what people have written by reading out the qualities on the slips of paper and sorting them into piles of similar qualities.

- Which are the most popular qualities?

Ask the class to design and create badges to reward people who have shown these qualities the most during a week. They could include: helping someone else on the computer, explaining the SMART rules to a friend, sorting out a problem another child had on the computer, sending friendly messages to a classmate who was ill. Create a chart to enter the names of your pupil of the week.

The badge can be designed on computers with Publisher or drawn and coloured in by hand. Badges can be made up using cheap badge-making kits, or stickers can be used to avoid sharp pins.

Songs that can inspire, bring courage and raise awareness

Listen to or look up all lyrics first to ensure they are suitable for the age group with whom you plan this activity. In some, one verse is ideal whereas another is not. In others you will want the chorus only.

- Katy Perry's 'Roar' is an empowering anti-bullying song.
- 'Don't Laugh at Me' by Mark Willis is another song that can be used to support children who have been bullied. It tells of a child bullied for wearing glasses and teeth braces or with physical difficulties.
- Bette Midler's 'The Wind beneath My Wings' can be adapted to the theme of friendship.
- Selena Gomez's 'Who Says?' is useful for raising girls' self-esteem and fighting the appearance police.
- Taylor Swift's 'Mean' encourages victims of bullying to make a great life.
- Jessie J's 'Who's Laughing Now' is a hip-hop empowerment anthem.

Other songs you may want to use include:

- Journey's 'Don't Stop Believing'
- Christina Aguilera's 'Can't Hold Us Down'
- Avril Lavigne's 'Keep Holding on'
- Demi Lovato's 'Skyscraper'
- Kesha's 'Love into the Light'
- Simon and Garfunkel's 'Bridge over Troubled Water'.

More suggestions can be found at www.songsforteaching.com/charactereducationsongs/anti-bullying-songs.htm.

Empathy – bullying linked with disability group activity

This is for children in Year 6 and lasts for one hour. The film can be upsetting for younger viewers.

View the DCSF DVD *Make Them Go Away* (www.youtube.com/watch?v=Cw0VrC5ODKA). See the accompanying resource pack, available at www.inclusivechoice.com/Make%20them%20go%20away.pdf; use the DVD chapter People Who Have Been Bullied.

You will need: digital cameras, pictures, poetry, songs, a selection of 'junk' art materials such as scissors, tissue paper, balloons, large boards, coloured paper (including black) and computers, and magazines.

1. As a whole group, listen to the interviews on the DVD in which young people describe how being bullied made them feel.

2. Divide the class into four smaller groups. Allocate each group one speaker in these interviews and then invite them to create a presentation using music, images, colours, art or poetry to illustrate how their interviewee (in the film) was made to feel as a result of bullying. (Replay the interviews as needed.) Each group will then be asked to present these ideas to the whole class or wider group and explain their choices.

You could use a painting such as *The Scream* by Munch or a song such as 'Don't Laugh at Me' by Shamblin and Seskin, performed by Mark Willis (there are numerous versions of this on YouTube). A collage could be made using magazine or news pictures and other materials including words to illustrate feelings.

Discuss how the rainbow has come to represent equality – lots of different colours but beautiful and harmonious together. Encourage ideas for posters and songs.

Figure 9.5, a diagram of advice on how to act if you are bullied, can be used on a classroom wall after children have acted out some examples of walking like a victim or walking strong.

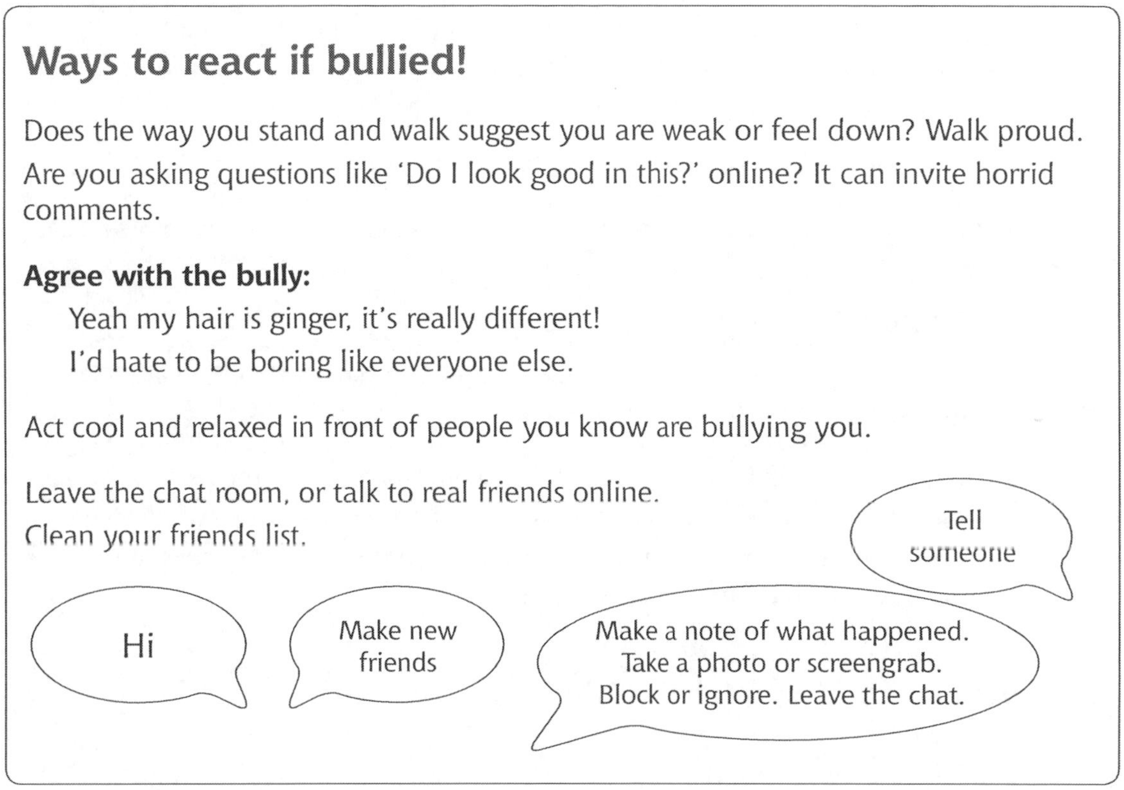

Ways to react if bullied!

Does the way you stand and walk suggest you are weak or feel down? Walk proud. Are you asking questions like 'Do I look good in this?' online? It can invite horrid comments.

Agree with the bully:
> Yeah my hair is ginger, it's really different!
> I'd hate to be boring like everyone else.

Act cool and relaxed in front of people you know are bullying you.

Leave the chat room, or talk to real friends online. Clean your friends list.

Tell someone

Hi

Make new friends

Make a note of what happened. Take a photo or screengrab. Block or ignore. Leave the chat.

Figure 9.5 Ways to act if you are bullied

Activity: The real me

This is for children at Key Stage 2 and explores behaviour on- and offline and the ways in which it differs (see earlier handout).

Aim

- To explore children's behaviour on- and offline and the ways in which it differs

Learning objective

- To encourage children to avoid common pitfalls found in personal profiles, online communications and reputation management such as exaggeration, risk taking, poor privacy settings and acting anonymously

Use the following to engage with the pupils.

Sometimes it can feel as though we are two different people – our online persona and the real me.

- Why do you think this is?

- Can you give some examples? (e.g. People can have a thousand friends on social networks.)

Draw two large boxes. Fill in things about 'Me online' and 'Me in the real world'. Compare and spot the differences. Colour in a mask each and display the masks to illustrate the false 'Me' online behind which all of us hide. Fold your own sheet with boxes in half and post it into this box. Do not put your name on it.

Me online

- I have 253 friends.

- I look cool and popular and busy.

- My photos are a little more bold than I really am.

- It looks as if I am always out and about at exciting places.

- I take lots of risks online because I don't say who I am.

Me in the real world

- I have eight friends.

- I am sometimes bored and lonely.

- I dream about having lots more friends.

- I never feel that I really fit in.

- Lots of my time is spent in my room.

- I am quite cautious in real life.

Use the messages that the children have put into their boxes to develop another session based on different behaviour online. Consider following this session with the digital footprint (see earlier handout).

Activity: Cyberquiz

Use the following to quiz children at Key Stage 2.

Could I be a cyberbully?

Have you ever:

1. used/stolen someone else's password?

2. sent a nasty message using someone else's phone?

3. pretended to be someone else using text, IM or BBM?

4. teased and scared someone using messaging?

5. forwarded a message not meant for others to see?

6. posted photos of someone without asking them?

7. altered someone's online photos in order to upset them?

8. created an online ratings poll about someone else without their consent?

9. spread rumours about someone in cyberspace?

10. made threats to someone in cyberspace?

11. sent rude and abusive material to someone online/by phone?

12. used information about someone to harass, scare or embarrass them?

13. created or forwarded a chain letter with threats about what will happen if people don't pass it on?

14. signed someone up for something online without asking them?

15. altered someone's profile without his or her consent?

16. created a cruel web page about someone and invited others to comment?

17. hacked into someone's computer?

18. sent a virus to someone else deliberately?

19. insulted players in online games?

20. joined in with insulting chat room talk that is racist or abusive about religion or culture?

21. joined in with insulting chat room talk that is homophobic?

22. signed on to a website and lied about your age?

Rough guide to how you did

- If you answered yes to more than 15 questions, what you are doing could be a matter for the police.

- If you answered yes in 12–15 cases, you could be a cyberbully.

- If you answered yes in 10 cases, you are on your way to being a full-blown cyberbully.

- If you answered yes in 5 cases, take a deep breath and think about where this is heading before it is too late.

Did you know that it is against the law to send malicious communications or to incite hatred?

Activities that encourage and explore friendship and inclusion
Old-fashioned skills meet new technology

The old-fashioned work on friendship and inclusion is needed now more than ever. It sets the foundations of how we treat one another, what is acceptable and how most people behave positively. This can then be translated to life on the Internet. Children are unlikely to be good digital citizens if they cannot behave in the real world. Empathy, sharing and kindness need to dominate trolls, attacks and hacks. Where better to start than on friendship? These activities are all commonly used in bullying intervention work and they are a good place to start with young children. Your school is doubtless already doing similar activities. Could you harness them and extend the conversation to include how we want to be treated online and offline? Values and vision are more emotionally satisfying to discuss than rules and scary dangers. Would you rather discuss friendship or rules? Once you can agree on friendship values, it is easy to draw up an agreement or a manifesto – this is what we have agreed, and we are all going to try to behave this way. This is the opposite of imposed rules and is true democracy in action. In my view it has a better chance of being acted upon than the 58 per cent of 10–11-year-olds who say they always follow the e-safety guidelines they have been taught.

Group work

Group work is needed to enhance the following:

- working together to solve problems

- making friends

- listening to and understanding others

- sharing feelings with others

- providing help and support to others, not just within the group – e.g. in the playground

- dealing with bullying (behaviour we've decided we do not want in this class).

Getting to know someone in this class you know very little about

You need cards and a hat or box. Each person writes one interesting thing about themselves on a card and throws it into a hat. Each person then draws out one card and sets off to find the person who wrote it. When they have found the person, they have a short conversation and try to find out some more about this person before moving on.

Everyone sits in a circle and you engage them in a discussion:

- What one interesting thing can you tell us about the person you had to find?

- What did you learn about someone that you did not know before?

Activities that require a partner to help you – any game where two heads are better than one

Computer keyboard

Give out blank representations of a computer keyboard and ask each child to try and fill it in. Then move them into pairs and see how much better most people do when they are with a partner. Keep reinforcing the idea of *support*. The message is that sharing = success. Reward children who cooperate well.

Treasure hunts, quick quizzes and word searches

These provide a similar type of experience – friends can help one another. Together you achieve differently. Count off partners so people cannot choose their partner and leave someone out.

Quick circles

- Sit in a circle and pass a ball around the outside of the circle (behind the pupils' backs). Everyone has to cooperate.

- Sit in a circle. A leader claps a new rhythm, which is copied around the circle by everyone in turn. Try to create ripples of sound or a storm ending with a quiet round of soft clapping.

None of the above will work without cooperation. This illustrates how we need each other.

Positive behaviour reward programmes

Involve the whole class – if one person lets the others down, everyone will lose out. Agree on the behaviour that is acceptable within the class. Via a circle time starting 'I don't like it when…', have people describe the types of behaviour they don't think are acceptable. No pupils' names are to be used.

The reward

Describe the treat or outing that will be given at the end of term if everyone helps the whole class achieve a certain number of award points for positive behaviour. Explain how pupils can help one another to achieve this. They won't, for example, collude in jeering or bullying. They won't let people be left out. They won't call each other names or be nasty. They will support each other if someone seems to need friendship.

Set up a chart and each morning tell the class how they did yesterday. This includes reports from other teachers, dinner ladies or sports staff and teaching assistants, learning mentors, etc. Award points.

Drama/role play: How do I tell someone I am being bullied or cyberbullied?

Have some pupils act out a scene in which a child tries to tell his busy mother that he or she has been cyberbullied. The mother is rushing to work and has to drop off a baby sister at nursery. She is very busy. Then the pupil tries to tell a teacher he or she has been cyberbullied but the teacher is too busy marking and rushing around supervising other children.

Ask the whole group what the pupil could try. They give suggestions in secret to the person acting the pupil. Then the actors re-do the scene and try to show whether or not the suggestions are good ones. Aim to have a few tries before finally the mother and the teacher take notice. Now ask the group how the mother should react. What should the teacher do? Ask half the class to advise the mother and the other half to advise the teacher.

Coming together as the group gels

Over time, using various methods in a consistent approach, you want the children to develop a group identity. They should have developed their own rules, be able to discuss behaviour and challenge each other when behaviour is unacceptable to them. They should demonstrate the following improvements:

- making and sustaining positive friendships with peers
- making open and positive relationships with adults
- developing feelings of responsibility towards and care for others – the ability to empathise
- considering their own thoughts, feelings and behaviour and those of others.

Embed this work in the curriculum and reward people for positive behaviour.

Further Key Stage 2 activities are shown in the resource book inside the Make Them Go Away DVD pack by the DCSF. The DVD is a moving film about bullying someone with learning disabilities.[70]

Circle of friends

Also known as 'circles of support', the circle of friends approach provides emotional support to vulnerable pupils who may feel isolated and rejected by their peers. Pupils are trained to befriend and support another pupil identified as isolated or in other ways vulnerable to bullying.[71]. Encourage the group to think of ways to help a hypothetical person who is getting into difficulty online or on a mobile. Help them to explore what kind of behaviour they like or dislike. Then, when they are sufficiently skilled and confident, use the circle to elicit support when needed for other pupils. Encourage them to bring to the circle any worries they may have. They can talk to you first about this and together you will plan a way of asking the group for support.

Activity: A human friend

This is for children at Key Stages 1 and 2.

You will need sticky notes and adhesive and, if possible, large chunks of polystyrene made into a human figure. Alternatively, you could use large sheets of paper (e.g. sheets of flip chart paper taped together). Lay the paper on the floor and invite a child to lie on the paper and have others draw around their shape so that you have an outline of a child. Stick the paper shape onto the wall or set up the human figure.

Learning objectives

- To understand friendships and fallouts

- To increase resilience in relationships

- To raise awareness of values

- To explore how to navigate conflict

Introduction

Ask the children about why we need friends. Allow five minutes for discussion.

Activities

Ask the children to think about the qualities they look for in a friend. How do they choose friends? For example, 'She's kind', 'She helps me', 'He's fun', 'He plays nicely', 'He's fair', 'She is so funny' and 'He is never unkind'.

For Key Stage 2, elicit comments such as 'I can trust him', 'She's loyal', 'She is there for me', 'He stands up for me', 'We play games together', 'She is never horrible', 'We find the same things funny' and 'We like the same football team'.

Ask the children to write their chosen qualities onto coloured paper and pin them onto the polystyrene figure or attach sticky notes onto the flip chart paper.

Discuss:

- Which were the most popular attributes mentioned?

- When is a group of friends a clique?

- Sometimes people change as they grow up and they make different friends. If this happens to us, what should we do?

- When friendships go wrong, what is not OK?

Set up a circle time and start with 'I don't like it when friends…'.

Some suggested answers might be: 'get revenge', 'retaliate', 'spread rumours', 'say nasty things behind someone's back', 'hack your Facebook account or gaming accounts because they know your password', 'send you scary chain letters on your mobile' and 'leave you out'.

Being assertive, not aggressive: Scenarios to act out

- Joy and Chanelle have been friends for ages, but now they are ten they are beginning to argue a lot. Joy thinks she should not say what she thinks because she has always been taught to be quiet and kind. She cannot imagine herself shouting and yelling. How can she tell Chanelle what she is really feeling?

- Ollie and Devon are always at each other's throats. They irritate each other all the time and each always says the other boy started it. It has been going on for ages. They trip each other up, damage their things, always get in the way of the other and generally try to annoy the other person. Nobody wants to lose face or be seen as weak. How should they do something to change this? Act out what you think they should do.

- Jake and Damon are mates. They spend hours playing online games together. They talk to lots of other players. They know each other's passwords. One day they argue and the next day Damon finds that all the points he has won in his gaming account have disappeared and other gamers are saying horrid things to him in chat. He suspects Jake has hacked his account. What should he say to him?

Further ideas to reinforce ideas about friendships

- *Friendship tower*: Groups of children design a box that represents all the good things about positive friendships. Boxes are then placed on stage and a friendship tower will be built from them. Boxes are supported by other boxes; they all need each other.

- *Friendship bracelets*: Children make friendship bracelets in different shades of blue (Blue Friday is the last day of Anti-Bullying Week every year). Join the bracelets together at the end of the sessions to show that together students can make a difference. (Source: Consett Academy)

- *Friendship wall*: Each person creates a brick on which they draw or write things they believe make a friendship work. These are then built up to make the wall of friendship.

- *Anti-bullying wall*: Each brick represents a pledge. Bricks are built up to create a wall against prejudice or hate, or a wall against cyberbullying. (Source: Dudley Anti-bullying team).

What do you think is unacceptable in friendships?

Put ideas onto cards or sticky notes. Then ask everyone to rank them. What is the worst attribute?

What is acceptable in a relationship?

Tell the pupils we are talking here about the way the relationship works and how the two people treat one another. Use the following questions:

- What would be entirely unacceptable to you?

- What would make you feel uncomfortable?

- What do you find reassuring?

- What do you think really makes a relationship succeed?

- What do you think is unacceptable on mobiles?

- What do you think people should never do online to their friends?

A further activity: Friends online – are they who they seem to be?

Use the following to address the pupils.

Imagine a big bowl of sweets in their shiny wrappers – but when you unwrap them it turns out that they are not what they seem. Online you have to pick your friends in a careful way. People can pretend to be someone else entirely. The sweets could be wrapped in the wrong wrapper – could online friends be similar? The picture they give you of themselves could be like a wrapper, but inside they are not what they seem.

Discuss this idea and then make posters or slides in PowerPoint to warn your friends to be careful when they meet people online.

Activities that explore digi-dilemmas
Fixology

This is for children at Key Stage 2.

Set one of these 'digital dilemmas' once a week. Have the pupils work on what they would do if this happened to them and then discuss it in class. Create a wall display of good suggestions. Typical dilemmas:

What will you do if...?

- You get a message that seems to be selling you something.

- You get a message from someone you don't know.

- You get a message asking you to re-send your password and username.

- You get a message telling you that you've won a big prize – a holiday in the Caribbean and spending money.

- Someone who is bullying you in school begins to send you some scary threats or nasty messages.

- You've been searching for something for your homework or school project when you find you have landed on a page with very violent pictures on it.

- You forget your password for a message service you have been using.

- Your dad lets you use his credit card to buy and download an app game but now the app or game says you must choose and buy things for your online pet or your online warrior.

- Your friend is really upset because someone has hacked into his account on a game.

- One of your friends has seen your password for a message service you use.

Extension

Ask the children to add a few new dilemmas by doing an anonymous survey of their classmates or other classes asking what has happened to them. They can set up a 'digital dilemma' suggestion box into which pupils can drop ideas for future fixology lessons. They can design posters with all the advice (e.g. page 000).

Digi-dilemmas board game

In a similar vein to Fixology but taken to another level is the board game Digi-dilemmas, another activity that is for children at Key Stage 2. In this game there are two sets of cards, one set marked 'safe' on which are written some safe actions, and another set marked 'unsafe' on which are written some risky actions. Using throws of the dice, players try to advance and win the game by getting to the end first. Players are rewarded if they pick up a 'safe' card and are sent back several places if they pick up an 'unsafe' card. There are discussions to be had on each card. If players can explain the reason why their action is safe or unsafe they could be awarded a 'free pass' card. This card could help them avoid being sent backwards or avoid going forward and landing on an unsafe spot. The teacher could adjudicate, or why not set up a panel of people (an uneven number for successful voting) and have them decide whether the explanations are worth a free pass card?

While I have given a lot of ideas for the cards, it would be invaluable to work with your class to create more dilemmas. In addition, older students could be encouraged to make cards for use with younger pupils. Their insider knowledge of what pupils a year younger are accessing online will make it seem true to life and relevant.

In the world of computer gaming, the struggle, challenge and failure that often make children so disheartened in the classroom act as drivers of entertainment and achievement. So, turning e-safety into an old-fashioned competitive board game might be more attractive than top-down learning!

How to play

Photocopy or print out copies of the board; it is best to laminate it if possible. Have pairs of dice available and counters or little charms to represent the players. Make cards in two colours, one for 'safe' and one for 'unsafe', and print each of the sentences below onto an appropriate card.

Players begin at Start, and as they throw the dice they advance by the number on the dice when it is their turn. If they land on an 'unsafe' stop they must pick up a card from the 'unsafe' pile. It may tell them to go back a number of spaces. The only way to escape this fate is if they can explain the risks successfully and win a 'free pass' card, or if they already have one from an earlier success.

If they land on a 'safe' stop, they pick up a 'safe' card, which might advance them a few spaces if they can explain why this action is safe. If the panel thinks their explanation is not good enough they may have to stay where they are. The first player to reach 'End' wins.

Another layer of this game is to discuss the following each time a card is picked up:

- Why is this action unsafe – what is the risk or harm?
- Why is this action safe – what have you avoided?
- Are there other options you might have chosen?

Adjudication panel

Select a panel of three players to adjudicate. If the panel consider the answer is correct they can award a 'free pass' card, which the player can use to get themselves out of trouble when they next land on an 'unsafe' card spot. By using the card they can escape having to go back.

Making the cards

Print the following sentences on the 'safe' cards:

- You did not open the email with the subject 'You have won a prize'. Go forward two spaces.

- You did not open an attachment in a message from someone you've never heard of. Go forward two spaces.

- When you shopped with your mum's credit card online you helped her check that the site was safe before using the card. Go forward six spaces.

- You have a strong password, using letters and numbers. Go forward five spaces.

- You use different passwords for different clubs and services. Go forward five spaces.

- You remembered to turn off the location service on your phone's camera. Go forward three spaces.

- A friend sent you a message saying, 'You must try this game.' But before you clicked on the link he sent, you checked the URL of this game so that you did not land on a fake site. Go forward three spaces.

Print the following sentences on the 'unsafe' cards:

- You have hundreds of friends on your SNS account. Go back four spaces.

- You post photos online without making sure only your friends and family can see them. Go back four spaces.

- You post webcam shots of yourself online. Go back five spaces.

- You carelessly gave away the name of your school when you posted photos of you and your friends in school uniform online. Go back three spaces.

- You keep logged on to your favourite apps on your phone all the time. Go back two spaces.

- You use the same password on lots of different sites or services. Go back three spaces.

- You agreed to meet up with someone you only knew online. Go back six spaces.

Digi-Dilemmas Board Game

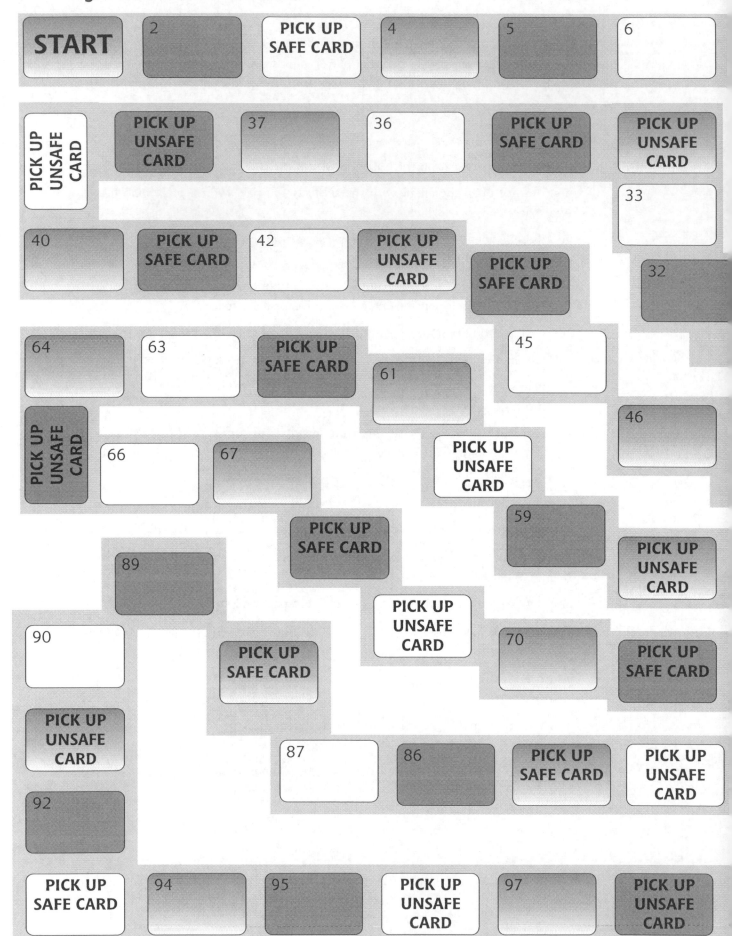

| PICK UP UNSAFE CARD | PICK UP SAFE CARD | 9 | 10 | 11 | PICK UP SAFE CARD |

| PICK UP UNSAFE CARD | 18 | 17 | PICK UP SAFE CARD | 15 | 14 | PICK UP UNSAFE CARD |

| 20 | PICK UP SAFE CARD | 22 | PICK UP UNSAFE CARD | 24 | 25 | 26 |

| PICK UP UNSAFE CARD | 30 | PICK UP UNSAFE CARD | 28 | PICK UP UNSAFE CARD | |

| PICK UP UNSAFE CARD | PICK UP SAFE CARD | 49 | PICK UP UNSAFE CARD | 51 | PICK UP SAFE CARD |

| 57 | 56 | PICK UP SAFE CARD | 54 | PICK UP UNSAFE CARD | |

| PICK UP UNSAFE CARD | 73 | 74 | PICK UP SAFE CARD | 76 | PICK UP UNSAFE CARD |

| 83 | PICK UP UNSAFE CARD | 81 | 80 | PICK UP SAFE CARD | 78 |

| PICK UP SAFE CARD | 100 | 101 | 102 | 103 | END |

Digi-Dilemmas Board Game Cards

You did not open the email with the subject 'You have won a prize.' (Go forward two spaces.)	What is the risk if you open this type of message? Hoax messages like this are usually phishing to get your email address.
You did not open an attachment in a message from someone you've never heard of. (Go forward two spaces.)	What is the risk if you open attachments from people you have never heard of? Clicking on the attachment can let a virus or malware into your computer.
When you shopped with your mum's credit card online you helped her check that the site was safe before using the card. (Go forward six spaces.)	What is the risk if you do not check the website is secure? Having her credit card details stolen or hacked.
You have a strong password, using letters and numbers. (Go forward five spaces.)	What is the point of a strong password? It is harder for people or software to guess it and get into your account.
You use different passwords for different clubs and services. (Go forward five spaces.)	What is the reason you should have different passwords when it is easier to remember just one? If one of your passwords is hacked at least your other accounts will be safe.
You remembered to turn off the location service on your phone's camera. (Go forward three spaces.)	Why should I turn off the location service on my phone's camera? Because when you post the photo online or send it, people can click on it and find out exactly where you are. This is not a safe situation.

A friend sent you a message saying, 'You must try this game.' But before you clicked on the link he sent, you checked the URL of the game so that you did not land on a fake site. (Go forward three spaces.)	Why can't I just click on the link? I know him.
	If this is a virus email using his address, it might be taking you to a fake site made to look like the game, but in fact it is a 'skin' only there to capture your details when it asks you to sign in. Always check the URL first.
You did not share a photo sent to you of someone in your class because you can see it was meant to be private – between them only. (Go forward six spaces.)	Why shouldn't I share it with friends? Everyone else is doing it. It's a joke.
	No private photos should be shared.
You reported abuse to a website or service after keeping evidence. (Go forward five spaces.)	Why should I bother to report abuse? Nobody ever does anything about it.
	Actually, that is not true. If the behaviour is against the rules of the web site the person can be stopped and the material taken down. If a lot of people think someone is behaving badly online then it will be noticed.
You have hundreds of friends on your SNS account. (Go back four spaces.)	I like to look popular, so why shouldn't I accept friend requests?
	But you do not know more than 20 of these 'friends' and you are revealing your personal life and photos to all these people who might misuse the material. Nothing is private.
You post photos online without making sure only your friends and family can see them. (Go back four spaces.)	Why does it matter who sees my photos?
	Not everyone means well and people could misuse your photos in many ways. They could also share them with even more people. You might give away a lot about yourself in your photos without realising it. One day someone you care about might see a photo you are desperately ashamed about when they do a search about you.
You post webcam shots of yourself looking cute online. Go back five spaces.	But I like sharing photos of myself!
	Your photos could be misused or collected by people you do not know or shared by people you know. Your photos will be out there always. You could be blackmailed to post more and more.

You carelessly gave away the name of your school when you posted photos of you and your friends in school uniform online. Go back three spaces.	Who cares what school I go to? This gives away your location to anyone, making you less safe. Now they know where you are each day.
You keep logged on to your favourite apps or message services on your phone all the time. Go back two spaces.	Why should you make sure your phone is protected by pin or password and apps and message services are not left open? If you put your phone down, anyone can pick it up and pretend to be you, use your account, send messages or insult other people.
You use the same password on lots of different sites or services. Go back three spaces.	But it is easier for me to remember If someone cracks your password they can get in to all your accounts, sites and services.
You agreed to meet up with someone you only knew online. Go back six spaces.	Why should you never agree to meet up with someone you only know online? People are often not who they say they are. This could be a trap. An adult could pretend to be a young person in order to meet children.

Activities that promote e-safety to the whole school
Making e-safety posters and leaflets

This is for children at Key Stage 2.

Teaching objectives

All pupils must be able to show that they understand what e-safety is and produce a poster that explains this. Most pupils should be able to show appropriate information that could be used in a leaflet or poster to explain e-safety to other children. Some pupils will be able to explain in further detail about e-safety tips and successful ways of communicating these using colour, images and text, either using software or by hand.

Learning outcomes

How will you know that pupils have achieved these objectives?

- All must take part in the discussions and show that they have understood what e-safety is and why they need to know these messages.

- Most should produce a poster using graphic or word-processing software.

- Some could introduce or suggest other risks online and suggest solutions.

- Some could plan good communication methods to get these messages across to other pupils and parents using ICT.

Activity 1

Ask:

- What do we mean by e-safety?

- Should we choose five key messages to get across? What is most important?

Activity 2

Show a PowerPoint presentation of various e-safety posters.

Activity 3

Discuss:

- What makes a good poster or leaflet?

- What should we avoid in a poster or leaflet?

Activity 4

Create posters using Publisher or other software, or make them by hand.

Activity 5

Print, display and share posters.

Cyberspace: stuff to know

- Keep your personal information and profile private!

- Only add friends you know in real life.

- Share your profile and photos only with people on your friends list.

- Don't give clues to your location or the school or clubs you go to.

- Never meet up alone with anyone you met and only know online.

- If someone hacks your account or makes a page in your name, **report** it to the site.

- Remove any identifying information from photos and videos **before you post.**

- Don't share all your plans and say where you will be next.

- Ignore harassing or rude comments posted on your profile but keep a record, block and report.

- Think how information and photos you post could cause you embarrassment or harm one day.

Never post sexually provocative photos and if you have made any kind of mistake and someone uses this to make threats, please report it and get help. Police can often trace abusive people.

GAMES

When you play games you may talk to people you do not know.

Are you spending too much time on games?

Some games can be scary—talk to a grown-up if you feel scared.

Are you on the right games for your age?

FOOTPRINT

Did you know—everything you do online stays on the internet and other people can find it. We call this leaving a footprint, just as you do when you walk on wet sand. Would that photo you posted embarrass you one day?

LIFE ONLINE

Going online is fun and gives you lots to do and see.

But sometimes it can be risky. Stop and think about it—are you talking to strangers? Never agree to meet up.

Be careful when you shop.

You don't have to answer questions about who or where you are.

CREDIT CARDS ONLINE

Check you are on the real website of the place you want to shop in.

Some websites are fakes so do another search and check it out!

Look for the 'https' before the URL of the website before entering card details. Keep your parent or carer's card details really safe, never give them to anyone without permission.

PASSWORDS

Create strong ones with numbers and letters

Change them often

Never give them to other people

Don't use the same one all the time

Avoid 12345! Millions of people use it.

Login
Username ....
Password....................

The BAD agency: A PR and advertising agency project

This is for children at Key Stage 2.

Learning objectives

- To communicate anti-bullying messages to the school community
- To engage and involve all pupils in the school's anti-bullying approach
- To develop child-friendly anti-bullying resources
- To create materials to use to engage parents
- To reinforce key messages about bullying

You will need flip chart paper, computers with graphic design software such as Publisher, felt tips, paint brushes and paint. Have available for consultation any school policy that is child friendly, such as anti-bullying messages, e-safety policy, Acceptable Use of ICT policy or school vision statement. Use the following to engage with the pupils.

Introduction

Nowadays, every company or music artist needs to have a public relations or media manager or an advertising agency. Can you explain what these people do? Today we are going to imagine we are the BAD agency – Bullying Ad(vertising) Agency. Our job is to make the school's plan to prevent and tackle bullying clear to everyone in the school. Now we have to make it clear what cyberbullying is and what we want pupils, parents and teachers to do about it.

- *Who?* Plan on flip chart paper the different groups your messages are aimed at.
- *How?* Think about how you will get the message across to these different groups of people.
- *What?* What is the message?
- *In what way?* Younger children may need simpler language, people who cannot see may need a sound version of the message and parents may need a different sort of message. We call these the different media.
- *Agree your messages* for your different audiences and test them out.
- *Create your adverts and posters*: Use computers or your paint brushes.
- *Plan your public relations campaign*: What will you release first and why? How will you check whether your messages are reaching the right people?
- *Include in your thinking*: School plasma screens, messages to appear on school computers, in homework books, given to new pupils and their families when they first start school, displays on walls, songs, assemblies, drama, stories and real demonstrations on computers of what to do.

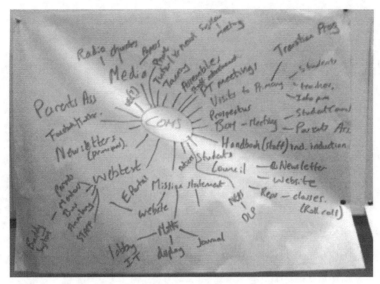

Figure 9.6 Communications diagram: The different people who need to hear messages about cyberbullying

Figure 9.7 Word cloud (www.wordle.net) made by pupils from John Keble School

Figure 9.8 An exhibition of children's artwork: Art against bullying in Birmingham

Activities that help children spot danger signs
Detective game
Use the following to engage with the pupils.
What should make you suspicious?

If someone:

- you have only met online tries to force you to give them your phone number or tell them where you live or what school you go to

- sends you photos or videos which make you feel shocked, worried or uncomfortable

- you have only met online suggests you should keep your chats with them a secret from your parents

- you are talking to online or on your mobile says you will get into trouble if you tell a grown up what is happening

- you are talking to online suggests or tries to force you to send photos or videos of yourself that you think should be private

- you met online tries to arrange to meet up with you offline and tells you not to tell anyone or bring anyone with you

please tell someone you trust right away.

What would you do? What can you check? What can you find out about them?

True or false? Are they who they say they are?

This activity for children at the upper end of Key Stage 2, is vital for teaching children how to recognise when they are being pressured to give away information and to learn ways to resist this.

Objectives

- To explore ways in which people online may not be who they say they are
- To practise not giving away personal details online

Advance preparation

It may be necessary to obtain permission from parents for their children to use something like a Google Hangout and to do this exercise. Parents can do their part by reinforcing these messages at home.

Set up a messaging group (e.g. Google Hangout) as a learning tool for a group. Use the privacy settings to ensure that only pupils in this class are able to access the page or messaging group.

Divide the pupils into two groups, A and B. Ask each child to create an online name and write it on a piece of paper with their group letter, then fold it in half without anyone else seeing it and hand it to you. Using their online names, set them all up as members of this messaging group.

Children in Group A ask those in Group B questions and try to work out whether they are who they say they are from the answers. Group B pupils can answer with true or false answers. Group B's task is to try to get pupils in Group A to give away personal information.

Swap roles. All the children need to practise not giving away too much identifying information about themselves.

Some question ideas to start them off:

- What sports do you do?

- Do you have Skype?

- What is your favourite colour?

- What pets do you have?

- Is your school near mine?

- Do you have brothers or sisters?

- Which football club do you support?

- Did you see that amazing goal X scored yesterday (mentioning a key player in the team)?

- Are you about the same age as me?

- What is your favourite food?

Discuss:

- How many of you could tell who you were talking to online?

- Is it easy to tell when someone is telling the truth when you are together in the real world talking face to face?

- How easy is it when you are talking to people online and you are not sure who they are?

- We put a high value on telling the truth in our lives and in the way we behave with other people around us. But online we need to be careful to keep some things private. So while we are not suggesting you actually do not tell the truth there are some things it is best not to share.

- What are the things you think are most important to keep private? List these as a group and discuss.

- What are some snappy or witty answers to get you out of an awkward situation when you do not want to answer a question someone is asking you online?

Figure 9.9 Cartoon: Two dogs talking

Gaming online and staying safe

Use the following to address the pupils.

Introduction

You have probably found that when you are playing online games you meet up with other players who could be anywhere. Even in other countries. When playing games like *World of Warcraft* and *Clash of the Clans* or using a gaming portal like Miniclip it is exciting to be able to 'chat' and 'meet' other people when you play with them. But, of course, just as in the offline world, you need to be careful when playing with people you do not actually know. They may be dodgy or be trying to make friends with kids for bad reasons.

Not everyone is really who they seem to be! It's easy to hide your real identity online and lie about how old you are. Some people, who want you to think they are 'friends' in your online game, may actually want to harm you in some way. So, to be on your guard, what should you watch for?

- *Someone who tries to get you to trust them and 'make friends' with you.* They might start by trying to make you think they like the same things as you – hobbies or the game that you're playing with them. They find out what music you like or which team you support and say they are your age.

- *They might try to get you to do things that make you uncomfortable.* A player might ask you to add them to your friends on SNS, to give them your phone number, send them photos or chat on a webcam. If they talk about things which make you uncomfortable or ask you to do things you don't want to do, you can turn off voice chat, you can activate 'ignore' or leave a chat room.

- *They might offer to tell you 'cheats' to help you do well in a game.* If they ask for something in return, stop! Think about why they are doing this – are they a 'real' friend or trying to build your trust? Be alert!

- *They might try to share a link with you which is a computer virus or spyware.* This could tell them your personal information without you knowing – so be careful and don't click on links from people you don't know!

- *They may encourage you to tell them personal information.* This could be where you live and what school you go to. This is part of their attempt to get your trust and will tell them how to find you in the real world. Never give out your phone number or address.

Find out more at www.thinkuknow.co.uk/11_13/Need-advice/Staying-secure-online.

Breck Bednar, a tragic case: Can we learn from it?

It is so important to discuss gaming with pupils. While it is generally a leisure activity and takes place at home, there cannot be too much advice on not meeting people in real life whom you only know online.

Breck, a boy of 14, was playing games regularly with his friends and another 'boy' joined the game without showing his face, only using his avatar. Over months they played often and chatted. Slowly this new person began to influence the boy in many ways and tell him not to spend time with his parents and family as he used to, or go to church on Sundays with them. Then he suggested that if they met up he could help upgrade Breck's computer. Breck now trusted this person without ever having met him. He went to meet him on his own after telling his mum he was going to sleep over at a friend's home. This case ended tragically in murder; the 'boy' was not who or what he said he was. In a further cruel twist, the murderer posted images of Breck's body online so that his friends and sisters found out before the police or their parents could break the news to them. His parents have set up the Breck Bednar Memorial Foundation (www.breckbednar.com) to raise awareness of the dangers Internet relationships can pose for teenagers.

Can you spot the differences?

The following handout is for children at Key Stage 2.

In this exercise we are asking you to carefully compare the two boxes and try to spot any differences. Then think about what the differences mean. Can you think why there are there? What could happen differently because of some of the actions people take?

- Put the children into pairs and hand out the 'Spot the difference' sheet.

- Ask them what differences they spotted and why they think each one could make a difference to the e-safety of the children in the mini stories.

Can you spot the differences?

Susie had been playing with friends on her Bebo account using her mobile. They got bored with this and ran off to watch TV.

Susie had been playing with her friends on her Bebo account. They got bored with this, she logged off, switched off her mobile and they ran off to watch TV.

Her friend Sam got a message from Aisha and they all started laughing at Aisha and planning to play a joke on her.

Her friend Sam got a message from Aisha and they all started laughing at Aisha and planning to play a joke on her. This grew and soon they were spreading rumours about her.

Joey got a text from his friend saying 'You must try this game!' and he added a link.

Joey clicked on the link.

Joey got a text from his friend saying 'You must try this game!' and he added a link.

Joey first looked online to find the real URL of the site then he searched for the game.

Activities that explore ownership and evaluate search results

Whose work is this?

This is for children at Key Stages 1 and 2.

Aims

- To teach the concept of ownership and copyright

- To teach that pupils do not pass off other people's work as their own

- To foster respect for other people's work

Step 1	Take several pieces of work children have done recently with no names on them. Stuff them into a tennis ball tube or some other cardboard tube or, failing this, a large padded envelope. Put a label on the tube/envelope addressing it to your class in your school.
Step 2	Show the children the tube that has arrived at your school. Class 1a Dreamborough Primary School
Step 3	Ask: *What do we know about this parcel? Is it for our class? Is it the right school? Do we know who sent it?* Open up the tube and take out the nameless sheets. *I wonder where they came from?* (Someone might claim one.) *Could some people pretend this is their work if they had not done their own work? What would the person feel who had done this work? Would it have been better if their names had been on the work? That is why it is a good idea to put your name on your work, and sometimes even the day you made it. That way we can see how your work changes during the term and as you get older.* *On the Internet we make lots of pieces of work and other people do too.* *These are easy for other people to find and maybe use.* Discussion.
Step 4	*Can you think of things that people create (make)? Music, art, writing, games, films, programmes. So they need to put their name on things and we need to respect that other people's work is the result of their hard effort.*
Step 5	*Has anyone ever seen this sign © on something? Take a look at some of the books in this room. This is the sign that tells us that this book is the copyright of the person who wrote it.* *So who wrote The Gruffalo? Julia Donaldson – and she should be famous because so many people like her stories. But if her work did not have her name on it, people could say it was their work and she would not be noticed for her lovely work. So Julia has the copyright of her own work.* *When you are surfing the net and you see ideas for your work in school like homework, you need to say whose work or picture it is and you may need to ask if you can use it.* *Always put your name on your own work and always respect other people's work and don't pretend it is yours!*
Step 6	Make some decorated labels to tie or stick onto work (see figure 9.10).

Step 6

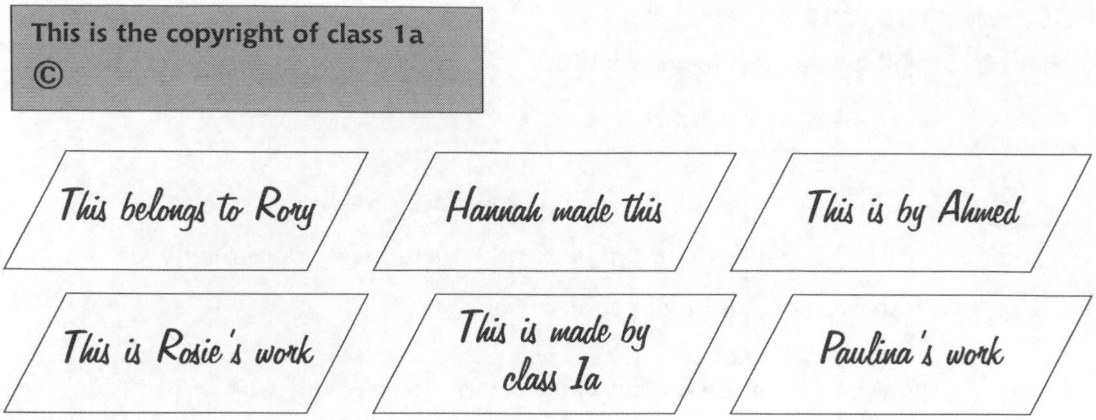

This is the copyright of class 1a
©

This belongs to Rory

Hannah made this

This is by Ahmed

This is Rosie's work

This is made by class 1a

Paulina's work

Figure 9.10 Copyright

Spiders and search engines

This is for children at Key Stage 2.

Learning objectives

- To understand the concept of safe search

- To know we have to evaluate search results

Use the following to engage with the pupils.

A search engine has three software programs working to try to find what you are searching for:

1. the 'spider' which crawls around the web (or searches)

2. the index which stores information

3. the search query software.

The spider does not actually crawl anywhere – it is really software that gathers in new information – but it is an easy way to understand what is happening if we imagine a spider crawling over the web.

As McGaffin *et al.* writes 'when you type in your search words and hit search, then the search engine will try to match your words with the best, most relevant web pages it can find by "searching the web"'[67]. It does this by checking through zillions of records that its index software has collected. These might be text or links that the 'spider' collects. 'The search engine has done all the hard work of collecting, analyzing and indexing web pages, BUT it only makes that information available when someone does a search by entering words in the search query box and hitting the return key. The words people use – what words they type into the query box – when they search will therefore determine the results the search engine presents.'[68] These words that people use when they search are called key words. So the choices you are shown might be any site that has rather a lot of the key words on it. It does not mean that the site at the top of the list is the most reliable or the best – in fact it could be a paid-for advert. So, how do we decide which of the sites in the search might be the best one to try? Are there clues in the name? Are there clues in the address? We might have to try a few and compare before deciding. Could we compare the facts in a few different sites?

Activity: Debating

This is for children at the upper end of Key Stage 2.

A debate is a structured contest about an issue or a resolution we call the motion. A formal debate involves two sides: one supports a resolution and one opposes it. The rules are agreed beforehand. Debates are judged in order to declare a winning side. Those in the room will vote at the end. In some cases you might like to take a vote at the start and at the end, in order to measure how many people have had their views changed by the persuasive debaters.

Why are debates useful to young people?

We use debates in democratic societies to explore and resolve issues and problems. There are many different kinds of debates, and this skill will be useful to every citizen in various situations where decisions are taken or influenced, such as at a board meeting, a public hearing, and at local council or national government level.

I have found them an inspirational way to explore with young people issues related to the Internet, whether we are debating who is responsible for children's safety online, or whether gaming is bad for children, or issues related to violence in relationships. Teachers listening to the debate can find out how much their pupils know about an issue and prepare lessons to fill in any gaps they note during the discussions.

Structure for debates

In a formal debate there are two teams: one consisting of three people supporting a resolution (affirmative team), and another consisting of three people opposing the resolution (opposing team). The audience judges the quality of the evidence and arguments and the performance in the debate. A chairperson is required.

Preparing for the debate

- Develop the motion to be debated.
- Ideas for debates.
   o Children and young people are responsible for making the internet a safe place for themselves
   o Gaming is good for you
   o Small children should not be online
   o Cyberbullying could be stopped if there were online police
   o It would be easy to live without the Internet
   o Children should teach adults about the Internet
   o Nothing is really free online
   o People behave differently if they think they are anonymous

- Organise the teams.

- Establish the rules of the debate–how long will each speaker in each team get to speak? (No more than three to five minutes each is suggested.) Who will speak first, second and third? The first speaker introduces the team's argument, the second speaker backs this up with further evidence and the third speaker can strongly sum up the argument for the whole team when it is their turn.

- Research and prepare the arguments on both sides.

- Try to imagine what the other side will argue and prepare your counterarguments or rebuttals.

- Prepare the room for the debate. The most successful debates I have enjoyed with young people have taken place in the council chamber of some local authorities. There was electronic voting with the results instantly visible on screens (try voting via Twitter and relay to a screen where the Twitter feed is displayed). Another feature of the council chamber venues is that they have microphones at each seat and a button for an audience member to press to show they wish to speak. One person controls it all, and when it is your turn to speak the light flashes green at your seat and your microphone is live. Each speaker is shown on screen and everyone can see and hear them.

The debate

There are no interruptions while anyone is speaking. However, the chair can tell someone their time is up.

1. One speaker from the team speaking for the motion presents their arguments first, followed by the first speaker from the opposing team.

2. Then the second speaker from each team follows next – the second speakers will try to argue against anything said by the first speaker from the team opposing them as well as reinforcing their team's argument strongly. Any conflicting issues are outlined.

3. The third speaker from each team tries to present the total argument of their team persuasively.

4. Audience members and teachers can take notes as the discussion is going on. Audience members can note down any questions they wish to ask later.

5. During a short break, the two teams prepare for the second round called the rebuttal round.

6. This time it is the turn of the opposing team to have their first speaker go first, followed by the first speaker of the team speaking for the motion.

7. Second and third speakers take their turns. The team speaking for the motion get the last word. The final round of the third speaker in each team should sum up for their side after their first and second speakers have demolished the arguments of the opposition.

8. A vote is taken on the motion.

9. Then the discussion is open to the floor. Audience members may speak, challenge or ask a question for no more than one minute when they are called by the chair.

10. Finally, choose some of the points raised by the audience and put them to the vote.

Post-debate

Discuss with each team what they considered worked well and where they could have done something differently. Take note of points raised in the debate and ensure that you cover these in future e-safety or citizenship lessons (or other lessons as appropriate – social studies, moral, cultural, health).

- You may wish to give a prize to the winning team.

- Ask the audience for ideas for future motions they would like to debate.

- Praise pupils for working collaboratively and handling conflict in a formal, controlled manner.

10

Supporting and Working with Parents

Too little supervision or moral panic? Can parents be helped to take a middle path?

We are living in an era when parents have intense fears about safety if their children roam around outside, yet they are often pleased or relieved that they are absorbed and quiet indoors, 'where I know where they are'. Yet those same children are accessing the Internet unsupervised or playing computer games that are not intended for their age group, or talking to unknown people anywhere on Earth.

Parents might be:

- unwilling to address online safety, feeling they know less than their child about the digital world

- suffering from a lack of time to take children to places to play outside

- convinced their children can't go out to play unsupervised

- living where it is not safe for their child to walk to school alone but allowing them to roam the global Internet unsupervised.

While this gaping hole in parental awareness of online risk needs to be understood and addressed by schools, the other extreme – delusional public panic or DPP – is blinding many to what is needed. Every now and then we see a huge moral panic about the dangers of too much screen time, the content children might see and a whole deluge of media horror headlines. These might be about screen time affecting children's brains or a specific social networking site as parents campaign to have it closed down because it is linked with a tragic case. But closing down one site simply means the kids will go to another to communicate. It does not of itself educate children. What it can do is give publicity to the site. After the panics about Ask.fm in the summer of 2013, their user numbers soared as children and teens flocked to see what it was all about. It was only when the site was acquired by new owners more than a year later that they committed to setting up new moderation and safety measures.

Professor Tanya Byron, who led an independent review on this issue, has argued that 'moral panic' about the Internet among middle-class parents is stunting children's development. She believes that 'unless parents let their children explore and make mistakes – both in the real-world and online – they will never become "digitally responsible"'.[69]

However, she added that 'managing these risks, and guiding children through them, is ultimately the responsibility of the adults in their lives, both at home and school.[70]

The challenge is to equip parents with the knowledge they need when many primary teachers are not confident about this themselves and parents are not always willing or able to attend e-safety evenings. Thinking about how we might engage parents, it seems that DPPs should be avoided, even though it is tempting to invite parents in while a DPP is raging in the media. Instead we should aim for an incremental programme that develops with the age and stage of the child and supports a pupil's entire school career. Starting with some facts about what we know of parents' views might be helpful in constructing a programme to suit their needs.

There are a number of paradoxes:

- *Games are seen as violent, but few parents look at ratings.* Few parents look at PEGI ratings on games they buy their children, yet many are worried about the level of violence in some games. Some parents even play unsuitable games with young children.

- *Parents fear inappropriate searches but there is low take-up of parental controls.* Some parents are aware of what their child might encounter online. In a survey of 2000 UK parents of 7–14-year-olds by Bullguard in 2014, 36 per cent of parents said they think their child gets together with friends and searches for inappropriate terms or images, and 18 per cent put the source of this content largely down to children 'simply Googling things they don't understand'. But Ofcom has found that take-up of the new parental controls that could prevent this, and which parents are offered when signing up to a new provider, are incredibly low.

- *Parents shop online with children using credit cards but set few rules about safe shopping.* Children tell us of how they shop with a parent – often managing the process or helping, other times using the credit card themselves to purchase items or book tickets. Too often a child proudly tells me he has memorised his mum's credit card pin or security code and asks if I would like a demonstration! One ten-year-old boy explained how he and his dad run a mini business on eBay, buying and selling games together. He is involved at all levels.

So parents are shopping online with even their youngest children, but not always teaching them how to do this safely. This can have unintended consequences as Kaspersky Lab and B2B found: One in five families said they had lost money or important information thanks to their kids' online activity. What is more their report shows that:

> 44% of respondents believe their children know little about computer technology and 35% thought their kids know nothing of cyberthreats. That same lack of awareness poses risks for parents who allow their children to use their online devices. 12% of respondents said their children had accidentally deleted important information, while 6% faced unexpected bills from app stores after the youngsters got online. All in all, every fifth polled parent confessed they had had an experience of losing money or important data because of their children's actions … [But] just 32% are concerned that their children may spend money online without parental consent, and only 27% are worried that their kids share confidential information too freely online.[71]

Schools want to develop partnerships with parents to help keep all children safe. But they need figures like these to engage parents. It is difficult in some schools to get parents to come in for a dedicated e-safety session. Those who work with computers all day at work, or shop and get their evening entertainment on a tablet, can feel they know it all already, while those who are not very confident online may not want to be shown up in front of others, so they stay away. So the trick is to make these messages engaging and supportive – sprinkling them into other events when parents are in school, and into the messages that are sent home.

It helps to have:

- a dedicated web page of e-safety advice on your school website

- a series of Frequently Asked Questions for parents

- a series of group emails sent out every fortnight, each with one bright idea on it

- a handout for parents

- trained local secondary pupils giving practical demonstrations to parents

- a coding demonstration by primary pupils followed by a quiz for parents (see page 190)

- up-to-date figures on parents' use of parental controls (see Ofcom's website for regular reports)

- prizes and challenges for pupils, with prize-giving events for parents

- well-informed governors.

Some of the tools in this section can be used at parents' evenings or in guides sent home to parents. What has worked successfully in primary schools are sessions in which trained secondary pupils from a local or partner school are on hand to work one to one with parents and show them what primary school pupils are likely to be doing online and some safety steps parents can take. This requires a bank of computers or tablets – so that everyone can have a practical demonstration on screen.

Further below is a quiz you might use as a warm-up exercise if parents have come into school, perhaps for a prize-giving to pupils who have done some exceptional work helping others to be safe online or using the Internet for social good.

The issue of children accessing pornography

In 2005, research by the London School of Economics suggested that more than half of children and young people had intentionally or accidentally come into contact with pornography online.[72] The age group looked at was aged 9–19. Around ten years later, after a wave of new devices, the end of dial-up and the arrival of 'always on' broadband and wi-fi, and unlimited data packages, it was forecast that far more children would be exposed to pornography online. At the same time, pop music videos and even billboard advertising and talent shows on TV are all far more explicit than would have been acceptable ten years ago. The figure is therefore likely to be much higher now due to increasing ownership of Internet-enabled devices by young people.

In Britain, people were alerted to the problem when in 2008 the Byron Review *Safer Children in a Digital World*[73] highlighted the following fact: 'The Internet has undoubtedly made it easier to distribute, obtain and for children to come across pornography either accidentally or on purpose.' This seminal review concluded, 'There is a small but accumulating body of evidence showing a link between exposure to sexually explicit material and negative beliefs and attitudes.' Two years later, Professor Byron's 2010 update report[74] found that parents' 'top digital concern is easy access to pornography and inappropriate adult content'. In 2008 the Cybersurvey showed that large numbers of children and young people could get round blocks set up to prevent them visiting adult sites. Some even said, 'I don't have to cos my brother can.'

In the same year as the Byron update, the Papadopoulos Review looked at *The Sexualisation of Young People*,[75] confirming the view that viewing pornography could be detrimental to the development of many young people. This idea of the 'pornification of society' was further explored in the Bailey Review[76] a year later, pointing out the way adult material and age-restricted material was easily accessed by young people on the Internet and via video on-demand services.

This led to an agreement between the UK's major Internet service providers and the government to offer parents a choice of whether they wanted adult content to be automatically streamed into their homes or to be automatically filtered at source. The take-up has been remarkably poor.

But what about the children? Have they gone to hell in a handcart? Not really! After a worrying period in which exposure to pornography revealed itself in unrealistic expectations of relationships, how girls should look and early sexual awareness, it seems that the kids are beginning to calm things down a little. Teenage pregnancy rates and drug taking is down, and surveys show that, despite the media focus on selfies and some explicit cases leading to high-profile suicides, every single one a dreadful tragedy for families and those working to keep children safe, in fact the percentage of teens who have been pressured into sending a nude or explicit selfie is very low – around 4 per cent. The percentage of those who have been blackmailed as a result is even lower, and the percentage of teens trying to get around blocks or filters is down. (I have been measuring this annually since 2008.)

This relief despite a relentless tsunami of sexualised imagery shows in a more clued-up teen population, better school-based e-safety education and possibly more parents having 'the talk' with their children. In general, there is an overall trend of risky behaviours like unprotected sex, smoking, drug use and alcohol consumption reducing among teens. Maybe their e-safety behaviour is part of this trend?

Children from disadvantaged backgrounds

The EU Kids Online research programme points out that children of less educated parents are often left alone when dealing with the Internet. Children in some families use media more intensively than others and their socialisation is dominated by media. 'Furthermore, their parents use more restrictive measures to influence their children's Internet use instead of trying to actively support and facilitate a safe and profitable way of dealing with media.'[77]

> In particular, children who grow up in socially disadvantaged families often find it difficult to take advantage of the opportunities offered by media or to cope adequately with the risks that they might encounter while using them. Therefore every societal stakeholder needs to develop approaches that enable all citizens to use media for actively participating in society.[78]

So the EU Kids Online research shows a need to support children who have parents with a lower secondary education or less, children whose parents do not use the Internet and children who use the Internet less than once per week.

These children tend to encounter slightly fewer online risks than their peers in Europe, but they are more upset if they experience them. Furthermore, their online skills are noticeably below the European average. This is illustrated by the following findings that compare children from households with lower, medium, and higher socio-economic status, which has been defined on the basis of parents' formal education. Children from families with lower socio-economic status use the Internet slightly less and more often not at home than children from higher socio-economic groups.[79] Furthermore, they also have significantly less access to the Internet through mobile devices and their parents tend to use less active mediation strategies. However, in terms of their age when they first used the Internet and in relation to the average time spent online, there is hardly any difference between children and adolescents in low, medium and high SES families.[80]

Keeping parents informed and involved
'Different childhoods?' quiz for parents

This quiz is a light-hearted attempt to get parents to think about the lives their children lead. The answers are based on a variety of sources and are not intended to represent a scientific or definitive analysis.

- How much less do children play outside than their mums and dads did?

- What percentage of children get their entertainment from a screen compared to the percentage in the 1980s?

- How many parents think their child gets together with friends and searches for inappropriate terms or images?

- How many parents put this largely down to children simply Googling things they don't understand?

- How many parents believe their children know little about computer technology?

- How many believe their kids know nothing of cyberthreats?

- What percentage had lost money or important information due to their kids' online activity?

- What percentage said their children had accidentally deleted important information?

- What percentage faced unexpected bills from app stores after the youngsters got online?

- What percentage worry that their children may spend money online without consent?

- What percentage are worried that their kids share confidential information too freely online?

- What percentage personally control how their children use devices?

- What percentage had asked their Internet provider to block access to certain sites?

- What percentage of parents regularly remind their children about the dangers of the Internet?

- What percentage opted to befriend their children on social networks?

- What percentage of parents use specialised software to regulate their children's activities online?

- How many parents are aware of the new offers of parental controls from broadband/ wi-fi providers?

'Different childhoods?' quiz answers

- Children in 2014 play outside two-thirds less than their mums and dads did in the 1980s.

- 36 per cent of children get their entertainment from a screen compared to 8 per cent in the 1980s.

- 36 per cent of parents also said they think their child gets together with friends and searches for inappropriate terms or images.

- 18 per cent put this down largely to children simply Googling things they don't understand.

- 44 per cent of respondents believe their children know little about computer technology.

- 35 per cent believe their kids know nothing of cyberthreats.

- 21 per cent had lost money or important information due to their kids' online activity.

- 12 per cent said their children had accidentally deleted important information.

- 6 per cent faced unexpected bills from app stores after the youngsters got online.

- 32 per cent are concerned that their children may spend money online without parental consent.

- 27 per cent are worried that their kids share confidential information too freely online.

- 39 per cent personally control how their children use devices.

- 13 per cent asked their Internet provider to block access to certain sites.

- 38 per cent of parents regularly remind their children about the dangers of the Internet.

- 19 per cent opted to befriend their children on social networks.

- Only 23 per cent of parents use specialised software to regulate their children's activities online.

- 14 per cent check who their children are friends with on SNS.

When offered parental controls at sign-up with phone and broadband providers, parents are reluctant. In 2013, the government asked providers to offer an opt-out filtering system at sign-up, but an Ofcom report[81] shows that only 5 per cent of new BT customers signed up, 8 per cent opted in for Sky and 4 per cent for Virgin Media. TalkTalk rolled out a parental-control system two years earlier and has had much better take-up of its offering, with 36 per cent of customers signing up for it.[82]

A schedule of emails to parents

Pre-prepare a series of engaging short emails which will automatically go to parents once a fortnight. Make them attractive and easily recognised. Give them a recognisable 'brand' that includes your school's name, for example 'Dreamstime School ENews'. Then archive them on the school's website where parents can access them later. These might include ideas such as those below, for example a regular digi-drama twice a term. Use a fictional or old case and discuss what parents should do – the case could vary each time. There should be no identifying details – anonymity is vital. Below is an example.

Example of a digi-drama

Tallulah is distraught that her best friend Emma has become friends with Keisha and is now leaving her out. But the last straw came when Emma, who knew Tallulah's password on Facebook, had been into her account and sent some mean messages to other girls in the class to isolate her further. Emma simply laughed when Talullah asked her if she was the one who did this. Tallulah is convinced it was her. But she feels anxious and suspicious of other people in her class too. Now she cannot concentrate for worrying about who it was. Emma has never apologised.

What should her parents do?

- Go round to Emma's house and give her a piece of their mind?
- Start shouting at Emma's parents in the supermarket?
- Tell Tallulah to forget about Emma and make some new friends?
- Keep the evidence and note the date and times the messages were sent and ask to see Tallulah's teacher?
- Reconsider allowing under-13s onto Facebook?
- Demand the school deals with it and leave it to them?

Privacy and passwords

The following can be used to engage with parents.

Your child has used this password – his middle name and the numbers '123' – since he first went on to Moshi Monsters. It was easy to remember and lots of his friends did the same. Now he is a little older he is going onto new sites and services. What advice would you give him?

Parental controls

These are a few scenarios in which parents frequently forget to re-set parental controls:

- You have just switched to a new service for your phone and broadband/wi-fi in the hope that this will be a cheaper service. About this time your child gets a mobile phone.

- You buy a tablet for your family and sign up to a new broadband/wi-fi provider.

- You bring back from work a used laptop that you have managed to buy for very little. You plan to give it to your children to use for their schoolwork and entertainment.

- Everyone is very excited at the faster speeds, the fact that you can now download movies and watch TV programmes so easily on the tablet with such a great clear picture.

What do you need to do about making sure the child or children are protected from unwanted content?

What are young children doing online?

Entertainment and games and photos

Young children love watching favourite TV characters in stories online, on tablets and mobile phones as well as on TV screens. Peppa Pig or Thomas are found on all these devices along with new characters like the Octonauts. Even three-year-olds love taking photos with a mobile. If a parent takes a shot or video of them, they understand that they can view it on the phone and often ask to see it before the phone is put down. They also know that they can ask to see it over and over again.

Games and apps that appear to be free

Small children, especially around seven or eight years old, enjoy games and might easily fall victim to games that appear at first to be free, but then pressure players to acquire 'boosters' to go faster or to buy special items – for a virtual pet, for example. There could be hidden costs, and heavy marketing to children can entice them to buy items for their game. They will play happily for hours on games on their mum's smartphone. Indeed one little lad of two even sat stock still having his hair cut the other day simply because his mum gave him the phone with a game open on the screen!

Is the filter set on this phone to protect them from mistakenly clicking onto the 'wrong' sites?

Social clubs and groups

Children may enjoy a club or a social networking site for children; Moshi Monsters is popular, as is Club Penguin. Complaints made about Moshi Monsters, however, point out that these 'monsters' are drawn like disfigured faces and children with facial abnormalities or impairments are often deeply distressed at being called the names of the monsters. Some argue that this is encouraging children to bully children with facial problems or disabilities. This could be deeply distressing to a child with any form of disability or facial difference.

Google Hangouts are popular with some groups of friends, but nobody will go on any networking site without their friends, and children tend to migrate to sites simply because their friends are moving there and it is the fashion of the moment. Some begin and quickly become bored with Hangouts.

Young children enjoy searching the net for homework and projects, or to find out about a favourite footballer or pop star. They may inadvertently come across violent or sexual content and parents should set parental controls and filters to try to prevent this happening. But no filter is entirely reliable and parents should talk to their children and make it clear that if they see something upsetting they should move away and tell an adult. Explain that the world of the Internet has good people and bad people in it just like the real world and sometimes people are nasty. We should enjoy it, but be careful just the same. Innocent searches may call up surprising content, so do not blame the child if they come across inappropriate material while doing homework on the Victorians or Easter hot cross buns!

What are juniors doing online?

At ages 10–11 many children in the UK acquire a mobile phone. They may also have a games console. Both could have access to the Internet. Parental controls/filters should be set wherever available. These may be supplied by a parent's search engine, your phone provider or anti-virus software. Software programs can also be purchased separately.

Although parents like to feel that if their child is going to school alone now they can stay in contact through the phone, there has been a marked switch to tablets with a drop in phone ownership, as families have opted for one family tablet for use by everyone rather than buying a smartphone for a pre-teen child.

They might chat with friends on instant messaging services, BBM or apps like Whatsapp or Instagram; or upload photos to share using Pinterest, Vine or Tumblr. They love making videos and posting them on YouTube. Their games now involve other players who might be online and unknown to them. They may start shopping online with a parent from time to time and could use the Internet to find out information about a holiday destination, their football club or events.

They get their entertainment, music and often films online and are adept at downloading a new game or music. Few understand that it is not right to download some music or films, for example, that appear to be free.

Their searches for information are now wider and more sophisticated. They use the Internet for homework far more and share with their friends in a new, exciting online world. They may use Twitter and many go onto Facebook before the age of 13, which is the intended barrier age, but many simply give a different birth date when signing up. Others memorise the password of their brother or sister and simply use their account.

At this age we see chain letters circulating, threats and name-calling. Bullying from school life can be amplified by going on phones or online after school and retaliating or ramping up the insults.

Get in first and talk to the child about what he or she would do if they received a nasty message or people were talking about them behind their back. Children who are prepared can become very resilient. As one boy said, 'It was just death threats – I ignored them.' It is both worrying that this is going on and must be investigated, and it also useful that he feels he can disregard it. Nevertheless, if the sender of the threat is in the school, some serious work needs to be done. Credible threats of harm should be considered for referral to the police. If banter of this kind is common in the school, it must be addressed with the whole class.

If the child is cyberbullied

- Keep evidence, including the date and time.

- Do not reply or tackle the parents of the other child.

- Tell an adult who can talk to the staff at the school or sports club, who can:

  o try to get the offensive material removed either by the perpetrator or the website concerned

  o contact the police if this is needed

  o contact the phone provider

  o block the sender

  o address the behaviour and try to get the perpetrator to understand the harm they have caused and help the pupils to find new ways of living alongside one another

  o consider effective approaches to bullying and restorative actions that might be appropriate

  o put a buddy group around the target

  o teach the whole class or group that this behaviour is wrong and how to report it

  o monitor how the targeted child is doing over the following weeks to ensure there is no retaliation for having reported it

  o increase the teaching on e-safety and responsible behaviour online and on mobiles

  o reinforce the school's anti-bullying policy and their Acceptable Use of ICT policy

  o ensure the school or club can do some work with the whole year group to challenge any prejudice-driven behaviour

  o reinforce the school's aim for every pupil to feel safe and respected

  o praise people for prosocial, positive behaviour and model it.

Activity for a parents' evening

Ask parents to turn to their neighbours and discuss the reasons they think parents gave for not having made use of parental controls. Then give them this list and ask them to discuss it. Do they recognise themselves? What next steps are they planning?

Reasons parents did not make use of parental controls[83]

The following reasons were given

- the idea that they are complex to install

- not understood

- lapsed and out of date

- new device bought and not re-installed

- switch to new ISP and forgot

- risks not a major worry for parent right now

- not got around to it

- more inclined to worry their child spent too long online or gaming than risk

- lack of awareness

- rules not strictly followed – busy life – path of least resistance

- forgetting to install if parental controls stopped working for some reason

- thinking you have to know a lot to choose or research it

- feel ill equipped to intervene due to own lack of digital competence

- child learns about this at school

- child is always supervised

- trust child to be sensible.

Help parents to develop clear and simple rules for young children with supportive messages

The following can be used to engage with children.

- *No means no*: Do not be forced into doing things you do not want to do by friends or people you meet online. The Cybersurvey showed that there are many coercive threats sent around among ten-year-olds.

- *Your body is your own*: A doctor or a nurse may ask you if they can look at your body to help fix it, but apart from parents and people who care for you like a childminder, or a grandma, a child can say no to unwanted touching or photos. The NSPCC's 'Talk PANTS' activity is useful here (www.nspcc.org.uk/preventing-abuse/keeping-children-safe/underwear-rule).

- *Tell someone about secrets that upset you*: Good secrets are when you plan to make a cake for your mum's birthday and give her a surprise. Bad secrets are when someone asks you to 'keep our little secret' and it is about something that makes you feel sad, scared or worried. You will not get into trouble if you tell us about something you are worried about.

- *Don't say cruel, nasty things to other people whether online or off*: Sometimes it is so easy to say horrible things to someone, especially if we are feeling angry ourselves.

- *Speak up so someone can help*: If you ever feel worried, sad or frightened you should talk to a grown-up you trust.

- *If I cannot help*: I can find someone who can or I can find out how to help.

- *You will not get into trouble* if you come to me with a problem.

- *Life is full of exciting things to do and see*: Most of the time it is all OK, but sometimes if things go wrong or we make a mistake, we need some help. This is OK.

Parents tell us that they turn to their child's school as a first point of call for advice. Be ready for this with factsheets and advice that have been carefully edited and prepared. Below is an example of advice to parents about social networking sites.

Action parents can take if their child uses social networking sites

Primary schools advise parents to discourage their children from going onto SNS while under 13. Yet we know that 39 per cent of 10–11-year-olds and 72 per cent of 12–13-year-olds are doing so.[84]

Forbidding the child to have a social networking page will work for a while with a very obedient, compliant child, but sooner or later the pull of the peer group will lead them to want to try it out, for they fear being left out of every social interaction their friends are sharing. They might also fear that others will talk about them behind their back and desperately want to view what is going on! In some situations a child may be bullied because he or she has not got an SNS page and is therefore shut out of the group. Children and young people appear to believe that life is not truly lived unless reported online, complete with photos to prove it. It is as though it were not fully experienced unless it is shared, rather like a living diary that is put in front of readers for their ongoing approval. Of course, if that approval is sought and instead they get offensive remarks and cruel put-downs, it can hurt. They tend to know this but go for it all the same. Online they create a persona they want to project, pink and fluffy or tough and cool, but in all cases they want to appear and be popular.

Where they have been totally forbidden to go onto a social network we often see that they do so with another name so that their parents do not find out. Some even set up two profiles, one in their real name that parents can view, and another that they actually use. In situations like this a child cannot or will not seek help from their parents if they get into difficulty for fear of their parents' reaction.

But if parents can talk through the situation in a reasonable way and encourage their child to wait until they are old enough then a good deal may be struck. Parents can also discuss this with parents of their child's friends and together as a group they might delay the age at which the children begin to use SNS. Many are digitally capable of using social networks but are certainly not emotionally old enough.

Once they are using SNS, parents can do the following:

- *Clean their friends list on SNS*: Help the child to remove anyone they do not know in the offline world – having 4000 friends is not a sign of true popularity!

- *Check photos are correctly tagged and privacy settings are all in place including old photos put up ages ago*: Talk to the child about inappropriate images that will still be out there years from now. While everyone posts photos that they believe show them as humorous, popular and attractive, every photo should be thought about carefully before posting online. What does it say about the child? How could it be viewed? How could it be misused? What is it giving away about their identity? Do photos give away too much about them such as which school or club they go to and where the photo was taken? Is the location feature switched off on the mobile phone they use to take photos?

- *Encourage them to avoid sites that offer anonymity*: e.g. Tumblr or Ask.fm.

- *Remind them that they can always leave a chat room.*

- *Talk through why they should never agree to meet anyone they have only met online.*

- *Make clear that you are not judgemental; they can tell you anything*: For this to be true, you will have had to show an open mind beforehand. Young people can be blackmailed over something they have done, such as once posting a sexy photo, because they are scared their parents will find out. It is surely better to have made a mistake and to learn from it and be safe than to be forced into inappropriate behaviour over the initial mistake through fear.

If they are vulnerable or isolated in the offline world, young people often seek intimacy and relationships online. These young people need extra e-safety advice and support.

If a young person is being bullied face to face in school, the addition of cyberbullying sets up a devastating environment in which there is no respite. Bullying can occur multiple times a day, and targeted young people need immediate support and intervention.

- Keep a copy of the abusive messages or images.

- Record the date and time – there will be a trail.

- Block the sender where possible. Don't reply.

- Get friends to post supportive messages and 'drown' out the negative messages.

- Don't give out personal details. Report abuse.

- ChildLine and Samaritans can be contacted in multiple ways. They are trained to help.

Communications and advice

Figure 10.1 outlines the different ways schools can communicate with parents

Connected kids: A communications plan with parents

Set up the automated emails so that they are ready to go out every fortnight

Online options

Safe suggestions

Connected and cared for

Cyber parents' roundup

Links to Childnet International

Report button for CEOP

Dear Parents/Carers

A series of eight handy hints emails to parents – one a fortnight.

1. A friendly reminder to set filters on your devices and home broadband or wi-fi system so that your young children do not accidentally come across unsuitable content. There are free options...

2. A friendly reminder to check the rating on the computer games your child is playing. This is what they mean...

3. A friendly reminder to chat to parents of your child's friends about their online safety rules and filters. Is your child safe online in their homes?

4. The digi-drama series (case examples) – what would you do?

5. Passwords and privacy – fun creating new passwords in a secret language...

6. Some ways to respond to unpleasant behaviour in texts and messaging...

7. A friendly reminder that you can agree some rules with your child about Internet use...

8. A useful list of resources you can use with your child.

Dear Parents/Carers

Handouts for parents – an attractive handout with useful advice can be sent to parents once a year or once a term.

If there is an incident, write to all parents alerting them to the risks of SNS for primary-age children, reminding them that you have advised that children should not use SNS as they are too young.

Figure 10.1 Connected kids: A communications plan with parents

Advice you can give the parents

- Start the conversation early.

- Little and often! Don't overwhelm them with advice or scare them off the Internet.

- Set your parental controls on every device.

- Reassure your child you are always there to help and support them.

- Explain what to do if your child ever feels unsafe or uncomfortable in any online situation. Explain that you will not be angry; you will help because you want your child to be safe.

- Give information in small chunks rather than a whole lot at once.

- Judge when you think your child is ready for it by asking what they are doing online. Join in games, help with searches and chat about what they are finding online. If you do not understand, ask them to show you.

- Do not ban them from accessing the Internet on a mobile phone – they will have many other opportunities to access the Internet and it would be better if they did so with your advice and support. Remember, if your child uses a mobile phone with parental controls set, there will be other children in their class who use phones that do not have controls set.

- Ask questions such as:

  o What do you enjoy most about being online?

  o Which are your favourite games?

  o How do you prefer to keep in touch with your friends?

  o Can you show me how this works?

  o Which websites would you recommend to a friend?

  o Who do you play games with? Are they good at these games?

  o How do you know whether the people in your friends list are all people you actually know?

  o How would you take someone off that list if you needed to?

  o Please show me how to set the privacy settings on Facebook or any other SNS.

  o If we are going to buy that with my credit card, how do we know that this website is safe and it is secure to use my card?

  o Do you know how to block someone?

  o Can you teach your little brother what he should be careful about?

  o You are so fast at this. How did you learn about it?

  o What would you do if you were worried about something?

  o What would you do if someone was nasty to you?

If your child knows more than you do about being online, remember you may know about life. Together you are a strong combination! Your parenting skills are needed as never before! Use your child's expertise to get them to show you around the net, their life and their games, so that you have a better idea of what controls to put in place.

Children show parents what to do

Children enjoy showing their parents what they know and can do, and it gives parents a way to support and encourage them while learning what they know. Here are a few ideas teachers might want to suggest to parents, to encourage them towards working with their child online and opening the way to having conversations about staying safe.

Build confidence and self-esteem along with digital skills!

Enjoy the excitement and ease of the Internet together to find things out. Explore things that relate to the family holiday or the next family day out. Your child can feel he or she is making a contribution to family life, planning for a holiday or outing, or being trusted to do a task like find a translation of some key phrase or how much the currency is worth.

Show them how to use timetables, maps and distance planners. Try converting sterling to euros before you go on holiday. Google it and options to do this free of charge appear. Plan your route to the park on Google Maps. Use your phone to follow the route and teach map reading.

Children can help each other and share what they know with your guidance

You can follow up with questions like:

- Where did you learn these steps?
- Do you enjoy this site/game? What is so special about it?
- What would you do if you were worried about anything?

Children can help you set up a profile on one of their favourite websites. This will give you the opportunity to ask lots of questions like 'What does that mean?' or 'Why did you choose that option?' or 'What if…?' You will have an opportunity to ask about safety features and this will reveal what your child knows about them.

Children can play a game with you online

Playing together will help you understand how the game works, if it's appropriate for their age and how they can communicate with other players. Games have ratings which parents often ignore, but they are there to help you select games suitable for your child's age and stage. Called PEGI ratings, they give you a guide rather like the ratings for movies.

Know who your child is talking to online – they could be people somewhere across the globe

Children don't think of people they've met online through social networking and online games as strangers; they are just online friends. They may even feel an obligation towards them if they play games with them online – rather like a team player. Have them show you how it all works.

Social networks

Explore together where the reporting button is on the sites they spend time on. Even though there is a watershed age of 13, we know that many children below 13 want nothing more than to have their own page and profile. They lie about their age and go onto Facebook before moving on to other SNS and messaging services. They may even use your birthdate! I have met parents who say their child shares their Facebook page.

Show them how to report abuse when they are old enough to do so. Explain that social networking sites have some rules about how people behave when using their service, and if someone sends abusive messages, the material could be removed by the site if it breaks these rules.

Questions to ask:

- Who do you know that has the most online friends?

- How can they know so many people?

- How do they choose who to become friends with online?

- Why is it a good idea to have so many friends?

- Can you think of reasons why it could be risky to have friends you do not really know?

You can also become 'friends' with your child so you can see their profile and posts. But your child may not want to have you as a friend on social networking sites, especially as they get older, but it may be that you agree that they can choose a trusted adult like an aunt or uncle, or an older sister who can feed back any worrying or upsetting behaviour and keep an eye on the child's social networking page.

Agreements

Agreements matter – they provide secure boundaries. Make an agreement about how they will use any new technology or spend time on the Internet. The agreement could cover issues such as:

- the amount of time they can spend online

- the websites they can visit or services/apps they can use

- sharing images and videos

- spending money online

- how to behave online respectfully and not to post anything they wouldn't say face to face

- the age rating of all games they play and movies or TV programmes they view

- how much information they are sharing with other players

- how often this agreement will be reviewed! This might be every birthday or every time a new device comes into the household.

It should not appear restrictive and limiting – but should be presented as an enabling way for a child to enjoy the exciting opportunities the net can offer. Think of it as a licence – like a driving licence – that gives the child permission to drive and enjoy new experiences.

Filters and controls

The following is addressed to parents.

No tool is 100 per cent effective and should not replace conversations with your child, but filters and controls are an important infrastructure step in protecting your child. Think of it as the scaffolding on which you hang your love, advice and support.

Parents can filter, restrict, monitor or report content using parental controls:

- Internet service providers (ISPs), such as Virgin Media, TalkTalk, Sky and BT, provide controls to help you filter or restrict content.

- Laptops, phones, tablets, games consoles and other devices that connect to the Internet will have settings to activate parental controls.

- Software packages are available – some are free – to help you filter, restrict or monitor what your child can see online.

Remember that if your child goes online away from home, the same controls might not be in place at other people's houses or on public wi-fi. New 'Friendly WiFi' provision in public spaces with controls to make it family friendly began in autumn 2014. Look out for the sign in coffee shops and shopping centres. Many high street names have become Friendly WiFi accredited. These can be identified by the Friendly WiFi logo. This will reassure consumers that the most worrying Internet content for children, including pornography, will have been placed behind filters. This could be useful for schools when on field trips with pupils using tablets or mobiles.

When your child is visiting friends' homes, let their parents know your rules and views on Internet use.

Which parental control system should I use?

Parental controls are reviewed by *PC Advisor* to help parents make their own choices. Many are free with other protection software or broadband/wi-fi provision. If you are unsure you might wish to read the reviews.

Know what connects to the Internet and how. We live in an age when connectivity is changing fast. Soon, even our houses will be wired up and we will be able to give them commands before we get home. But for now we are concerned with how your child can access the Internet. Make sure you're aware which devices your child uses can connect to the Internet, such as their phone, a tablet, laptop or games console. Do they watch TV content on a tablet or laptop too? Also, find out how they are accessing the Internet – is it your connection, or are they often using a neighbour's or public wi-fi? This will affect whether the safety settings and parental controls you set are being applied.

'Safety mode' is an opt-in setting that helps screen out potentially objectionable content that you may prefer not to see or don't want others in your family to stumble across while enjoying YouTube. You can think of this as a parental control setting for YouTube.

In the UK customers are automatically offered parental controls when signing up for broadband/wi-fi. This is an opt-out service – it is provided as standard unless customers choose not to use it. Paid-for parental controls may offer more features.

Reporting any concerns

If parents want to report inappropriate material or behaviour online they can find advice at Childnet International (www.childnet.com/resources/how-to-make-a-report). All online child sexual exploitation should be reported to CEOP (www.ceop.police.uk/Ceop-Report).

Do filters work?

Filters are only successful up to a point – their systems are as crude or as good as the dictionary of terms they will exclude. They cannot tell whether every search will be safe as some graphic material could be on a safe website, so it is not effective to rely only on filters. They also often block valid content, which might be useful for health advice or something entirely innocent or informative.

When adults relax because they 'leave it all to the filter', or block so much in fear, children and young people could be denied the chance to develop resilience to risk with adult help. It is also far more tempting for teenagers to try to get round this restriction and go online somewhere else – in a friend's house, a friend's filter-free smartphone or via some open wi-fi. Relying entirely on blocking can hamper learning, and even with the filters there will be sudden unexplained images that the filter missed. So, while parents should set appropriate filters, especially if they have young children at home, on its own this is not enough. Filtering will of course not stop cyberbullying from taking place: this is a behaviour, and the social networking sites or messaging apps are only the communication tools. Block one and bullies will use another. Children are in any case migrating to new sites all the time. It is more productive to teach civil behaviour and what to do if things go wrong.

The handout that follows has some checklists for parents set out by age.

Checklists for parents – What should your child know?

Under-5s	6–9-year-olds	10–11-year-olds
Set boundaries on how long they can spend on tablets, computers and Mum's phone	Teach your children to search safely with key words	Those agreements on use of technology need revising now as many youngsters get a smartphone or use a tablet even more widely
Check filters are in place	Show them that not everything the search engine provides is true, accurate or appropriate	Chain letters and threats are common at this age – pre-empt this by talking about it before it happens
Put passwords or PINs on all devices	Ensure they know how to get help if they need it for any reason	Show your child how to set a really strong password and don't give them yours!
Check age ratings on games and apps and also on TV programmes they can access on mobiles or tablets	Create a family shopping email account	Warn them about risks of theft with a fancy phone
Set home page on family computer to a child-friendly website like CBeebies	Create a user account for your child on a family tablet or computer with a good filter and use parental controls and tools like Google Safe Search	Ramp up the discussion on identity and personal details by playing detective and showing a video
	Agree on a few popular websites, clubs or TV programmes they can visit	Introduce the idea of a digital footprint and the fact that what you post can live forever online Digital citizenship can be discussed now
	Explore the kind of personal information and identity details they should not share	How do we behave towards one another?
	Help them create strong passwords they can remember	How do we avoid seeing unpleasant stuff? If something you see upsets you…
	Discuss with any older siblings the issue of them showing their younger siblings sites or games unsuitable for the age group	Not everything online is true! Don't believe all you see or are told
	Negotiate rules for the family	SNS are for over-13s
	Talk to other parents about their approach, especially when your child is going to a sleepover	Turn off the location feature on the camera of their mobile phone if they have one
	Do you understand age ratings on games, apps and videos and TV content?	Agree rules on how long they can spend on games
	Agree rules on how long they can spend on games	Turn off chat features on online games
	Turn off chat features on online games	
	Turn off the location feature on the camera of their mobile phone if they have one	
	They may begin to use email, messaging or Hangouts	

So should you post your adorable child's photo online?

It's a birthday or the first day of school and you are dying to share your child's picture. But think for a second before giving away to the world the date of his birthday so that it's out there attached to his name for anyone to get hold of.

Check you do not show the school uniform to all and sundry – along with your child's preferences for princess dresses. Limit who can see each picture. Check carefully that they are seen only by close friends and encourage them not to share them without your permission. Avoid those cute toddler-in-the-bath shots – they can be misused and your child might be embarrassed in years to come when his girlfriend finds them.

It is tempting to offload your memory card onto Flickr, but please, think about it first! Lots of photos can give away where they were taken – have you switched off the location feature on your phone's camera? If not, it is safer to delay before uploading the photos of your children on a big adventure along the beach on a sunny afternoon. This location data can tell anyone what your child looks like and where he or she is. When you do post the pictures you should be safely back at home.

Parents worry that people with ill intent could misuse their child's image in some way, but this is the least likely outcome, although it is possible and more likely if you post nude shots of your child. One blogger found her child passed off as someone else's child, which is weird. Employers, potential girlfriends and academic institutions may search for information on your child one day – what will a search turn up? You are inadvertently creating your child's digital identity without her permission.

What about future developments? Face recognition software already exists and websites are mining our information for details about our preferences to sell us stuff. What might be next? You might like to post pictures that do not directly show the face. It is a fact that everything you post will hang around on the net and there may be unforeseen ripples. If you are a well-known individual be even more careful with your child's image.

Bullying and cyberbullying – entwined and feeding off one another

Parents and teachers need to be able to recognise the signs that may indicate a child is being bullied. Bullying at school migrates to cyberspace, and in the primary years most cyberbullying is the result of something happening at school. Obvious signs are:

- cuts, bruises or aches and pains that are not adequately explained
- clothes or possessions that are damaged or lost
- the child requests extra money or starts stealing
- the child starts going to school, or returns from school, at earlier or later times
- the child uses a different route to school
- the child starts to refuse to go outside at break times, or refuses to stay at school for dinners
- the child requests to change classes, options or school
- the child is not with his or her usual friends
- the child is reluctant to attend school or refuses to.

Any marked change in a child's behaviour may indicate that the child is under stress:

- immature behaviour (e.g. reverts to thumb-sucking or tantrums)

- the child may become withdrawn, clingy, moody, aggressive, uncooperative or non-communicative
- school performance and ability deteriorate
- sleep or appetite problems or other issues such as bed-wetting
- obsessive checking of mobile phone or SNS/messaging service
- avoids playing an online game they used to love
- spends an excessive time using a webcam in their bedroom and is secretive about this.

Early signs that a child is being bullied could be:

- the child becoming withdrawn
- a deterioration in the child's work
- erratic attendance or spurious illness
- persistently arriving late at school
- general unhappiness or anxiety
- the child wanting to remain with adults
- sudden outbursts not consistent with the child's normal behaviour
- usual friends not seen around the child.

Physical symptoms could include headaches, stomach aches, fainting, fits, vomiting or hyperventilation. Victims can become depressed or anxious and this can continue into their adult lives.

In extreme cases a young person may express feelings of hopelessness, suggest life is not worth living, or state they are 'hanging by a thread'. They may insist it is not worth doing anything about the bullying. Be alert to self-harm or suicidal intentions.

Patterns of thinking

Some victims of bullying begin to believe that they 'deserve it'. They can internalise what people are saying about them and come to think that there really is something wrong with them or that they are at fault, fat, ugly or unlovable. This view must be picked up immediately and the child supported. Nobody deserves to be bullied.

Victims turn to the net to retaliate

If you were a small or shy person being bullied by another or others who seem to be all powerful, how tempting it would be to go online and, with a cloak of anonymity, send some threats to your tormentors. This is so common, but it leads victims into new problems as they almost always get discovered. They are then at greater risk.

Victims turn to the net for new friends

Another pattern is when a young victim feels isolated and friendless. She might look online for new friends – and make herself more vulnerable to grooming. If someone says 'You are lovely' or 'I love you', she will agree to meet up and is suggestible in so many ways as she is eager to please.

11

Real Life Cases

Case example

A deputy headteacher of a primary school talked about a situation involving two girls – one in Year 5 and the other in Year 6. They each appeared to wield power over other girls in their year group and there were endless fallings out which destabilised the entire class in each case. This situation is often described as the Queen Bee scenario. There were also problems with the parents. As is common, one set of parents could not believe that their child, 'always so quiet at home' and popular at school, was bullying others. Unsurprisingly, the girls denied they were doing anything wrong.

The mother of one of the targeted girls had frequently been to see her child's class teacher and reported that her child was being bullied. She maintained that the school was not doing enough and she was becoming extremely upset and angry. This mother was over-sensitive and thought every slight or bit of banter was bullying and she was over-protective of her daughter.

The class teacher had escalated the case up to senior management and a considerable amount of staff time was spent trying to investigate and administer punishments or 'sanctions'. Despite all this involvement, the same behaviour was repeated again and again and the school went through the same processes once more, but there was no change. Everyone was worried at the effect this was having on morale and ethos. Indeed it was affecting the pupils' ability to learn and disrupting others. The deputy head mentioned that there were also several other bullying problems involving girls in the school at the moment.

It was so time consuming that the deputy head said he had no time to implement new programmes. He sounded at the end of his tether. But this was not all. Things were worsening as the feuds had migrated to Facebook and every Monday brought a stream of complaints after nasty messages had been sent at the weekend. The girls texted threats to their victims and used various messaging apps. They talked about the targeted girls behind their backs on their mobiles. They said when challenged that it was just 'joking'.

Why persist with an approach that does not work?

At our training sessions we often present a case and the delegates discuss it and plan what they might do in such a situation. The fascinating fact is that few groups come up with the same solutions. Many are likely to be effective. This shows that there is always more than one approach to be tried. If the approach you are using is not bearing fruit – why continue with it?

This seemingly heretical viewpoint often causes people to feel shocked or nervous. But there are other approaches to try, and if you are keeping a close eye on a persistent case you will soon notice what works despite the occasional setback. The main principles still apply, but how you go about it can vary.

Below are the strategies recommended by a group following a presentation on this case, and it shows the breadth of ideas a group can offer to address complex bullying situations involving girls.

Focus on creating a positive school ethos

- Develop a school culture in which children get opportunities to know each other well and interact positively together.

- Teach children the strategies needed to become 'defenders'. Create a culture where it is OK to tell and staff respond appropriately when told.

- Consider training peer supporters or buddies and running a full peer support programme.

- Intervene earlier – before the eruption wherever possible.

- Increase e-safety education on Acceptable Use of ICT.

- Increase friendships and relationships education.

- Promote gender equality and reduce emphasis on appearance.

- Teach children how to save evidence if they receive threats via mobiles and not to pass on rumours but to report to an adult if asked to do so.

- Offer a wide range of ways to report any concerns or worries.

Classroom dynamics

- Manage the classroom dynamics – choose people to work together, draw up a new seating plan and insist on it. Pick teams rather than let pupils pick who they want on teams. Integrate targeted girls into other groups.

- Praise the girls daily for not being involved in falling out so they get more attention for this behaviour than from falling out.

- Offer a chart to measure how the class is behaving – if sufficient stars are achieved for prosocial (kind) behaviour, the whole class will go on an outing at the end of term. If anyone lets the class down this may be cancelled. The group will help enforce good behaviour.

- Agree with a targeted fragile girl that she has a set of signals so that if she is feeling upset she can signal you. Teachers can send a child out of the room on a prearranged errand to the office to remove them from the aggressive looks or whispering of a group of girls. She can also let you know how she is feeling today with an emotions chart. This can be used for those children who bully too – if they are poor at handling their own anger, an emotions chart can help you to know before they reach boiling point so that you can plan an activity or move them to another task.

Curricular work

- Set up circle time, delivered by a teacher, to focus on cyberbullying.

- Create time in the curriculum to maintain a PSHE or spiritual, social, moral and cultural subject.

- Try the structured social and emotional aspects of learning modules (SEAL).

- Introduce R Time, a structure for teaching mutual respect.

- Do group work on friendship and consider the qualities children look for in a friend.

- Use stories to illustrate bullying and cyberbullying situations and show positive outcomes (e.g. *Maggot Moon* or Carol Gray's *Social Stories,* where appropriate.)

- Ensure that the curricular work runs across the entire school.

- Invite pupils to prepare an assembly and other activities on cyberbullying/friendship. This could include a mass sing-along to an anthem such as Katy Perry's 'Roar'.

Responses to cyber/bullying incidents among primary pupils

These well-known approaches are successfully used in real-world bullying situations. In the primary years they can be very successful in tackling cyberbullying, which is seldom happening in isolation; there is almost always some face-to-face bullying happening too. When bullying is reduced, cyberbullying is frequently responsive too.

Circle of friends or a nurture group

Set up a circle of friends, a mix of girls with an adult mediator, to analyse situations relating to friendships. Or try a peer mentor, or a buddy from your trained buddy scheme.

Shared group approach (previously known as the no blame approach)

This approach involves a staged procedure in which the victim's situation is presented to the bullies along with other group representatives from the year group/school, and the group as a whole come up with ideas of how to help the person who has been targeted. There is no blame directly attached to those who have been involved in the bullying. The emphasis is on moving forward in new ways.[85] It is assumed they will behave well and they are given a chance to change. If they do not change their behaviour, have ready a plan for next steps in which they are not included in class activities and outings/treats but have to do some community service tasks. They may have to undertake specially chosen visits such as to help out at a special school if they have shown prejudice towards people with special needs.

- Dispel the girls' negative reputation with staff by giving them a positive project – e.g. creating a video which gets them working collaboratively with others or supporting younger pupils and teaching them to be kind.

Working with the families involved

- Meet all parents/carers and listen to them to identify the children's underlying needs.

- Try to get the family involved in some way in a partnership with the school.

- Remind parents that children of this age should not be on Facebook at all and that they have a responsibility to keep their children safe online.

- Clarify the definition of bullying and explain that fallings out are incredibly painful for children even if not actually classed as bullying and you are working on a longer-term action plan to change the behaviour. It did not arise overnight and will not necessarily disappear overnight either, but with the help of all families you hope to see real progress in the right direction. All parents will be asked to give regular reports on how their daughters are doing and how they seem at home. All will be asked to stay calm and help their daughters see what harm they have caused to others and explore how they might put this right. Parents of the targeted girls are encouraged to build their resilience in a number of ways. They might be offered clubs to join where they could be semi-supervised at lunch times, meet other children and make friends. The classroom seating plan will be changed and managed. Playground staff will be alerted.

- Ask to see the mobiles of all parties. Establish who has been sending threatening messages if possible. (Ask targeted children's parents to keep the evidence and bring it in.)

- Keep written notes of everything agreed at meetings with parents and provide a written action plan.

- Arrange for regular feedback times with parents, such as every fortnight. Tell them that if anything occurs in between those times they can email you.

Address cyberbullying and e-safety

- Write to all parents reminding them that Facebook has a lower cut-off age of 13 and it is not advisable for their children to be on this social networking site – it suggests they have lied about their age. If they have lied, it is likely that others have done so, and they may be talking to people who pretend to be their age in order to groom children.

- If anyone experiences a distressing or nasty message or threat online or on a mobile they should keep the evidence, not reply, and report it to an adult.

- Parents should familiarise themselves with the 'report abuse' buttons on these major websites and also the CEOP button to be used only in serious cases of exploitation of children.

- Do group work with pupils on e-safety – exploring with practical demonstrations the steps they should take to stay safe. Chain letters are very common at this age and so are threats.

- Work on what it means to be a good citizen of the digital world.

In a recent follow up, this deputy headteacher reported that, although there are still occasional bullying situations involving these two and other girls, they are fewer in number and he believes this is to do with the work which has focused on teaching other pupils assertiveness skills and how to support each other.

Always expect that a new approach may take a little while to have an effect, with some backsliding. However, if the general direction of travel is positive, it is worth continuing. If it is having no effect, do not continue. Try another tactic. You are more likely to get success if you implement a multifaceted approach as outlined here. All staff should be made aware of the action plan and their part in it as well as their ability to report both good and negative behaviour from those who have been using bullying behaviour.

Real life cases to use in staff training discussions

- A boy complains to you that he is being bullied with racist texts. What steps has your school put into place to deal with this complaint and what, if any, action would be taken against the bully? What will be done to confront prejudice more widely? How do you monitor this?

- After a lesson you have delivered, a pupil approaches you and says that they are being pestered by someone via instant messaging who keeps asking to meet them. What steps should you take and how could you reassure the pupil?

- A parent alerts you to a Facebook page on which a group of parents are saying nasty things about a teacher, including false information and statements. What action would you take and who is responsible for dealing with this in your school?

- A pupil with special needs is found to have stolen cigarettes from a newsagent. He reveals that he has been forced to do this by other pupils using texts and Facebook messages which threaten him if he does not do what they say. How will you approach this case? What digital trail will you examine among the group of pupils? How will you ensure the evidence of coercion is preserved? How will you work with the newsagent to put things right? What next steps will you put in place to ensure the class learn from this incident and challenge attitudes towards pupils with special needs?

- There are rumours that a girl has posed nude and her photo is being circulated online. You investigate. It appears that she was coerced into posing for this photo by an older man. What are your duties and who would you turn to from outside agencies?

- A boy reports being homophobically bullied. He does not want his parents to know. Messages and rumours are circulating online. He is too embarrassed to show you the images he was sent, but asks for help. He has never thought about his sexuality before. How would you proceed?

- A young person contacts you anonymously saying they are being cyberbullied because of the music they like (EMO) and they are desperate. 'Life is not worth living' are the words used. They have worried all summer about going back to school. This pupil left a message on your school's bully text system. What can you do? You do not know their name, gender, age or whereabouts.

- A young boy who was bullied badly sets up a website for young people to help each other with a live, unmoderated forum in which young people give each other advice. What are the risks and how would you handle this?

Questions to consider

- Which of these cases is a matter for the police?

- Are there any you would report to the IWF?

- Are there any that are appropriate for CEOP?

- When would you involve outside agencies?

- How would you retain evidence?

- How would you work with the parents/carers?

'What if...?' Scenarios
Scenario One

Parents of child A in Year 6 reported that child B had been bullying her for a long time and now she had sent her a death threat via Facebook. Parents of child B are known to services due to their substance misuse and your school has done all it can for child B during the past three years. Her home circumstances are poor and she wanders in and out of flats on her estate, sometimes into the homes of people thought to be a risk to children. She has a learning mentor and her behaviour is a cause for concern, although you have provided intensive support. You are at your wit's end to think of something new to try. Now you have to make child A and all other children safe, but also provide for child B. Parents are increasingly complaining and insist you act at once. Your school is graded 'outstanding' by Ofsted.

- What do you need to consider?

- How should you work with other agencies?

- What data should be recorded?

- What steps should we take with the rest of this class and their parents?

- Do your safeguarding and serious incident management procedures work sufficiently well for you in this situation?

Scenario two

Two boys have been at each other's throats for 18 months, since the start of Year 5. It is more serious in fact, as one has been injured by the other a few times and his parents produce letters they have sent to the school saying they have had to take their child to hospital for stitches due to the endless bullying, fighting and picking on him caused by a boy called Damian. Damian has a plan showing he is on the autistic spectrum and you suspect that Steve might also require special needs help, but his parents are very keen to avoid this route as they have a daughter at your school who does have special needs and they wish to see Steve as 'normal'.

But Steve, though academically bright, is struggling socially. He cannot cope when anything goes wrong or he loses at a game, or is not picked for a team. He has been a target for so long now that the whole class take it for granted that he is the 'victim' and they make fun of him on instant messaging and also take photos of him sometimes when he kicks off – outside of school at the park or on the playing field. They know how to 'press his buttons' say his parents. Steve's parents produce a range of letters they have written to the school over several months but there appear to be no written replies from the school, and no emails. The school says they have had meetings with the parents, but there is no action plan, nor are there arrangements for any feedback to parents.

- What steps should have been taken earlier?

- What would you do now?

- What formal procedures are required?

Scenario three

Most parents support your school, but one or two have formed a little clique. They are talking on a social networking site about specific teachers in a very demeaning way. This could be damaging to these teachers' careers. Another parent alerts you to this page and you are horrified at what you read. The comments are defamatory and sexual.

- What actions could have been taken earlier to try to prevent this situation developing?

- What will you do now?

- Where can you get help fast?

- Do your policies and procedures assist you in this case or do they need updating?

Scheme of Work by Year

I am grateful to a number of sources such as published schemes of work, but I take responsibility for the ideas expressed in this suggested programme and wish to thank children who have given their views via the Cybersurvey. This is a fast-changing field, and any educator will need to adapt their scheme of work according to new devices and services and changing patterns of behaviour among children and their families. These are suggestions only. Please feel free to extend or expand these ideas to suit your target audience and to meet the needs of the national curriculum.

Early years foundation stage: E-safety

	Concepts	Messages to convey and learning to achieve
Commu-nicate	Children know that they can use the Internet and new devices to communicate with family and friends	Children understand that they can share information online, e.g. via email or the school learning platform, or via parents' mobiles, tablets or computers Children understand that there is a right and wrong way to communicate and this may be different in some situations Children are unlikely to distinguish between online communication and mobile phone communication and all advice should cover both
Explore and enjoy with an adult	Children are aware that they can use the Internet to play, be entertained and learn, supported by a trusted adult/teacher Children begin to understand the difference between real and online experiences	Children need help from their teacher or trusted adult before they go online Children watch their favourite TV programmes online (e.g. CBeebies) Children enjoy music, videos and stories online Children can recognise logos of favourite sites/programmes/apps/games Children talk about the differences between real-world and online experiences Children understand how to use touch on screens to get to a permitted favourite Children understand that phones can be used to take photographs

Year 1: E-safety

	Concepts	Messages to convey and learning to achieve
E-awareness	Children begin to think about what marks out a person they can trust Children understand that some information is personal and should be carefully looked after Some things about us are private	Children understand there are some people they would feel safe talking to about anything that worried them Children know that things about them (full name, address, birthday, etc.) are theirs alone Children know that these special things about them matter as much online as offline and that they should not be shared without a parent, carer or teacher's permission There are rules for using the Internet and mobile phones to be able to enjoy them more. One rule is that some things are private
Safe search	Children understand that they can find all sorts of information on the Internet Children learn to visit and navigate selected websites Children know what to do if something makes them uneasy online	Introduce Hector's World Safety Button (www.thinkuknow.co.uk/5_7/hectorsworld) Children understand that just like in the real world there can be people or things that make them feel scared or worried. If that happens they should always talk to a grown-up or use the safety button Teach children how to navigate to a selected website using a shortcut or favourites link Introduce the idea of buttons for moving forward or back or within a website Know how to return to the home page of a teacher-directed website Visit sites to find out about things like animals or plants
Communicate and work with others	Children know that the Internet and mobiles can be used to communicate with other people Children know that they can send a message or do work with others	Show that email and texting are ways we can use to send and receive messages Send a group message to a classmate who is off school sick or far away Send a group message to the headteacher

Year 2: E-safety

	Concepts	Messages to convey and learning to achieve
E-awareness	Children understand that there are ways to keep safe online Children know what marks out a person they can trust	Children understand that not everyone they meet online is who they say they are, or safe to befriend Children know that things about them (full name, address, birthday etc.) are theirs alone and should be kept private Children know that these special things about them matter as much online as offline and that they should not be shared without a parent, carer or teacher's permission Children understand that there are some people they would feel safe talking to about anything that worried them. How would they decide who to trust?
Safe search	Children use the Internet for clear-cut tasks to find out useful and interesting things Children know that not everything they encounter on the Internet is true	Remind the children of the Hector's World Safety Button (www.thinkuknow.co.uk/5_7/hectorsworld) and discuss possible Internet dangers, including what to do if they find something upsetting or worrying online Children are given opportunities to explore carefully selected online sites, films and images Children know that they can question what they find online, because it is not always good quality and some of it may tell you what them need to know, while other information may not be true. Teachers and parents will guide children to places where they can find useful and interesting things. Always ask, 'Who wrote it? Could anyone have changed it?' Children understand that some of what they see online is there to sell something. They learn to recognise and ignore adverts Children discuss, understand and abide by the school's e-safety and acceptable use policies. They learn to 'Think before you click' or 'Click safe'
Communicate and work with others	Children know the difference between email and a discussion forum Children are aware of the different forms of online communication (email, forums, instant messaging and social networking sites, message or bulletin boards and Hangouts)	Children are able to send simple emails, using the right kind of language Children are able to text simple messages using the right kind of language Children are able to join in a group discussion using a discussion board or forum, message board or Hangout Children learn about passwords – secret codes that help to keep some information safe Children learn to 'Think before you click' on messages they receive Children can answer the question, 'What information about myself should I not give out?'

Year 3: E-safety

	Concepts	Messages to convey and learning to achieve
E-awareness	Children are aware of bullying of all kinds, including cyberbullying, and know what to do if they see it Agreements on how we treat one another are made with the whole class Children develop awareness of online protocols in order to stay safe on the web	Children agree to treat one another kindly, fairly and with respect both on- and offline Children learn to recognise forms of cyberbullying, rumour-spreading, nasty texts and threats Children understand and comply with the school's acceptable use policy because they understand its purpose is to keep children safe Children understand what personal information should be kept private Children know that passwords keep information secure and that they should be kept private Children know that it is better not to use the same password too often Children know how to make a password strong Children learn the SMART rules Children are aware of the NSPCC's PANTS rule (www.nspcc.org.uk/preventing-abuse/keeping-children-safe/underwear-rule)
Safe search	Children develop strategies for staying safe when using the Internet Children use the Internet to undertake independent and appropriate research and attempt to distinguish between fact and fiction	Children can confidently use child-friendly search engines independently to find information through key words Children learn not to simply accept the first piece of information that appears in a search, but to look at others and decide which is better for their needs Children learn that the Internet can offer a remarkable amount of information. Lots of it is really useful, but some of it could be untrue and some of it is dodgy. Just as in the offline world we have to decide what we think. Children understand that if anything worries them or they have a question, they can ask an adult they trust Children learn to recognise adverts and distinguish them from content
Communicate and work with others	Children begin to use a range of online communication tools, such as forums, email and polls, in order to formulate, develop and exchange ideas	Children learn to use a variety of communication tools online Children know how to deal with a nasty or worrying message (save the message and speak to a trusted adult) Children should know that they can report any text or email chain letters to a teacher and don't let chain letters frighten them Children should be able to recognise when an email is not from someone they know and could be spam or phishing Children should know how to block a sender The class can create a simple poll and pupils can answer it – and discuss the results Examples of questions could be: Do you know how to send a message to a friend using email? Yes /No Do you know how to tell if something online is trying to sell you something? Yes/Sometimes/No Do you know what to do if you get a scary message? Yes/No Do you know what the SMART rules are? Yes/Sort of/No Children are able to design simple posters with e-safety messages Children can spot the personal information in the stories given in the three lessons plans of Chapter 9 (Findlay, Kayla and Sarvendra) and contribute advice on what the protagonists should do

Year 4: E-safety

	Concepts	Messages to convey and learning to achieve
E-awareness	Children understand and abide by the school's acceptable use policy Children are aware of the need to develop a set of online protocols in order to stay safe online Children develop awareness of relevant e-safety issues	Children fully own and understand the school's acceptable use policy and understand the purpose of this 'agreement' Children are consulted and can contribute to the review of this policy as and when rapid changes in technology or incidents make it necessary Children understand that a password can keep information secure and they are aware of the need to keep it a secret. They also know how to make a strong, effective password and not to use the same one for everything Children fully understand and can explain the SMART rules to a younger child or to a parent Children develop digital skills and are able to use different software programs safely Children can describe common forms of attack such as hacking, phishing, spam and scams Children can do the security word search (see page 151) Children take an active role in an anti-bullying focus group or school council meeting where they can contribute on e-safety matters Children help organise a school campaign on e-safety and against cyberbullying
Safe search	Children can search online safely Children understand what search engines do and the importance of using correct search criteria Children use the Internet to support their work, and begin to understand plagiarism and copyright Children know that not everything they find on the Internet is true and know what to do if they come across anything that makes them uncomfortable	Children can use the Internet confidently to search for material for homework or projects or to follow their interests and hobbies (see page 182) Children know about different search engines and understand how to search for images or use YouTube (with safety features on) Children understand how to pick key words for their search or to create a suitable question they want answered Children are aware that not everything they find online is accurate or true and that information needs to be cross-checked and evaluated. They know how to do this and when to ask for help Children learn to acknowledge the creator of the work and not to pass it off as their own (see page 181)
Communication and work with others	Children can safely use a range of communication tools to collaborate and exchange information with others – e.g. email, blogs, forums	Children can communicate using a range of tools and can collaborate with other pupils on group work projects, blogs, comments and edits Children understand that, just as there is language we use for letter-writing, there is appropriate language to be used when using online tools. They learn about formal and informal language. They learn that capital letters = shouting. They understand that a digital footprint can be around forever and that some language is offensive Children can add attachments and photos to an email or a text message. Children can tag photos correctly, they can set their privacy settings and know why this is needed Children are aware that it may not be safe to open an email attachment and look for the security software check that might indicate risk Children can participate in online polls and discussions

Year 5: E-safety

	Concepts	Messages to convey and learning to achieve
E-awareness	Children understand the potential risks of providing personal information across all devices, apps and services in an increasing range of online technologies both within and outside school	Children have learned a set of values. They know they have a right to be respected and they respect the rights of others both on- and offline Children understand what being a good digital citizen entails Children understand the potential risks of giving away personal information even inadvertently Children fully own and understand the school's acceptable use policy and understand the purpose of this 'agreement' Children are consulted and can contribute to the review of this policy as and when rapid changes in technology or incidents make it necessary Children can create strong passwords and keep them safe Children fully understand and can explain the SMART rules to a younger child or to a parent Children understand that some people are not who they say they are online, and some have harmful intentions Children develop digital skills and are able to use different software programs safely Children can describe common forms of attack such as hacking, phishing, spam and scams. They understand risks when gaming online and communicating with strangers Children can do the security word search (see page 151) Children can spot the security risks in the story about Red Riding Hood (see page 147) and have completed lessons 1 and 2 (see pages 147 and 149) Children take an active role in an anti-bullying focus group or school council meeting where they can contribute on e-safety matters and cyberbullying concerns Children help organise school campaigns on e-safety and against cyberbullying Children are trained and supported as peer supporters or buddies, with a component of e-safety
Safe search	Children develop a clear idea of what to do in order to keep safe online Children recognise inaccuracy and bias on the web and evaluate websites for their validity	Children know the difference between interpreting online information and simply copying other people's work Children are able to use what they have read and put it into their own words Children are able to carry out more refined web searches by using and changing or testing key words Children can evaluate search results and refine their search to achieve the most useful results Children know that information found on websites may be inaccurate or one-sided and they know how to check the validity of a website Children are able to ignore, delete or select as junk, unsolicited advertising (spam, pop-ups, banners, videos or audio) Children use websites where resources can be downloaded without infringing copyright Children understand how important it is to acknowledge the sources used in their work (see page 181) Children are aware of what to do if they come across something that makes them feel uncomfortable when searching
Communicate and work with others	Children use a variety of online tools to exchange information and collaborate with others within and beyond their school Children understand risks and can take steps to avoid them If children are at risk of harm they know how to report abuse and get help	Children can experiment with different forms of technology to access the Internet and communicate with others Children are aware of apps and service providers offering messaging systems and they know how to stay safe when using these. They also know that some apps appear free but contain hidden charges Children can collaborate with other pupils on group work projects, blogs, comments and edits Children understand that, just as there is language we use for letter-writing, there is appropriate language to be used when using online tools. They learn about formal and informal language. They learn that capital letters = shouting. They understand that a digital footprint can be around forever and that some language is offensive Children can add attachments and photos to an email or a text message. Children can tag photos correctly, they can set their privacy settings and know why this is needed Children are aware that it may not be safe to open an email attachment and look for the security software check that might indicate risk Children can participate in online polls and discussions, work together with classmates and edit documents together online Children can create artwork and drop it into documents or add photos to work

Year 6: E-safety

	Concepts	Messages to convey and learning to achieve
E-awareness	Evaluate children's use of technology including the use of email, social networking, online gaming and mobile phones and consider how they present themselves online. Consolidate their e-safety knowledge to prepare them before secondary school Encourage children to lead the school on preventing cyberbullying and devising campaigns	Children are aware of cyberbullying and other online aggression or abuse. They know the problems that can occur as a result of sending or uploading unkind or inappropriate content. They play a full lead role within the school in helping to prevent cyberbullying Children understand that adults can use the Internet with intent to harm children. They are alert to this and aware of how to report abuse, can recognise 'report abuse' buttons and know how to report problems within school Children have learned a set of values. They know they have a right to be respected and they respect the rights of others both on- and offline. Children understand what being a good digital citizen entails and practise these values. They understand the risks of selfies and the need to post only photos they would not mind their family viewing Children understand the potential risks of giving away personal information even inadvertently and why this is important Children can check the security of a website retailer when shopping online Children fully own and understand the school's acceptable use policy and understand the purpose of this 'agreement' Children are consulted and can contribute to the review of this policy as and when rapid changes in technology or incidents make it necessary Children can create strong passwords and keep them safe; they use a variety of passwords and change them from time to time Children fully understand and can explain the SMART rules to a younger child or to a parent Children develop digital skills and are able to use different software program safely Children can describe common forms of attack such as hacking, phishing, spam and scams. They understand risks when gaming online and communicating with strangers Children can spot the security risks in scenarios such as those given on pages 148 Children take an active role in an anti-bullying focus group or school council meeting where they can contribute on e-safety matters and cyberbullying concerns Children help organise and run school campaigns on e-safety and against cyberbullying; they lead on events such as flashmobs, drama, assemblies and posters to help other pupils learn about e-safety Children are trained and supported as peer supporters or buddies, with a component of e-safety. They are trusted by younger pupils
Safe search	Children confidently and competently use the Internet as a tool for research and critically evaluate websites for their use Children understand there is inaccuracy and bias in some online information Children are aware of copyright issues and know that not all resources they find on the Internet are legal to use or copy (even if sources are acknowledged)	Children understand that work belongs to the owner. They have learned about plagiarism, copyright and data protection and take care when reproducing other people's work. They know that there are often fees payable Children select copyright-free images and sounds Children know the difference between interpreting online information and simply quoting other people's work. They are able to use what they have read and put it into their own words Children are able to carry out more refined web searches by using and changing or testing key words Children can evaluate search results and refine their search to achieve the most useful results Children know that information found on websites may be inaccurate or one-sided Children are able to ignore, delete or select as junk, unsolicited advertising (spam, pop-ups, banners, videos or audio). Children are aware of what to do if they come across something that makes them feel uncomfortable when searching Children are now confident searchers
Communication and working with others	Children use a variety of online tools to exchange information and collaborate with others within and beyond their school Children understand risks and can take steps to avoid them If they are at risk of harm they know how to report abuse and get help	Children can use different forms of technology to access the Internet and communicate with others Children are aware of apps and service providers offering messaging systems and they know how to stay safe when using these. They also know that some apps appear free but contain hidden charges Children collaborate with other pupils on group work projects, blogs, comments and edits Children understand that, just as there is language we use for letter-writing, there is appropriate language to be used when using online tools. They learn about formal and informal language. They learn that capital letters = shouting. They understand that a digital footprint can be around forever and that some language is offensive Children can add attachments and photos to an email or a text message. Children can tag photos correctly, they can set their privacy settings and know why this is needed Children are aware that it may not be safe to open an email attachment and look for the security software check that might indicate risk Children can participate in online polls and discussions, comments and podcasts and work together with classmates to edit documents together online Children can create artwork and drop it into documents or add photos to their work Children can communicate e-safety messages confidently to other pupils

Appendix B

E-safety Checklist for Schools

Policies, practice and monitoring	Yes	No	Action
Does the school have an up-to-date e-safety policy in place?			
Are there 'Acceptable Use Policies' for both pupils and adults? Is the pupil version child friendly? Are sanctions made clear?			
Is cyberbullying addressed in the school's anti-bullying policy? Does teaching about e-safety form part of the strategy to prevent bullying?			
Is there a structured e-safety curriculum embedded across all aspects of the school?			
Has the school appointed an e-safety lead?			
Is e-safety provision rigorously and regularly reviewed?			
Does the school record and monitor e-safety incidents and survey data to inform practice?			
Has an evaluative comment on e-safety been included in the safeguarding self-review assessment?			

Infrastructure	Yes	No	Action
Is the school network safe and secure? When was it last updated?			
Does the school use an accredited Internet service provider? If your school has left the local authority provider, who is providing this service now?			
Does the school use efficient, updated Internet filtering/monitoring?			
Who oversees the school's network and who can authorise development or change?			

Learners	Yes	No	Action
Do pupils understand e-safety guidelines and do you have evidence on levels of adherence?			
Are learners offered an evolving e-safety curriculum appropriate to their age and stage?			
Do learners know how to recognise and report anything that makes them feel uncomfortable or worried online? (Designated staff, peer mentors and report abuse buttons.)			
Are learners confident about identifying risks when given fictional scenarios?			

Staff	Yes	No	Action
Do teaching staff understand e-safety issues and risks, privacy and the code of conduct expected of professionals?			
Are all staff trained in the school's policy and practice with regard to e-safety? Are staff aware of how to report any concerns or disclosures?			
Are all staff, teaching and non-teaching, trained in safeguarding issues related to e-safety?			
Is data handled with care and encrypted when taken off premises?			
Do staff understand the rules about using photos of pupils online?			
Are staff trained to preserve evidence where this might be needed?			
Parents/governors	**Yes**	**No**	**Action**
Is there a designated governor with responsibility for e-safety?			
Are parents engaged as partners with the school on helping to keep their children e-safe?			

Source: This checklist was developed for *Safeguarding Children Online – How E-safe Are Your School and Your Learners?* (BECTA) and the work of e-Safer Suffolk and the Bullying Intervention Group.

Useful Websites

Cyberbullying

BIG Award

For advice on Twitter, Ask.fm, SNS, mobiles, Snapchat, etc., general advice on bullying for young people and a separate page for parents.

www.bullyinginterventiongroup.co.uk/bighelp.php

Bullying UK

Bullying UK is part of the organisation *Family Lives* and offers advice and support.

www.bullying.co.uk/cyberbullying/how-to-stay-safe-online

ChildLine

Offers many ways to communicate and get help.

www.childline.org.uk/Pages/Home.aspx

Thinkuknow

Thinkuknow is a site by CEOP. It offers advice to age groups 5–7, 8–10 and 11–13 and 14+. It also offers advice to parents or carers.

www.thinkuknow.co.uk/11_16/control/cyberbullying

Safety settings

Google Safety Centre

www.google.co.uk/familysafety

The googlefamilysafety channel

www.youtube.com/user/googlefamilysafety

Yahoo safety information

http://safely.yahoo.com

YouTube educator resources

www.google.com/support/youtube/bin/answer.py?answer=157105

YouTube film clip on how to turn on safety mode

www.youtube.com/watch?v=gkI3e0P3S5E

YouTube policy and safety hub

Short film clip and advice.

www.google.com/support/youtube/bin/request.py?contact_type=abuse

Online safety information and websites

CEOP

The Child Exploitation and Online Protection Centre (CEOP) is a command of the UK's National Crime Agency (NCA), and works both nationally and internationally to bring online child sex offenders to the UK courts.

www.ceop.gov.uk

Childnet International

Childnet International provides a wide range of resources for children and young people and educators or parents.
www.childnet-int.org

Click clever, click safe

'Click Clever. Click Safe' is a campaign to help children to be safe online. Aimed at the young it teachers them a code Zip it, flag it, block it. to deal with problems they encounter.
www.thinkuknow.co.uk/safeinternetday/clickcleverclicksafe

Connect safely

www.connectsafely.org

Digizen

Digizen's website provides information for educators, parents, carers, and young people, it encourages users of technology to be and become responsible DIGItal citiZENS. It is run by Childnet International.
www.digizen.org.uk

Gardai

In the Republic of Ireland the Gardai provide online advice.
www.webwise.ie/teachers/connect-with-respect-programme-z

Thinkyuknow

www.thinkuknow.co.uk

Watch your space

'Watch your space' is a website set up in Ireland to help tackle cyberbullying.
www.watchyourspace.ie

Webwise

'Webwise' is the Irish Internet Safety Awareness Centre. It provides teaching resources and advice on Internet safety topics, including cyberbullying and privacy.
www.webwise.ie

Facebook

Facebook Help Centre

www.facebook.com/help/?hq=report+abuse

Facebook: Safety advice online

www.facebook.com/about/basics

Sexting

ACPO (Association of Chief Police Officers)

ACPO Good Practice Guide for Digital Evidence
www.acpo.police.uk/documents/crime/2011/201110-cba-digital-evidence-v5.pdf

ACPO has also published a position statement on the prosecution of young people who have posted self-generated images.
http://ceop.police.uk/Documents/ceopdocs/externaldocs/ACPO_Lead_position_on_Self_Taken_Images.pdf

ChildLine

ChildLine is able to help get explicit images removed by working with the Internet Watch Foundation (IWF). They also provide Zippit, an app which offers some useful images to send back if asked to send an intimate photo.
www.childline.org.uk/explore/onlinesafety/pages/sexting.aspx?utm_source=google&utm_medium=cpc&utm_campaign=NSPCC_Sexting&utm_term=advice_on_sexting

Cumbria Constabulary

Useful videos.
www.cumbria.police.uk/advice-and-information/online-safety/sexting-issues

NSPCC

Advice for parents.
www.nspcc.org.uk/preventing-abuse/keeping-children-safe/sexting

Securus

A useful booklet to help determine the type of case you are dealing with
www.securus-software.com/wp-content/uploads/2013/03/Sexting-Booklet-FINAL.pdf

Songs for Teaching

A list of anti-bullying songs for teachers to use.
www.songsforteaching.com/charactereducationsongs/anti-bullying-songs.htm

UK Safer Internet Centre

Resources for teachers and other professionals.
www.saferinternet.org.uk/advice-and-resources/teachers-and-professionals

Useful sources of materials

Audio Networks and NEN image gallery

Free, safe and royalty-free images and sounds for use in education.
https://audionetwork.lgfl.org.uk/terms.aspx
http://gallery.nen.gov.uk/index.php

Bullying Intervention Group

The Bullying Intervention Group or BIG offers a BIG Help page on all aspects of bullying and cyberbullying, with resources for teachers in schools from infants to further education colleges. It runs a national award programme for recognising excellence in bullying intervention.
www.bullyinginterventiongroup.co.uk/bighelp.php

CBeebies

Children's TV stay safe link.
www.bbc.co.uk/cbbc/topics/stay-safe

Childnet International

Information for primary teachers.
www.childnet.com/teachers-and-professionals

Am I making myself clear?

www.accessible.info.co.uk/pdfs/making-myself-clear.pdf
Questionnaire about bullying in images
www.anti-bullyingalliance.org.uk/media/1047/mencap-questionnaire.pdf

Toca Boca

Lots of safe games
http://tocaboca.com/games

UK Safer Internet Centre

The UK Safer Internet Centre hosts the Professionals' Hotline and offers advice for parents and carers, teachers and young people. It also carries resources for Safer Internet Day and a range of regularly updated resources.
www.saferinternet.org.uk

Endnotes

1   *Health Behaviour in School-Aged Children* report, cited in *The Times*, May 2014.

2   *Can I Tell You Something?*, ChildLine.

3   http://media.ofcom.org.uk/news/2014/cmr-uk-2014

4   All figures are from the Cybersurvey. Reports on the survey are available on www.youthworksconsulting. co.uk. Youthworks Consulting runs the survey, consulting children and young people annually since 2008 about their online experiences and their e-safety education. Currently there are over 20,000 young people who have given their views. I am deeply grateful to all of these young people for the insights their participation has yielded. Without them I could not have had these valuable snapshots of their lives online. But this survey cannot happen without the hard work of those who recruit the schools, administer the programme and help in so many ways. Furthermore there are volunteers who test the questions and over the years there have been several researchers who have worked on the data alongside me.

5   Holloway, D., Green, L. and Livingstone, S. (2013) *Zero to Eight: Young Children and their Internet Use*. London: EU Kids Online, p.7.

6   *Inspecting E-safety in Schools*. Ofsted (2014), Section 5 Briefing.

7   The SMART rules, devised by Childnet International and the Safer Internet Centre (www.childnet.com/ resources/be-smart-on-the-internet), have long been considered the basics to be taught to all children. See the student handout in Chapter 9.

8   www.gov.uk/government/publications/personal-social-health-and-economic-education-pshe

9   Ofsted (2013) *Not Yet Good Enough: Personal, Social, Health and Economic Education in Schools*. Available at www.gov. uk/government/uploads/system/uploads/attachment_data/file/370024/ Not_yet_good_enough_personal_social_health_and_economic_education_in_schools_-_report_summary.pdf, accessed on 20 March 2014.

10 Brook, PSHE Association and Sex Education Forum (2014) *Sex and Relationships Education for the 21st Century*. Available at www.pshe-association.org.uk/uploads/media/17/7910.pdf, accessed on 20 March 2014.

11 www.gov.uk/government/uploads/system/uploads/attachment_data/file/283599/sex_and_ relationship_education_guidance.pdf

12 *Am I Making Myself Clear?* Mencap. Available at www. mencap.org.uk/node/6040, accessed on 20 March 2014.

13 Communication tools such as illustrations, pictures and symbols, communication charts or boards, signing and, above all, practical demonstrations and role-play are important for conveying messages on e-safety to this group of pupils. To find out more see www. communicationmatters.org.uk

14 *Flaming* is to incite or provoke arguments in a debate; *trolling* is a deliberate attack on another user, ranging from disrupting a conversation to threats of harm.

15 Adapted from a ten point guide by Lightspeed systems for NAACE www.naace.co.uk/2086 and advice by RM.

16 In creating this list I would like to acknowledge a guide by RM (www.rm.com/generic.asp?cref=GP2406455) and NAACE (www.naace.co.uk/2086) for their information, plus the schools trying this approach for their advice.

17 'Blended learning' describes the way independent online learning is being combined with traditional classroom methods to create a new hybrid teaching methodology that can be customised to students' learning style and needs, energising learning in new ways.

18 Cartwright, N. (2007) *Peer Support Works: A Step by Step Guide to Long Term Success*. London: Continuum.

19 https://ico.org.uk

20 *Keeping Children Safe in Education*: 'Statutory Guidance for Schools and Colleges', DFE-00341-2014, April 2014; 'Information for All School and College Staff', DFE-00585-2014, April 2014.

21 The helpline provided by UKCCIS is 0844 381 4772 (helpline@saferinternet.org).

22 DfE (2013) *Behaviour and Discipline in Schools*. London: DfE. Available at www.gov.uk/government/uploads/system/uploads/attachment_data/file/392489/behaviour_and_discipline_in_schools_statutory_guidance.pdf, accessed July 2013.

23 Internet Watch Foundation, 'Record reports for online child sexual abuse charity' (www.iwf.org.uk/about-iwf/news/post/389-record-reports-for-online-child-sexual-abuse-charity), and Operational Trends 2013 (www.iwf.org.uk/resources/trends).

24 An IP address is a unique series of numbers that identifies each computer using the Internet Protocol to communicate over a network.

25 www.nspcc.org.uk/preventing-abuse/research-and-resources/provision-young-people-displayed-harmful-sexual-behaviour

26 Described by Simon Hackett in his 2010 work 'A continuum of children and young people's sexual behaviours'.

27 Quoted from Hackett, S. (2014) *Children and Young People with Harmful Sexual Behaviours: Research Review*. Research in Practice. AIM has addressed the under-12s on http://aimproject.org.uk.

28   Department for Children, Schools and Families (2009) *Guidance for Safer Working Practice for Adults Who Work with Children and Young People in Education Settings*. London: DCSF, p.16.

29   Quoted from Point 6.11 of the memorandum prepared for parliament by the Anti-Bullying Alliance in 2007 (www.publications.parliament.uk/pa/cm200607/cmselect/cmeduski/85/6112210.htm).

30   Unicef (2014) 'Understanding the CRC.' Available at www.unicef.org/crc/index_understanding.html, accessed on 16 January 2015.

31   Ofsted (2003) *Bullying: Effective Action in Secondary Schools*. London: Ofsted. For more information, see Suckling, A. and Temple, C. (2002) *Bullying: A Wholeschool Approach*. London: Jessica Kingsley Publishers; The BIG Award: The National Award for Excellence in Bullying Intervention, www.bullyinginterventiongroup.co.uk; Katz , A. (2012) *Cyberbullying and E-safety: What Educators and Other Professionals Need to Know*. London:Jessica Kingsley Publishers.

32   NCB Spotlight briefing November 2004: 'Making schools safer using effective anti-bullying strategies.'

33   Peer support is described in depth in Cowie, H. and Wallace, P. (2000) *Peer Support in Action: From Bystanding to Standing by*. London: Sage.

34   Peer Support Forum (2002) *Bullying and Peer Support*. Peer Support Forum Briefing Paper, PSHE and Citizenship Spotlight Series. London: National Children's Bureau; Hartley-Brewer, E. (2002) *Stepping Forward: Working Together through Peer Support*. London: National Children's Bureau.

35   Peer advocacy is described on www.pacer.org/bullying/resources/students-with-disabilities/peer-advocacy.asp.

36   For more information, see Cowie, H. (2002) 'Not bystanding, but standing by: strategies for pupils to cope with bullying.' *New Era in Education 83*, 2, 41–43; Cowie, H. and Berdondini, L. (2001) 'Children's reactions to co-operative group work: strategies for enhancing peer relationships among bullies, victims and bystanders.' *Learning and Instruction 11*, 517–530; Cowie, H. (2006) 'Young People Themselves Tackle the Problem of School Violence.' In Österman, K. and Björkqvist, K. (eds) *Contemporary Research on Aggression. Volume I: School Violence*. Proceedings of the XVI World Meeting of the International Society for Research on Aggression, Santorini, Greece, 2004. Åbo, Finland: Åbo Akade University, pp.108–114.

37   For more information, see www.circle-time.co.uk.

38   For more information see the Welsh Assembly guidance of 2003 (http://wales.gov.uk/topics/Educationandskills/publications/circulars/antibullying/?lang=en) and Thompson, F. and Smith, P.K. (2011) *The Use and Effectiveness of Anti-Bullying Strategies in Schools*, Research Report DFE-RR098 (www.gov.uk/government/uploads/system/uploads/attachment_data/file/182421/DFE-RR098.pdf).

39   For further information, see Field, F.M. (2003) *Bully Busting*. Lane Cove, NSW: Finch Publishing; Rigby, K. (2010) 'Strengthening the Victim.' In *Bullying Interventions in Schools: Six Basic Methods*. Camberwell: ACER.

40   For more information, see Robinson, G. and Maines, B. (2000) *Crying for Help: The No Blame Approach to Bullying*. Bristol: Lucky Duck Publishing; Robinson, G. and Maines, B. (2008) *Bullying: A Complete Guide to the Support Method*. London: Sage; Brown, D. *Bullying: From Reaction to Prevention: A Support Group Approach*. Surrey: Young Voice. (Available from Youthworks Consulting.)

41   For further information, see Thompson, D., Arora, T. and Sharp, S. (2002) *Bullying: Effective Strategies for Longterm Improvement*. London: RoutledgeFalmer; see also Ken Rigby's *Bullying Interventions in Schools: Six Major Approaches* (www.bullyingawarenessweek.org/pdf/Bullying_Prevention_Strategies_in_Schools_Ken_Rigby.pdf).

42   For more information, see Sharp, S. and Smith, P.K. (1994) *Tackling Bullying in Your School: A Practical Handbook for Teachers*. London: Routledge.

43   www.rootsofempathy.org

44   Kidscape provide assertiveness workshops for young people. To find out more see www.kidscape.org.uk/what-we-do/zap-anti-bullying-and-assertiveness-workshops.

45   www.kivaprogram.net/Program

46   For more information, see www.persona-doll-training.org/ukhome.html.

47   Department for Education and Skills (2002) *Bullying: Don't Suffer in Silence*. London: DfES, p.22.

48   For more information: see www.rtime.info.

49   Williams, K (2001) *Ostracism: The Power of Silence*. New York: Guilford Press.

50   Wilson Jr, R.E. (2014) 'Bully victims are created by unstable households: parents unwittingly groom children to be victims of bullies.' The Main Ingredient, *Psychology Today*, 11 August.

51   Katz, A., Buchanan, A. and Bream, V. (2001) *Bullying in Britain: Testimonies from Teenagers*. London: Young Voice.

52   Ofsted (2014) *Inspecting E-safety in Schools: Section 5 Briefing* p.9.

53   Bullying Intervention Group, Teen Thousand Teens Series 2014. Adrienne Katz for BIG Award.

54   Palacio, R.J. (2012) *Wonder*. London: Corgi; Gardner, S. (2012) *Maggot Moon*. London: Hot Key Books.

55   It applies to all schools (whether maintained, nonmaintained or independent), including academies and pupil referral units, governing bodies and headteachers of maintained schools including aided and foundation schools). It does not include maintained nursery schools.

56   Department for Education (2015) *Keeping Children Safe in Education*. London: DfE. Available atwww.gov.uk/government/uploads/system/uploads/attachment_data/file/418686/Keeping_children_safe_in_education.pdf, accessed on 20 May 2015.

57   Department for Education (2015) *Keeping Children Safe in Education*. London: DfE. Available at www.gov.uk/government/uploads/system/uploads/attachment_data/file/418687/Keeping_children_safe_in_education_part_1_only.pdf, accessed on 20 May 2015.

58 HM Government (2015) *Working Together to Safeguard Children: A Guide to Inter-agency Working to Safeguard and Promote the Welfare of Children*. London: DfE. Available at www.gov.uk/government/uploads/system/uploads/attachment_data/file/419595/Working_Together_to_Safeguard_Children.pdf, accessed on 20 May 2015.

59 Schools may choose appropriate training and may take advice from their Local Safeguarding Children Board (LSCB) in doing so. The training should cover, as a minimum, the content of *Keeping Children Safe in Education* (March 2015).

60 Ofsted (2015) *School Inspection Handbook*. London: Ofsted, Section 157.

61 The 2014 Cybersurvey, Adrienne Katz, Youthworks Consulting.

62 https://gsmaintelligence.com/research/2014/05/measuring-mobile-penetration/430

63 The 2014 Cybersurvey, Suffolk, February 2015 (www.suffolk.gov.uk/assets/suffolk.gov.uk/Your%20Community/2015-02-09%20Cybersurvey%202014_FINAL.pdf).

64 The Living Image Camera Museum has a very useful timeline on their website (www.licm.org.uk) showing the history of photography by Philip Greenspun.

65 http://splashdata.com/press/worst-passwords-of-2014.htm

66 https://nakedsecurity.sophos.com/2014/10/01/how-to-pick-a-proper-password

67 McGaffin, K., Darwen, M. and Powis, O. (2012) *Keyword Basics*, p.8 (www.wordtracker.com/attachments/keyword-basics-final.pdf).

68 McGaffin *et al.* (2012) *Keyword Basics*, p.9.

69 http://schoolsimprovement.net/tag/tanya-byron

70 Tanya Byron led an independent review. Her report, *Safer Children in a Digital World* (commonly called the Byron Review: available at http://webarchive.nationalarchives.gov.uk/20101021152907/dcsf.gov.uk/byronreview, accessed April 2013), was published in March 2008.

71 www.kaspersky.com/about/news/virus/2014/costlykids.

72 Livingstone, S. and Bober, M. (2005) *UK Children Go Online: Final Report of Key Project Findings*. London: LSE.

73 http://webarchive.nationalarchives.gov.uk/20101021152907/dcsf.gov.uk/byronreview.

74 Byron, T. (2010) *Do We Have Safer Children in a Digital World?* (DCSF 00290-2010BKT-EN).

75 https://shareweb.kent.gov.uk/Documents/healthand-wellbeing/teenpregnancy/Sexualisation_young_people.pdf

76 Bailey, R. (2011) *'Letting Children be Children': Report of an Independent Review on the Commercialisation and Sexualisation of Children*. London: DfE.

77 Paus-Hasebrink, Ponte, Dürager and Bauwens (2012), p. 267. Quoted by Ingrid Paus-Hasebrink, Philip Sinner and Fabian Prochazka (2014) in *Children's Online Experiences in Socially Disadvantaged Families: European Evidence and Policy Recommendations*, p.2. Available at http://eprints.lse.ac.uk/57878/1/EU_Kids_Online_Disadvantaged_children.pdf, accessed on 16 January 2015.

78 Paus-Hasebrink, Sinner and Prochazka (2014) in Children's Online Experiences in Socially Disadvantaged Families: European Evidence and Policy Recommendations, p.1. Available at http://eprints.lse.ac.uk/57878/1/EU_Kids_Online_Disadvantaged_children.pdf, accessed on 16 January 2015.

79 Livingstone, S., Haddon, L., Görzig, A. and Olafsson, K. (2011) *Risks and Safety on the Internet*. Available at www.lse.ac.uk/media%40lse/research/EUKidsOnline/EU%20Kids%20II%20(2009-11)/EUKidsOnlineIIReports/D4FullFindings.pdf, accessed in March 2011.

80 Paus-Hasebrink, Sinner and Prochazka (2014) in *Children's Online Experiences in Socially Disadvantaged Families: European Evidence and Policy Recommendations*, p.3. Available at http://eprints.lse.ac.uk/57878/1/EU_Kids_Online_Disadvantaged_children.pdf, accessed on 16 January 2015.

81 Ofcom (2014) *Ofcom Report on Internet Safety Measures: Internet Service Providers: Network Level Filtering Measures*. Available at http://stakeholders.ofcom.org.uk/binaries/internet/internet_safety_measures_2.pdf, accessed on 14 January 2015.

82 Kobie, N. (2014) 'Those parental-control filters? As few as 4% are signing up.' PC PRO, 22 July. Available at www.pcpro.co.uk/news/broadband/389926/those-parental-control-filters-as-few-as-4-are-signingup#ixzz3DCdttKiB, accessed on 16 January 2015; The Co-operative Childcare (2014) 'Modern children play outside over 65% less than their parents did', 10 February. Available at www.thecooperativechildcare.coop/news/February-2014/Modern-Children-Play-Outside-Over-65-Less-Than-Their-Parents-Did, accessed on 16 January 2015; Kaspersky Lab (2014) 'Costly kids – one in five families lose money or data due to children on the Internet', 9 September. Available at www.kaspersky.com/about/news/virus/2014/costly-kids, accessed on 16 January 2015; BullGuard (no date) 'One in seven parents has found unsuitable content on their child's mobile device.' Press release available at www.bullguard.com/press/latest-press-releases/2014/18-06.aspx, accessed on 16 January 2015.

83 Ofcom (2014) *Parents' Views on Parental Controls: Findings of Qualitative Research* (http://stakeholders.ofcom.org.uk/binaries/research/research-publications/childrens/oct2012/Annex_1.pdf).

84 The 2012 and 2013 Cybersurvey, Adrienne Katz, Youthworks Consulting.

85 See Robinson, G. and Maines, B. (1997) *Crying for Help: The No Blame Approach to Bullying*. Bristol: Lucky Duck.

Index